Teaching FUNdamental Gymnastics Skills

Debby Mitchell
Barbara Davis
Raim Lopez

illustrated by
Stormy Gunter

Human Kinetics

Library of Congress Cataloging-in-Publication Data

Mitchell, Debby, 1953-
    Teaching FUNdamental Gymnastics Skills / Debby Mitchell,
Barbara Davis, Raim Lopez; illustrated by Stormy Gunter.
      p. cm.
    ISBN 0-7360-0124-7
    1. Gymnastics--Study and teaching. I. Davis, Barbara, 1953- II. Lopez, Raim, 1960-
III. Title.

GV461.M54 2002
796.44--dc21

2002017324

ISBN-10: 0-7360-0124-7
ISBN-13: 978-0-7360-0124-3

Acquisitions Editor: Judy Patterson Wright, PhD
Developmental Editor: Rebecca Crist
Assistant Editor: Mark E. Zulauf
Copyeditor: Jan Feeney
Proofreader: Jennifer L. Davis
Graphic Designer: Nancy Rasmus
Graphic Artist: Angela K. Snyder
Cover Designer: Keith Blomberg
Photographer (cover): Les Woodrum
Art Manager: Carl Johnson
Illustrator: Stormy Gunter
Printer: Versa

Printed in the United States of America   10 9 8 7 6

Human Kinetics
Web site: www.HumanKinetics.com

United States: Human Kinetics
P.O. Box 5076
Champaign, IL 61825-5076
800-747-4457
e-mail: humank@hkusa.com

Canada: Human Kinetics
475 Devonshire Road, Unit 100
Windsor, ON N8Y 2L5
800-465-7301 (in Canada only)
e-mail: info@hkcanada.com

Europe: Human Kinetics
107 Bradford Road
Stanningley
Leeds LS28 6AT, United Kingdom
+44 (0)113 255 5665
e-mail: hk@hkeurope.com

Australia: Human Kinetics
57A Price Avenue
Lower Mitcham, South Australia 5062
08 8372 0999
e-mail: info@hkaustralia.com

New Zealand: Human Kinetics
Division of Sports Distributors NZ Ltd.
P.O. Box 300 226 Albany
North Shore City, Auckland
0064 9 448 1207
e-mail: info@humankinetics.co.nz

Contents

Preface

Gymnastics can be a wonderful asset to any physical education program. What better way to teach children balance, strength, poise, and power than by letting them run, jump, swing, and pose? But gymnastics can also be dangerous if you're unsure of what you're doing. We wrote this book to provide physical education teachers and gymnastics coaches the opportunity to explore fundamental gymnastics skills with the proper instructional and safety information.

We began developing this project because there was no comprehensive book or teaching resource available that adequately prepared teachers and coaches to teach gymnastics in public schools or private clubs. Many club owners are looking for an efficient way to train new coaches. This text presents an innovative way to deliver quality, consistent instruction to those who teach gymnastics classes.

During the evolution and development of this text, we gathered—and used—input from gymnastics experts and public school teachers. Teachers who did not teach gymnastics because they lacked knowledge or a comfort level were very influential. They suggested the need for complete descriptions of the skill, common errors, and spotting information. They wanted some means to see the skill visually—high-quality illustrations to accompany the descriptions. The inexperienced teachers and coaches also wanted these questions answered:

- How do you move from exploratory, or educational, gymnastics to formal gymnastics skills?
- What lead-ups or progressions should you teach to prepare children for more advanced skills?
- How do you provide experiences to develop the psychomotor domain (such as strength, endurance, balance) and build students' confidence for higher-level skills?
- If you don't have apparatus at your school or gym or if you're concerned about liability, are there activities you can teach using just mats?
- Is there more than one way to provide verbal cues to help students who have different learning styles?
- Can task cards be used at stations so that students can follow and evaluate their own skills?
- How can you assess these skills?

This book provides complete information and tools for anyone who would teach or coach basic gymnastics skills. The objective behind the development of this teaching manual is to motivate physical education teachers—especially those that lack a gymnastics background—to add gymnastics to their curriculum. But we want everyone to enjoy the benefits of clear gymnastics instruction. Anyone involved in teaching or learning gymnastics—public school teachers, gymnasium owners and coaches, parents who desire to help their children, and the gymnasts themselves—can benefit from the teaching concepts we've compiled here.

There are several unique aspects of this book. One is the introduction and use of teaching cues for different learning styles. Not all students learn best by hearing the same coaching cues we've always used, so we include cues for verbal/linguistic, logical/mathematical, visual/spatial, bodily/kinesthetic, and musical learning styles. Kinder cues are also included for some skills for younger children. This allows the parent, teacher, or coach to provide information in different ways to help all students understand the instructions.

Another unique aspect of this resource is the guidance in the progression from exploratory gymnastics to formal gymnastics. Many instructors teach only exploratory gymnastics or only formal gymnastics. The information in this book will help teachers make the transition from one form of gymnastics to another.

The book is organized into seven chapters. The first two chapters provide background and safety information; the remaining five provide information on specific gymnastics skills. Chapter 1 focuses on teaching strategies to ensure student success in learning gymnastics skills. Development of the "whole" child, NASPE recommendations, Rudolf von Laban's concept of a movement chart, a movement chart specific to gymnastics, transition from exploratory to formal gymnastics, proper progressions, pedagogy, teaching methodology, multiple intelligence and learning cues, class organization, and biomechanics are topics discussed in this chapter. And of course, we cover safety issues in teaching gymnastics. Topics include proper warm-up and stretching, contraindicated exercises, conditioning, proper care of equipment, safety rules, safe landings, and spotting techniques.

Chapter 2, "Exploratory Gymnastics," helps beginners find the joy of movement and sets the stage for "real" gymnastics. Chapter 3, "Foundational Positions and Movements," is the most important of the skill chapters because it introduces the fundamentals of teaching beginning gymnastics skills, and it includes positions and movements that are the building blocks for all gymnastics skills. The final four chapters include skills for floor, beam, springboard and vault, and bars. The skills text can be used for individuals or small groups working at stations.

The following are unique features of the skill chapters:

- Exploratory gymnastics challenges that aid gymnasts in the transition to formal gymnastics skills
- Beginning skills that use only mats to aid in developing gymnasts' proficiency as well as strength, balance, flexibility, agility, spatial awareness, and the confidence to attempt skills on the apparatus
- Lists of skills to be reviewed before instructors progress to new skills
- Thorough descriptions of beginning skills along with progressions and lead-ups to intermediate or more advanced skills
- Descriptions of other challenges and variations of skills
- Illustrations of skills

We love teaching gymnastics, and we know you will, too. We hope this reference provides all the tools you need to be a successful gymnastics instructor!

ACKNOWLEDGMENTS

Any project this size takes the help of many people to accomplish. Special thanks to Lititia Levi, who was a major contributor to the writing of the text. She added her special touch and helped provide a fresh perspective to the book. Also, to Stormy Gunter for the beautiful and detailed illustrations and Stephanie and Tom Savas, owners of Broadway—Gymnastics for all your time and support. Thanks to all of the teachers and coaches for their input and advice. Finally, a special thanks to my family, Van, Michael, Mark and Tot, who was supportive and understanding through the long hours of preparation and work at the computer.

On the cover.   Review the Round-Off and the Handstand Snapdown on page 152, and then examine the skill depicted on the front cover. Can you spot any errors in movement?

Skill Finder

Gymnastics Basics: Teaching Safely, Teaching Well

Gymnastics is perhaps the best activity to use for teaching children overall body-management skills. Gymnastics reinforces and improves posture; it increases strength, flexibility, and overall fitness; it builds skills that apply to other sports; it builds confidence and self-discipline; it develops children's spatial awareness; and it helps develop children's awareness of body mechanics. All children should have some exposure to exploratory and beginning gymnastics skills, which are defined and presented later in this book.

As great as gymnastics is, it is also a sport with risks. This is especially true as gymnasts move on to intermediate and advanced skills. And like any other sport, gymnastics requires special effort to be taught properly.

SAFETY FIRST

Your most important task as a beginning gymnastics instructor is to keep the students safe by creating a safe environment and teaching developmentally appropriate skills. Gymnastics should provide a learning experience that is appropriate for each student's intelligence, skill, and maturity level. Therefore, safety and the prevention of injuries are important considerations in gymnastics. As a teacher, you must focus on physically preparing the athletes for skills, maintaining safe facilities, and carefully implementing safety procedures. Always keep in mind that every student does not have to perform every skill. What is easy for one person may be difficult for another person. For example, if a student is overweight or lacks strength or flexibility, he or she may not be able to perform backward rolls. Yet this student may be able to perform cartwheels. Therefore, don't be rigid; give each student options so that he or she can be successful in your class.

Safe Settings

The first step in keeping all students safely active is providing them with an environment free from unnecessary hazards. You can help by ensuring that all equipment is properly maintained and by ensuring that every participant knows—and follows—all rules and safety procedures.

Equipment and Apparatus

For optimal safety, your gym will need several pieces of apparatus that are in good condition.

Panel mats. Panel mats come in assorted sizes and colors. They range in thickness from 1 to 2 inches. These mats can be folded into panels approximately 2 feet wide. Panel mats measuring 5 feet by 10 feet or 6 feet by 12 feet work well and the mat colors should contrast with the walls and floor.

Incline mat (wedge). The incline mat (or wedge, as it is often called) is a mat filled with soft, shock-absorbent foam. It is used as a ramp for teaching skills that require gymnasts to gain momentum, such as backward rolls and back extension rolls. The wedge mat comes in various heights and widths. The recommended size is 5 feet wide, 6 feet long, and 18 to 20 inches high.

Skill and landing mats. These mats are thicker and more shock-absorbent than panel mats. They are often called "crash mats," "4-inchers," or "8-inchers," depending on their thickness. These mats are used for landings from beam, vault, and bars, and they're also used as safety devices for skill progressions on all pieces of apparatus.

Octagon mat. An octagon mat is a padded, eight-sided mat that is somewhat barrel shaped. The size and shape make this a useful mat for teaching front and back walkovers, backbends, and front handsprings. Use the mat to help support or spot a gymnast starting from a handstand base position.

Trapezoid or vaulting box. The trapezoid box is made of three to five stacked trapezoid-shaped pieces that are held together with Velcro™ strips. The base piece of the unit is larger than the top piece. You can add and remove pieces to the trapezoid to adjust the height when doing vaulting drills and progressions.

Single horizontal bar. A horizontal bar that adjusts from 3 feet to 5 feet from the floor is recommended. Beginners should never work with a bar that is higher than chest height.

Parallel bars. Bars that adjust from 3 feet to 5 feet from the floor are recommended.

Springboard. When using a springboard, follow the weight recommendations of the manufacturer.

Balance beam. For most skills, you should use beams that adjust from 6 inches for low beam to 12 to 24 inches for medium beam. The beam should be covered with a padded or nonslip surface. Gymnasts are ready to do skills on the high beam only when they have mastered the skills on the floor, then on the low and medium beams, if there is adequate matting and the beam can be adjusted.

As students begin to learn skills, it may be too challenging for them to perform the skills on the apparatus. Also, if the class is large, there may not be enough equipment to keep all students occupied at once. Fortunately, you can find good substitutes for apparatus as students begin to learn skills.

- A line on the floor can be used to simulate a balance beam.
- Carpet squares or poly spots (commercially-available small rubber circles for marking an area) can be used as an initial marker for the target when you teach the step-hurdle, landing, and jump for springboard.
- Folded mats, crates, and benches can be used for beginning mounts and dismounts for beam.
- Folded mats can be used for beginning vault skills.
- Drills on folded mats, crates, and benches can help gymnasts prepare for bar skills.

Rules and Guidelines

The safety of all gymnasts should be your primary concern when you establish a learning environment. Therefore, you must firmly establish all rules and guidelines.

Safety rules. Safety rules should be visibly posted on the gym wall. Each student should also have a typed copy of the safety rules. You must establish consequences for all rule violations, and you must make your students aware of the consequences. Sometimes a simple reminder is all that students need; other times, students may need time-outs.

Health form. Parents should fill out and sign a form that indicates the health status of each gymnast. In school settings, health forms are completed and turned in to the school administrators at the beginning of the year. Physical educators should review the forms and make necessary notes to ensure students' safety. Instructors need to know what conditions may limit each gymnast's participation or success. It is also a good idea to keep on file a waiver letter with each parent's signature. A waiver letter protects your club against any liability in case of accidents or injuries.

Traffic flow. Set up tumbling mats and approach pathways along walls to prevent students from stepping into the paths of other gymnasts. All areas surrounding apparatus should have ample room for landings; set up traffic patterns in these areas to prevent collisions. Keep clear pathways near doors, windows, walkways, and walls.

Starting, spotting, and stopping signals. Teach the gymnasts starting, spotting, and stopping signals. For example, when you prepare to spot a vault, the gymnast raises an arm overhead when he or she is ready to perform the skill. You would lift an arm overhead to acknowledge the gymnast's signal and bring your arm down to signal that you are ready to spot the skill.

Safety First Guidelines for Athletes

- Warm up and stretch properly before attempting any skills.
- Follow the traffic patterns.
- Start and stop on signal from instructor.
- For a skill that is to be spotted, wait for the signal from instructor before beginning the skill.
- Stay off equipment until instructor gives permission.
- Perform only those skills that you have been given permission to perform.
- Offer encouragement to others.

Safety First Guidelines for Instructors/Teachers

- Plan the lessons and protect gymnasts from any potential hazards or problems that might be encountered.
- Post safety rules and supervise activities closely.
- Stop any horseplay or misbehavior immediately.
- Designate traffic flow and identify approach and landing areas.
- Designate start and stop signals.
- Establish procedures for each station or skill.
- Provide a safe environment. Provide enough mats of appropriate sizes.
- Check equipment frequently. Is it properly positioned? Are there any obstacles? Is there proper matting sufficient for the weight of the gymnast and the force of a fall if one should occur?
- Reinforce proper landing techniques and falling techniques. Practice falling techniques early and frequently so that they are automatic.
- Evaluate each student prior to participation. Match each student's ability to the proper skill level.
- Follow proper skill progressions and make sure the gymnasts master basic skills.
- Know first aid and emergency procedures.

If you are not yet ready to spot the skill or if you want the gymnast to stop running, you can hold your arm out as a traffic officer would do.

Eliminating a skill. The following are instances in which a gymnast should not perform a skill:

- The equipment is faulty or there are not enough safety mats for safe landings.
- The gymnast cannot perform prerequisite skills.
- The gymnast does not want to try the skill. (Never force a student to perform.)
- The instructor does not have the size, strength, or knowledge to spot the skill properly.
- The gymnast has injuries or is hampered by excess weight, lack of flexibility, or lack of muscle strength to safely complete the skill.
- The gymnast is limited by ill health.

Safe Actions

In addition to providing a safe environment, make sure your actions keep your athletes as accident- and injury-free as possible. Any sport that requires athletes to stretch, exert force, or become airborne requires special consideration. Make sure your students and your club's instructors are aware of these considerations and know how to prepare for the activity to greatly reduce the risk of injury.

Warming Up

Warming up, stretching before and after activity, and developing flexibility and strength will reduce the risk of injury. Always warm up before stretching because cold muscles are not very flexible. To warm up the body, perform low-intensity aerobic exercises such as jogging or jumping rope for 5 to 10 minutes. This will elevate the core body temperature and cause slight perspiration, an indicator that the muscles are warm. Avoid extreme range of motion movements at any joint before the joint is thoroughly warm and stretched. If the muscle is warm and then stretched to its maximum, this reduces the likelihood of injury.

Make warm-ups fun! Use music that motivates the students and inspires movement. Use a variety of activities such as jumping rope, tag games, and follow the leader. This is also a good time to work on gymnastics locomotor skills such as stretch jumps, chassés, and low leaps.

Stretching

Three terms are often associated with stretching:

- Static—the muscle is stretched to mild tension and held still for 30–60 seconds
- Dynamic—the body is moving (for proper stretching always use slow, controlled movement)
- Ballistic—a movement that is performed quickly and with force; ballistic movements are not recommended for stretching because a joint may be taken past its normal range of motion

There are two main purposes of stretching in gymnastics. One purpose is to prevent injury. This type of stretch should be performed after a warm-up and before gymnastics skills to take the joints and muscles through their current range of motion. These stretches can be a little more dynamic but not ballistic.

The second purpose of stretching is to increase flexibility. Static flexibility stretches should be performed after gymnastics skills when the muscles are the warmest. Hold these stretches for a minimum of 60 seconds and perform two to three repetitions per stretch.

There are a few guidelines to remember when leading stretching exercises. Follow these rules to help your athletes increase their flexibility and avoid injury:

- Flexibility exercises should stretch every major joint and cover a full range of motion. Stretching one muscle group does not automatically stretch another muscle group or increase the flexibility of another joint. Therefore, gymnasts need to stretch all the muscles related to each joint.

- Remind the gymnasts to stretch the muscles to mild tension and consciously focus on relaxing each stretched muscle. As the muscles relax, the gymnasts should try to stretch a little farther. Gymnasts should not feel pain while stretching. Pain causes the muscles to contract, which may cause injury.

- There is a stretch reflex that automatically contracts, or tightens, the muscles when they are stretched too far. If a muscle is contracting, it is not stretching, which is counterproductive. If a ballistic movement is used for stretching before a muscle is fully warm, the momentum and force may take the joint past its normal range of motion before the stretch reflex can contract. This can cause immediate injury, or a cumulative injury over time.

- Gymnasts should use the joints' normal movement ranges and avoid putting unnecessary pressure, or torque, on joints while warming up and stretching. Many gymnastics skills place the body in unnatural positions—limit additional stress on the joint by avoiding unnecessarily taxing stretches. There are many safe ways to develop the muscles surrounding each joint, so limit the dangerous positions whenever possible.

- Each stretch should be smooth and slow. If a gymnast uses ballistic (bouncing) movements, gravity and momentum may take the muscles past their normal range. Although there is the stretch reflex, the damage has already been done to muscle tissue before the reflex can contract the muscle.

- Many injuries are cumulative. Improper stretching or stress to an area over a long period of time causes damage.

- Some warm-up stretches may be dynamic with slow, controlled movements. Gymnasts should stretch most positions until they feel a mild tension, then they should hold the position for 40 to 60 seconds.

- Encourage gymnasts to sit and stand with proper posture, even when performing stretching exercises.

Exercises to avoid.   Some exercises and skills place too much stress on joints, which can cause injury. Whenever possible, avoid or limit those positions.

Neck Exercises to Avoid
- Avoid extreme flexion of the neck.
- Do not bear any weight on the top of the head, which may result in neck flexion.
- Do not roll the head to the back.

Back Exercises to Avoid
- Avoid any unsupported bending forward at the waist from a standing position. If the back is unsupported, all the upper-body weight hangs on two vertebrae in the lower back. When bending forward from a standing position, support body weight by placing the hands on the thighs. The preferred way to stretch the back would be from a sitting or lying position.
- Avoid straight-leg sit-ups or straight leg lifts; these cause the lower back to arch, which places too much stress on the lower back.
- Avoid extreme back arching. When back arching is necessary, focus on an equal bending of the lower back and upper back. Avoid bending the lower back more than the upper back.

Knee Exercises to Avoid
- The knees should not be flexed more than 90 degrees while standing; the knees also should not be unsupported. The knees should not go past the toes when you are standing and supporting weight.

- During a runner's lunge, keep the knee over the ankle, which is the base of support.
- Do not perform the hurdler's stretch, which involves sitting with one leg extended in front and the other leg flexed and behind the body. This stretch puts too much torque on the bent knee. The same benefit can be achieved by sitting with the bent leg folded toward the body and the foot resting on the inner thigh.
- Do not lock (hyperextend) the legs. Keep the knee joint soft and slightly flexed.

Safe stretching exercises.   The following exercises are effective and safe when performed properly, and they make up a complete stretching routine.

Head and Neck

- Turn the head to the left and position the chin over the left shoulder. Then turn the head to the right and position the chin over the right shoulder.
- Tilt the head to the left, bringing the left ear toward the left shoulder. Tilt the head to the right and bring the right ear toward the right shoulder.
- Lift the head slowly and look at the ceiling. Drop the chin slowly toward the chest (no extreme forward or backward flexion of the neck).
- Roll the head from one side, to the front, and to the other side in a slow, controlled manner (do not roll the head to the back).

Torso

- Stand and slide the hands down the thighs to a supported pike position with the back flat. Round the back all the way up one vertebra at a time, sliding hands up the thighs and tightening the abdominal muscles. Repeat the flatback and rounded positions.
- In supported pike, slowly rotate the torso by pressing one shoulder down. Then rotate the other way and press the other shoulder down.
- Sit on the floor in a pike position with soft knees. Extend arms in the air over the head and slowly reach toward the toes with a straight back. Hold that position.
- Sit on the floor in a straddle. (See chapter 3, page 56 for a description of the straddle position.) Keep one leg extended with the knee soft and flex the other leg, bringing the foot in toward the body in a modified hurdle. Extend arms over the head, turn the body toward the outstretched leg, and slowly reach to the toes. Repeat with other leg.
- Sit on the floor with knees bent and feet together with soles touching (butterfly position). Place hands on the ankles, not the toes. Sit up tall and use the elbows to press the knees toward the floor. Then slide the feet away from the body and lean the chest forward toward the feet.
- In butterfly position, place the arms on the floor behind the body and lean back, stretching and slightly arching the back.
- Sit with left leg extended. Cross the right leg over the left leg, rotate torso to the right, place left elbow against the knee, and press, causing more rotation of the torso. Repeat on other side.
- Lie prone (face down) on the floor and place hands underneath shoulders in push-up position. Keep the lower body on the floor and extend the arms to lift shoulders and chest slowly off the floor, stretching the back. Only lift until mild tension is felt and then hold. Do not lift both upper body and lower body off the floor at the same time.

Arms and Shoulders

- Perform shoulder shrugs by lifting the shoulders toward the ears and then pressing the shoulders toward the floor. Repeat 8 to 10 times.
- Move shoulders forward, making the body hollow, then move the shoulders backward. Repeat 8 to 10 times.
- Perform shoulder rolls backward, then forward. Repeat 8 to 10 times.

- Perform arm circles forward from shoulders, starting with small circles and gradually increasing the size of the circles. Repeat with arm circles backward. Repeat 8 to 10 times.
- Place the arms overhead by the ears, extending from the shoulders and reaching as high as possible. Then, slowly place the arms in oblique (at a diagonal from the body) and hold.
- Cross one arm over in front of the body, keeping the shoulders down. Use the other hand on the outside of the upper arm to gently pull the arm in toward the chest. Repeat with other arm.
- Extend one arm up in the air and flex the arm, placing the hand into the middle of the back. Use the other hand at the elbow to gently push against the elbow so that the hand reaches farther down the back. Repeat with the other arm.
- Get in a crab position (hands and feet on the floor and abdomen facing the ceiling). Lift hips until torso is parallel with the floor. Shift the weight toward the feet to stretch the shoulders. (You may need to extend the feet so that the knees do not go past the toes.)
- Interlock the hands behind the back and lift the arms upward.

Wrists, Hands, and Fingers

- Perform wrist circles. Circle the wrists one way and then the other way.
- Interlock fingers and palms together. Alternately flex and rotate the wrists.
- Interlock fingers, turn the hands away from the body, and stretch the hands forward.
- Make fists with the hands and then open and spread the fingers as wide as possible. Repeat 8 to 10 times.
- Shake hands and fingers, then wave hands and fingers.
- Get on hands and knees and press hands to the floor, keeping elbows extended. Shift forward and place weight over hands. Position fingers in each direction: forward, sideward, and inward (toward knees).

Legs, Ankles, and Feet

- Perform a runner's lunge with the front knee bent at 90 degrees directly over the foot and the back leg extended to the back with toes on the floor. Place hands on the floor on either side of the front foot. Drop the hips as much as possible to make a backward diagonal straight line from the knee of the front leg to the toes of the back foot.
- In runner's lunge, place the knee of the back leg on the floor and gently push the hips forward. Place the hands on the floor or on the knee of the front leg for balance. Bring the back foot up to the buttocks and hold with the opposite hand.
- Stand in a lunge, keeping the back heel on the floor as the front foot moves forward to stretch the calf of the back leg (gastrocnemius and soleus muscles and Achilles tendon).
- Perform pliés by standing with legs shoulder-width apart, then bending the knees. Do not take the knees past the toes or bend more than 90 degrees. Repeat 8 to 10 times. Perform with feet parallel, then turned out.
- Stand in a lunge, then shift your weight over the back leg, flexing the weight-bearing knee (knee stays directly over the foot). Place hands on flexed knee for support. Keep the body weight on flexed knee and front leg extended with heel touching and foot flexed. Repeat with other leg.
- Sit in a straddle with the knees bent and the ankles flexed. Place forearms against bent knees and lean forward.
- Perform a straddle split by standing in a straddle support and slowly sliding the legs apart to lower the body until you feel mild tension in the legs. Put the hands on the floor for support. The insides of the feet should be against the floor.
- Perform a stride split by beginning in a runner's lunge position, touching the back knee to the floor. Place the hands on the floor on both sides of the forward leg. Slowly split the legs farther apart to open the angle of the legs. Hold in a static stretch until you feel mild

tension, not pain. Hold the position and relax the muscles, keeping the body weight supported with the arms. As the muscles relax, slide the legs a little farther apart.

- Stand facing a wall about 3 feet away. Lean forward and place the hands against the wall. Keep straight body position and bend the elbows, bringing the chest to the wall while leaving the feet flat on the floor.
- Perform heel raises by standing straight and extending ankles (relevé), lifting to the toes then lowering to flat feet. Repeat 8 to 10 times.
- Perform ankle rolls by sitting or standing and circling ankles one way and then the other way.
- Sitting in a pike with chest and abdomen lifted, point the toes and then flex the feet. Repeat 8 to 10 times.

Conditioning

Gymnasts must develop high levels of flexibility and cardiovascular and muscular conditioning to successfully perform gymnastics skills. This conditioning is more demanding than the warm-up and may be done immediately after the warm-up and stretch, during practice, or at the conclusion of practice.

As mentioned earlier, the best time to develop flexibility is after gymnastics activity, when the muscles are the warmest. The balance between flexibility and strength is especially important to the health of a joint. If a joint is very flexible but not protected by adequate musculature, injury may occur at that joint because there is too much movement and instability. Conversely, if the muscles surrounding a joint are very strong but lack flexibility, injury may occur.

When the muscles surrounding a joint are too strong, a joint may be stretched past its normal range due to a strong muscle contraction. For example, if a very powerful gymnast performs a split leap, she might "pull" a muscle by stretching past her normal range. Also, muscle bulk may limit a gymnast's pass through the range of motion necessary to perform a skill. For example, a gymnast will go through a lever position to a handstand. If muscle bulk limits flexibility, the gymnast will not be able to lever correctly into the handstand. Because she is strong, she might be able to "muscle" her way through to get into the handstand position. However, since the handstand is a prerequisite skill, this gymnast will eventually have difficulty in performing advanced skills.

It is also important to develop opposing muscle groups (adductors and abductors) to provide balance and stability during skills. For example, gymnasts need both strong biceps and triceps to do any handspring work.

To develop muscle strength and power, a person must do some form of resistance training three times per week on all the major muscle groups in the body. Gymnasts need to develop all major muscle groups, but they need to pay particular attention to the development of upper-body strength. Resistance training includes the use of free weights or machine weights (for adolescents and adults), bands, or a person's own body weight.

Here are some examples of resistance training that use a person's own body weight:

- Any movements in which the body weight is supported on the hands
- Any of the support skills on floor, beam, vault, or bars
- Push-ups or modified push-ups
- Abdominal crunches
- Tucked or straight leg lifts from a long hang on bars
- Jump series
- Dips or modified dips on bars
- Single leg lifts on floor while lying on side or sitting in pike

- V-sit exercises: flutter kicks, criss-cross
- Squats (knees not past 90 degrees)
- Mountain walks across floor (deep lunge walks with knees at less than 90 degrees)

Make the exercises fun! Most conditioning exercises can be made into games and entertaining activities for students. This way, students won't think of the conditioning exercises as work. Here are some suggestions, along with chapters in which the general descriptions appear):

- Seal tag (chapter 2).
- Water bugs ("hopping" in the front support, or push-up, position; chapters 2 and 3).
- Crab push-ups (chapter 3).
- Macarena push-ups: Begin in the push-up position; take one hand off floor, touch to opposite shoulder, place back on floor. Repeat with other hand. Continue performing a routine of taking one hand off the floor and balancing on three body parts.
- Open and close the X in a side support (chapter 2, page 32)
- Candle, stretch jump series (chapter 4, pages 139-140)

Landing and Falling

Proper landings are crucial to gymnasts' safety. Landing and falling are skills that should be practiced before the gymnasts need them.

Landing safely. Gymnasts must practice falling properly without hurting themselves, because inevitably through the learning process there will be times when the gymnasts land in unbalanced positions. When gymnasts first feel that they will lose balance, they should bend the knees. Sometimes this action alone will be enough to prevent a fall. Compare the gymnast's bent-knee position to a surfer's balance on a surfboard. You'll notice that if a surfer looks as if he will fall, he bends his knees to lower his center of gravity. But gymnasts will not always regain balance. When that happens, they should be prepared to land and roll out safely.

Gymnasts should practice falling drills until the drills become automatic reactions. Use this progression:

- Practice a safe landing position by bending the knees.
- Sit in a tuck on floor. Rock backward, roll forward, and learn how to stand without using the hands. Then roll back to the floor again without using the hands. This skill is called rock, roll, and stand.
- "Hug your teddy bear" and roll by bringing your arms, legs, and head in to a tucked position.

Up to this point children should perform skills at a height that allows them to perform the safe landing position or the teddy bear hug. Children should not progress to apparatus or skills that are any higher than they can jump until they can successfully perform forward and backward rolls. Then students can practice the following:

- Landings and recovery movements: side, forward, and backward rolls
- Recovery from inverted positions: twisting out of handstands for beam and floor skills
- Elevated drills for landing and falling from different heights
- Bar drills for landing and falling

Landing safely is one of the most important keys in the prevention of injury. The greater the height of the jump, the more important it is to utilize the safe landing position (SLP), especially the bending of the knees to absorb the force. Gymnasts should always try to land on their feet first.

Safe Landing Position

Follow this sequence for the safe landing of a jump:

- Come down on two feet without taking a step.
- Articulate (flex) through the toes, balls, and heels of the feet.
- Bend the knees softly in demi-plié to cushion the landing.
- Align knees directly over the center of the feet.
- Keep abdominal muscles tight and the upper body vertical.
- Arm positions vary for landings, but for practicing falls, keep the arms up and next to the ears, which helps protect the neck and head.

Recovery Movements: Rolls

It is a natural reaction to thrust the hands toward the floor to break the fall in an overrotated landing. When this happens, the arms, wrists, or hands are often injured. Train the gymnasts to perform the safe landing position: hands go over the head and the hips, knees, and ankles collapse to roll to the floor; hands do not stop the momentum. Also train the gymnasts to "hug the teddy bear" as they descend into an egg (side) roll.

Side Roll

Side rolls are necessary when gymnasts overrotate or lose balance in a vertical, forward, or sideward direction. Practice the side roll using this sequence:

- Begin in a lying tuck. Keep the arms up next to the ears or in hug position. Roll over sideways across the floor or down an incline mat.
- Perform the tuck and side roll from a kneeling position. Try rolling to both sides.
- Perform a small stretch jump. Land in safe landing position. As feet land, bend knees and hips to fall by tucking the body. In tuck, roll to your back or side. Then roll to your shins to protect yourself and stop the momentum. It is similar to the fire safety roll: "stop, drop, and roll."

Forward Shoulder Roll

- Stand with legs together.
- Fall forward, placing one arm diagonally across body (right arm to left side).
- Tilt head forward, tucking chin to the chest and to left side.
- Roll diagonally forward from right shoulder down and across back.
- Land sitting and continue rising to a stand.

Backward Shoulder Roll

- Begin in a squat or sitting position.
- Lower the back and lift legs upward with arms placed at the side of the body on the floor.
- Continue moving legs over the body until toes touch floor over right shoulder.
- Turn head and look toward knees.
- Bend knees while still looking at knees and bring left arm off floor to complete the backward roll.
- Transfer the remainder of body weight onto knees in kneeling position.
- Next, perform from a stand.

In addition, practice tuck forward roll (page 127) and tuck backward roll (page 135).

Recovering from inverted positions. Gymnasts may need to recover from handstands and other inverted skills. If a gymnast loses balance while the legs are in the air, he or she should cartwheel out (bring legs down one at a time to the side), twist out, or tuck the head and perform a roll out of the position.

Landing and Falling From Different Heights

Start with a low takeoff surface (6 inches) and have gymnasts perform the safe landing position for landings. Upon landing, gymnasts perform side, forward, and backward rolls. Gradually increase the elevation to 2 to 3 feet above the floor.

Safety note: Do not allow young children or inexperienced gymnasts to jump from any height greater than that which they can generate. As gymnasts gain experience, the apparatus can be raised to chest height.

Landing and Falling From Apparatus

When a gymnast falls from a piece of apparatus, she usually falls from a height and therefore has momentum. Also, the gymnast is likely to land off balance. One of the safest recoveries out of a fall from apparatus is a sideward roll. Teach gymnasts to close theirs fists when falling from a height. They should not try to roll with their hands or break falls with their hands.

Visual Techniques

The development and practice of eye contact is essential for safely and successfully completing gymnastics skills. Remind gymnasts of the importance of using their eyes in performing skills. They need to know where to look before and during skills and when landing. Teach visual techniques as part of every skill and sequence.

Teach gymnasts to maintain eye contact with apparatus or the floor in the intended direction of motion. Many times eye contact occurs in a gymnast's peripheral vision.

Spotting

The purpose of spotting is to assist and protect a gymnast in successfully completing a skill. There are essentially three levels of difficulty in spotting. It is easiest for you to spot when you can place your hands on the gymnast before the gymnast starts to move. A back walkover is an example of such a spot. The next level is when you put your hands on the gymnast before he or she moves but you must travel with the gymnast. An example of this is a back handspring series. The most difficult spot is when you cannot touch the gymnast until he or she starts moving; in this situation you must get into position quickly. An example of this is a round-off to back handspring. As a spotter, you must judge when to get into position. If you move in too early or too late, you risk getting in the way of the gymnast's movement and being unable to keep the gymnast safe.

Not all skills need spotting, however. Nor does spotting always involve putting the gymnast through the entire skill. The gymnast may only need assistance during one phase of a skill. You may need to give support to prevent injury or help the gymnast perfect the skill. Following are several examples of the degrees of spotting.

Facilitating spot. In this spot, the spotter actually completes the skill for the gymnast by supporting the entire weight of the gymnast. This spot is used when the gymnast is first learning a new movement or skill or when a skill needs a modification in direction, quality, or magnitude.

Safety spot. The safety, or hands-on, spot is used when the instructor is concerned about the safe completion of a skill. The spotter may support the weight for a portion of the skill.

Light spot. A light hands-on spot is used when the gymnast can perform the skill but lacks confidence. The gymnast feels more comfortable when he or she can feel a hand on the body at the start of the skill. This is the time to gradually reduce the amount of support.

Touch or tap. A touch or tap on a body part as a reminder that the spotter is there may be all that a gymnast needs to complete the skill.

Spotter ready. The spotter is standing ready to provide assistance if needed.

Spotters are facilitators of skills both in support and in timing, especially if there is danger or risk from incorrect placement of the head, hitting a piece of equipment, or falling on or from apparatus or in an inverted position. The head, neck, and spinal column must always be protected. The most common contact points for spotting are the gymnast's upper arms, wrists, back, abdomen, waist, hips, and legs.

When spotting, initially help throughout the complete skill. If the gymnast is safe, give some assistance but allow the gymnast to feel the skill. Spotting should gradually diminish in the amount of support as the gymnast learns a skill. If the spotter continues to do most of the work, the gymnast needs to perform more progressions and specific conditioning related to the skill.

Guidelines for Spotting

- Know the gymnast. Assess if the gymnast is developmentally ready to perform the skill. (Can the gymnast perform the prerequisites? Does he or she have the necessary strength and flexibility? Does he or she understand the skill? Is he or she mentally ready? Does he or she have any special physical conditions?) Be sure that the difficulty level of the skill is appropriate to the capabilities of the gymnast.

- Know the mechanics of the skill. What is the position of the body from the beginning to end of the skill? In what direction is the skill moving? What part of the body produces the force or momentum to initiate the skill? What parts of the body control the movement of the skill?

- Know the mechanics of the spot. What parts need to be supported? What force should the spotter give? What parts of the body are at risk? In what part of the skill are accidents most likely to occur? The spotter must understand the more critical aspects of the skill and how and where to spot.

- When you are first learning how to spot, practice with a gymnast who already knows how to perform the skill or is small and light. You must match your own capabilities to that of the gymnast.

- Decide how much of a spot will be needed and get in a ready position so that close physical contact can be maintained during the skill. Do not hinder or restrict the normal movement of the skill.

- Make sure that the gymnast is prepared physically through warm-up and conditioning.

- Be mentally and physically prepared. Know what skill the gymnast is going to perform. Be prepared for anything to happen. Be warmed up and physically strong enough to spot the skill.

- Communicate clearly. Establish a clear communication link with the gymnast. Establish eye contact, have the gymnast repeat the instructions, and use a signal to show that both the gymnast and spotter are ready.

- Always protect the gymnast's head, neck, and spinal column.

- As the gymnast's proficiency increases, reduce the spot.

- Stay alert! Have your hands ready!

TEACHING EFFECTIVELY

Successful gymnastics classes have a reliable structure and provide learners the opportunity to expand on what they already know. Gymnasts should move through three phases in gymnastics education: exploration, foundational skills, and formal gymnastics. *All* of the phases should be included in the physical education curriculum. Students should explore at least the beginning formal gymnastics skills in a physical education program. If the school has the proper facilities and equipment and you are highly trained to teach gymnastics, a physical education program may include intermediate and advanced skills. Typically, the private gym setting is where gymnasts perform intermediate and advanced skills. Good teachers know *what* they're teaching, and they also know *how* to present it effectively.

The Movement Chart

Rudolf von Laban, a leader in modern dance in the 1920s and '30s, was the first to chart movement and develop themes. Because of von Laban's influence, movement charts are used today as the basis for educational gymnastics as well as for dance and other areas of physical education. An example of part of a movement chart is shown in table 1.1.

Table 1.1   *SPATIAL AWARENESS*

DIRECTIONS	AREAS	PATHWAYS	LEVELS	DISTANCE	RANGES	PLANES
Forward	Upward	General	Straight	High	Near	Large	Horizontal
Backward	Downward	Personal	Curved	Medium	Away	Medium	Frontal
Left	Diagonal		Zigzag	Low	Toward	Small	Sagittal
Right							

Movement charts list the possible concepts or themes necessary to develop the psychomotor domain. Movement charts are helpful in planning lessons; they give students a variety of experiences to develop their repertoire of skills. A movement chart that utilizes general motor concepts should be used in the exploratory, or developmental, stages of gymnastics. Each chapter of this book contains a movement chart to assist instructors in planning and progressing through the skills.

Exploratory Gymnastics

Exploratory gymnastics may also be called educational or developmental gymnastics. This approach allows gymnasts to explore the different elements of the gymnastics movement chart such as body awareness, basic body positions, balance, support, locomotor skills, and circular movements. These skills simulate all the major movement patterns used in children's gymnastics development.

Exploratory gymnastics contrasts significantly with formal gymnastics in that it allows students to respond to a movement challenge in a variety of ways. An example of a movement challenge is "Find all the ways you can jump and land on two feet." There is no one correct way to solve the challenge and there is no exactness expected. This allows the learners to explore, discover how their bodies move, and respond in ways that are appropriate for their abilities. Everyone is able to solve the challenge; therefore, everyone feels successful. The focus of the lesson is on problem solving, which in turn allows gymnasts to develop body-management skills as they solve the movement problems. This method also allows for individual differences. When given the opportunity to solve a movement problem, a child will perform what is developmentally appropriate at his or her own stage of development. Children who are more physically developed will solve problems in ways that require more balance and coordination than less physically developed children would. Children who are less physically developed will "play it safe" and perform at their own ability levels.

Foundational Positions and Movements

Learners should acquire foundational positions and movements after exploring and discovering how their own bodies move. Foundational positions are the basic body positions known by their formal names, as well as basic balance, support, locomotor, and rotational movements. Children must spend time identifying, practicing, and perfecting these foundational positions and movements to develop strength, flexibility, kinesthetic and spatial awareness, balance, basic coordination, correct weight placement, and positioning. The foundational positions and movements will prepare gymnasts for beginning skills on floor, beam, bars, and springboard and vault.

Formal Gymnastics

Formal gymnastics skills are often called general or traditional gymnastics. An exact movement is expected when a gymnast performs a formal gymnastics skill. Lead-ups and floor skills should be the first formal gymnastics lesson. The purpose of lead-ups to formal gymnastics skills is to break down the skills into smaller, more manageable parts and then put the parts together as a whole. Unlike the activities in exploratory gymnastics, lead-ups are specific and correctness is expected. Teaching skills step by step in a progression is the safest and most productive way for children to learn because the skills build on previous learning. Lead-ups are the small, progressive steps that ensure the success of a formal gymnastics skill. Teachers should look for movement patterns that students can perform to help build the skills.

Drills are another important part of teaching gymnastics. A drill can be a lead-up or part of the movement pattern of a skill. It can also be an activity from the same movement family that helps develop strength, flexibility, and body awareness to better prepare gymnasts for a skill or series of skills.

After progressing through lead-ups, gymnasts should move on to beginning, intermediate, and advanced skills. Skill development is the focus in the floor, balance beam, vault, and bars chapters. Lead-ups and drills and beginning, intermediate, and advanced skills are illustrated and described in these chapters.

Progressions

Progressions allow students to develop skills at a gradual, natural pace. Provide plenty of opportunities for exploration and problem solving by making sure that students build on the skills they know.

- Spend part of each class reviewing previously taught skills. Repetition is an important part of skill development and will help gymnasts make connections from one skill to another in the progression.

- Add variety by changing approaches, body positions, and finishes. One simple change may help motivate the learners to continue to practice a skill.

- Break all the skills down into smaller parts. Practice the small parts one at a time. Then put small parts together before telling the students to attempt the entire skill. Another approach is to teach a general version of a skill first and add specifics or variations later.

- Master core skills and skills on the floor before moving to apparatus.

- Master the simple version of a skill before attempting a variation or challenge.

- Use a low piece of apparatus during the initial instruction of a skill. Gradually increase the height of the apparatus.

- Give students choices so that they can pick the activity in which they can succeed.

- Many times there will be a wide range of skill levels in one class. To keep more advanced gymnasts motivated while practicing a skill they already know, add variations and challenges. For example, while the entire class is practicing cartwheels, have the more advanced gymnasts add a second skill to the cartwheel to create a combination skill. Give choices so that the more advanced students will select the more advanced skill while the beginners will choose a skill they can perform. Both will feel a sense of challenge and accomplishment.

Combinations and Routines

No physical education teacher would dream of doing an entire basketball unit in which the students only do drills and never scrimmage or play a bit of the game. The gymnastics "game" is played by performing combinations or a routine: joining isolated skills together to create a unit greater than the sum of its parts. You must be observant and consider the interest level of the students. You could spend weeks of class time on gymnastics skills and lose many of your students to boredom! Therefore, you should offer a variety of made-up routines of different levels *and* a menu of skills that the students may pick from if they would rather make their own routines. Students may perform an individual routine or perform with a partner or group. This would add collaborative skills, which would help develop the affective domain (development of social/teamwork skills) for the students. The more choices you give the students, the better able they are to individualize their routines to fit their strengths and guarantee success. Think of it as a meal: one item from column A, one from column B. For example, one skill is the vegetable (an essential element, but the student's least favorite) and one skill is the dessert (the student's favorite skill). Combine locomotor skills, balances, rotation movements, and so on. Each person will be better at one category than he or she is at the other categories; you want to make sure that each child gets at least a taste of his or her preferred category at each lesson. We like to do what we do well; no one enjoys, forgets, or deserves embarrassment, especially in front of peers.

Pedagogy Tips

Teaching well means reaching every student and having a plan for success. It is the "science" of teaching, which is knowing your content, as well as the "art" of teaching, which is the delivery and teaching strategies incorporated into the teaching.

Success in teaching gymnastics also means creating an inviting environment so that students can learn. You've heard the saying "You can lead a horse to water but you can't make it drink." But you can make the water very inviting: make it clean, attractive, and free of pollution. This principle applies to a gymnastics setting. Make sure that every student can be successful every day. Make sure that no one performs solo or is embarrassed in front of peers. Students should be actively engaged during the class, not waiting in lines or listening to and watching long explanations and demonstrations.

Teaching in a School Setting

Physical education experts recommend that exploratory and beginning gymnastics make up one-third of the elementary curriculum. These activities build body awareness, strength, balance, and overall coordination that will lead to success not only in higher-level gymnastics skills but also in individual, team, and leisure sports and activities. In the secondary schools a unit in gymnastics should be taught annually. As a physical education teacher, you must be knowledgeable and establish credibility with those students who are involved in competitive gymnastics.

Schedule the gymnastics unit for the end of the school year, but start teaching toward it the very first day of school by including strength and conditioning activities as well as the locomotor activities that will prepare the student for gymnastics. Many of the strength-building, flexibility, and body-awareness activities listed in this book can be done in a regular physical education setting without special matting or equipment. You should spend 5 to 10 minutes on these developmental activities every class meeting; this will be appropriate for whatever unit you are currently teaching, and it will also prepare your students for success in the gymnastics unit later in the year. Most physical education classes spend 3 to 6 weeks on a unit. It is unrealistic to expect students to show dramatic improvement in flexibility and upper-body strength to allow good gymnastics skill growth if you don't address the developmental gymnastics issues until the gymnastics unit starts.

Once you introduce the gymnastics unit, you can apply the skills practiced all year to the gymnastics skills. Children who believe themselves incapable of ever doing gymnastics will have a wonderful revelation when they discover that they *have* been performing "gymnastics" all year.

Using these activities year-round will improve the entire physical education program at your school, not just improve the success of the gymnastics unit. Research is painfully clear about the poor physical condition of our children, and the weakest area is upper-body strength. Research also suggests that there is a window of opportunity in which to develop flexibility. After the onset of puberty it becomes much more difficult to increase range of motion, and gained flexibility is only temporary. A quality physical education program develops flexibility, muscular strength (especially upper-body strength), and body awareness—all the goals of the gymnastics preparation activities presented in this book.

Generally, in a school or recreational gymnastics setting, exploratory gymnastics would be taught in the primary grades, lead-ups and beginning skills in primary and intermediate grades, and intermediate and advanced skills in the upper grades. Each year you would build slowly and progressively add to the skill development of each child.

Choose Your Words

Choosing your words carefully can make a big difference to learners. Here are a few ways you can use words to better instruct and motivate your students:

- Begin each lesson or activity with an introduction. Tell students what skill they will be developing or practicing. Check for previous knowledge by asking questions. List the main points of the activity, including safety, to help the student make connections between prior knowledge and the activity of the day. For example: "Today we are going to practice a tuck jump. Last class we worked on the stretch jump. What do you remember about the landing? What did you do to jump high?"

- When in the exploratory stage, phrase challenges beginning with words that encourage problem solving: *explore, find another way, try,* and so on. For example, "Explore all the ways you can . . . (support, balance, move)."

- Use a variety of verbal cues to meet the needs of all learners. Begin by using the cues that are provided in this book. Eventually it will become more automatic, and you will start adding to and developing your own learning cues for the different learning styles. *Learning style* means the style that the learner prefers or learns best from. Most young children are visual learners and learn best by being able to see the skill performed, seeing a picture of the skill, or imagining the skill and how it would look. (See "Know Yoour Students" on page 22.)

- Have the gymnasts describe the skills to you or to another gymnast. Have the gymnasts personalize what they saw or felt while performing the skill. Ask them to tell you if they could see their hands, the apparatus, or the wall. Which muscles were tight or relaxed? How did other parts of the body feel while you performed the skill? Was the body vertical, horizontal, parallel, perpendicular, symmetrical, or asymmetrical? So many of the terms used every day are very abstract until we experience their meaning (for example, *on top of, beside, horizontal*). Asking students to verbalize, analyze, and describe the skills will help them develop the cognitive domain and enhance higher-order thinking skills as well as help them make more "connections" to be successful.

- Ask open-ended questions to engage gymnasts and make them aware of what is happening. Ask, "What do you need to do to get more height on that jump?"; "How does it feel when you are . . . ?"; "What do you see when you are . . . ?"; "How can you describe . . . part of the skill?"; "What are the lines the body makes when you are . . . ?"

- Use positive phrasing to tell the gymnasts what you want them to do. For example, say, "Keep your arms straight and your head neutral," instead of, "Don't bend your arms," or, "Stop lifting your head." Give immediate, specific positive reinforcement. For example, "That was good because you kept your legs together and toes pointed."

- Use a technique called the "compliment sandwich" by first stating a positive, then a suggestion or a correction, and ending with a positive:

1. Positive: "Great! You kept your arms straight."
2. Instruction: "Try turning a little earlier."
3. Positive: "I like the way you're focused and working today."

- Ask the gymnasts to analyze, compare, and describe the skills. For example, "What is different about the hand placement of the cartwheel and the round-off? What are the similarities and differences between the two skills?"

Break It Down

Many learners will understand complicated movements more easily if you can break skills down into more manageable bites. Use a variety of visuals such as charts, videos, CD-ROMs, digital video discs (DVDs), and real-life demonstrations to help you convey your message.

Also, be sure to show good transitions from one progression to another so that the learners can see the connections. For intermediate and advanced skills, tell the learners why a skill is a progression and explain the purpose of the formal lead-up. For example, "You need good hand placement for a good round-off. So, perform a cartwheel and change just one thing: the hand placement. This will keep your focus on the one change—hand placement—as you perform something familiar—the cartwheel."

When breaking skills down, utilize the part–whole method of teaching or the whole–part–whole method. In the whole–part–whole method, the skill is shown to the gymnast. They might even try the skill. Then they improve their performance by analyzing and performing each small part of the skill. Eventually, they will put all of the pieces together to perform the whole skill. In the part–whole method, the parts are introduced individually, then the parts are put together to form the whole skill. Here's an example:

Parts of a Forward Roll

- Back rocker
- Seated tuck, back rocker, seated tuck or squat
- Seated tuck, back rocker to tuck stand
- Seated tuck, back rocker, squat, stand
- Straight-body stand, pike support, roll to inverted tuck, tuck stand
- Straight-body stand, pike support, roll to inverted tuck, tuck stand, straight-body stand, salute

Keep learners engaged in learning a skill by varying it. For example, have students perform a forward roll on an incline and on the floor. Have them perform the forward roll from a different starting position. Have them perform a forward roll and, upon completion, perform a jump in straddle, pike, stretch, or tuck position.

Let the Learner Be Your Guide

Ensure that each learner experiences success during each class. Offer progressions, choices, and challenges that are appropriate to each gymnast's abilities. Do not put a gymnast in an embarrassing situation where they feel unsuccessful in front of their peers. Help all learners set appropriate goals for their abilities.

At the end of each lesson provide closure questions. This allows the student to reflect and think about what they have learned from the lesson. This provides an opportunity for the connections and reinforcement in their learning.

Structure in the Class

Classes need structure because students thrive on ordered classes. Structure also provides the element of safety that is necessary in the gymnastics setting. Structure comes from, among other things, the formations you use to divide students and the activity space. Many formations can be used during the warm-up and stretching phase of a lesson as well as the specific skill lesson.

Scattered Formation

Many exploratory gymnastics challenges, warm-up activities, and stretching activities usually do not require special equipment. Students may be scattered in a designated area for these activities. Encourage students to find their own personal space so that they cannot touch anyone else if they reach out in any direction.

Stations

Stations are an ideal way to organize a large number of students. Small groups of students (four to eight) rotate among stations and work on assigned learning tasks. For example, you may give students 5 minutes to work at a station with four or five tasks. Give a cue or signal to rotate to a new station after the time has elapsed.

Teaching in stations may take a little more planning. Here are some recommendations to help you make the most of teaching in stations.

- Select tasks that use proper progression and cover all the basic skills of an activity.
- Select tasks that provide students with success and challenge. The tasks should be varied to offer developmentally appropriate activities for the gymnasts' skill levels.
- Avoid activities that are excessively risky and could cause injury. One station could be the area where you give instruction and spot the activity. If this is the case, students must understand that you may change their group's activity if there is an interruption or if you need to attend to other students.
- Use task cards for each station. The task card gives instructions for the challenges to be accomplished at the station. Make the task cards easy to understand. Drawings, simple key words, and descriptions will explain what to do and how to do it.
- When students work in different areas, you must take extra safety precautions. You must position your body so that you can see all of the students in the class. Sometimes this is

Sample Stations With Beginning Skills

- **Balance beam station.** Walk forward with beanbag on head, backward with beanbag on shoulder, and sideward with beanbag on elbow. Find other ways to walk and balance a beanbag.
- **Low horizontal bar station.** Perform swings in tuck, straddle L, pike.
- **Body position.** Review standing body positions: hollow, arch, lunge, finishing lunge, straddle, stride, salute.
- **Flexibility and strength circuit.** Perform animal moves down the mat (bear, inchworm, frog). Perform different types of supports (on three body parts, two body parts).
- **Roll circuit.** Perform a straight-body roll. Perform a side tuck roll. Perform a tuck, back rocker to tuck, then stand.
- **Parallel bar station.** Perform supported hangs in tuck, straddle L, pike.
- **Balance station.** Perform arabesque, front scale, and V-sit.
- **Agility station.** Jump rope. Try the skier, straddle, and boxer.
- **Support station.** Between stacked mats, support the body in tuck, straddle, and pike, support walks (chimp, gorilla) then back to front of the mat stacks.
- **Springboard station (with instructor spotting).** Perform squat-on vault.

called the "back to the wall" position because you do not turn your back to the class. This may mean setting up stations so that you have a view of the class if you are spotting at one station.

- Another safety precaution is a stop signal. If you must take care of a situation, you can stop the class instead of putting yourself in a position where you cannot give your attention to the class or to a group you are working with. On your signal, all students would stop and sit at their station and wait for further instruction. You could also give the students a flexibility exercise to perform while they are waiting.

Challenge Course

A challenge course is similar to station teaching in that students follow a circuit to complete tasks. The course provides a pathway to be followed with different challenges along the way. The difference is that the gymnasts perform the task once and then move to the next activity without waiting for a signal to rotate. Each person works independently or with a partner to accomplish the tasks. Students can pass other students and complete the circuit more than once. This allows each student to perform at his or her own pace.

Instead of having all the students wait in line to begin the obstacle course, you can give each student a task number to start. Assign a number to each task on the challenge course. Have each student begin at his or her number on the course.

Tumbling Techniques With a Partner

Space the mats apart with three or four students assigned to each mat. Each gymnast works with a partner. One gymnast (the performer) is on the mat, and the other gives feedback. Then

Sample Challenge Course

1. Walk in a zigzag pattern to balance beam.
2. Walk across the beam in relevé.
3. Perform a crab walk to incline mat.
4. Roll down the incline.
5. Perform the inchworm to the tunnel.
6. Crawl through the tunnel.
7. Perform a gallop to mat stack.
8. Perform a straddle-on to the top of mat stack.
9. Perform a bear walk to push-up station.
10. Perform 10 modified push-ups.
11. Move backward to bar station.
12. Perform tuck, pike, and straddle hangs.
13. Jump inside each hoop to beam. Perform an arabesque on the beam.
14. Perform low leaps to the floor station.
15. Perform a backward roll down the incline.
16. Perform side chassés to the beam.
17. Perform a front support to straddle, V-sit, swing legs to squat, then stand. Perform a pivot turn. Stretch jump dismount on the end.
18. Perform a step-on mount then a straddle jump dismount.
19. Move on four body parts to vaulting box.
20. Climb over vaulting box.
21. Use 4 jumps to get to jump rope station.
22. Perform 20 jumps in a row as fast as you can.
23. Walk toe, ball, heel very slowly to floor station.
24. Perform a cartwheel over the jump rope.
25. Balance in scale or arabesque for the count of 15.
26. Jump over cones to next floor station.
27. Perform 5 consecutive tuck jumps.
28. Run to next station and jump on target with two feet.
29. Move to mat and perform a safety fall with shoulder roll.
30. Skip to start of runway for next station.
31. Wait for instructor's signal. Perform a straddle-through vault.

reverse the duties. To provide more structure, use the command style of teaching: "Number 1s, get on the mat. Get in ready position, place hands on mat in pike support, roll, stand. Now 1s off the mat, number 2s on the mat. Get in ready position, place hands on mat in pike support, roll, stand." Find ways to actively involve or engage the person who is waiting. That student could check the performer's body positioning, describe and analyze the movement, give feedback, or perform a balance activity such as a passé or coupé (see chapter 3 for basic dance positions).

Skills on Semicircle or Parallel Mats

Place mats in a semicircle or parallel to one another with no more than four students in line sitting at the end of each mat. State the skill to be accomplished. Give a starting signal for the skill to begin. (Be sure to tell students that this is not a race.) Only one person is to be on a mat at a time. On stopping signal, students return and sit behind mat and wait for instruction.

Biomechanics Related to Gymnastics

The whole body and individual body parts may be straight or bent, causing segmentation. If the gymnast's body is in a straight line, there is only one segment. If the gymnast bends at the waist to a pike position, there are two segments. Basically, gymnastics happens because of the body's movement into segments—going into small segments and going out. Typically, problems occur when a gymnast performs too many segments at once or the gymnast doesn't bend or straighten at the proper time during the skill. Segmentation is necessary for cause and effect—the longer the segment, the slower the body will rotate. When a segment is shortened (for example, arms that have been extended at side middle are flexed and brought in to the body), the rotation speeds up. However, each segment is usually slight.

Balance

Gymnastics is a sequence of starting with the body in balance, taking the body out of balance, and then bringing the body back into balance. One of the most difficult things that a gymnast must learn is to accept the momentary feeling of being out of balance. It is the loss of balance and learning the appropriate way to recapture the balance that forms the skill.

Here's an example: As a gymnast lowers her body for a forward roll, she is really falling and is out of balance until she tucks her head and rolls. Or when a gymnast shifts her weight to perform a back handspring, she has a moment when she is out of balance before and during the push from her feet backward into a handstand position.

Base of Support

The base of support is the body part(s) that supports the gymnast's body weight. Included in the base of support are the space between the body parts and apparatus if it is used to support the body. The larger the body surfaces (hips, back, shoulders) and the larger the base of support (two hands and two feet), the more stable the balance. Generally, a wide base of support will distribute the body weight over more space and will be more stable unless the base becomes too wide; then balance becomes a factor and the body becomes unstable.

Center of Gravity

The center of gravity is the center of the body or point at which the body would revolve if rotated by an outside force. If a person stands in a straight body position with the arms out to the side, the center of gravity would be somewhere between the hips and waist. There is a direct relationship between the base of support and the center of gravity.

- The center of gravity changes because of changes in body parts, body position, or base of support.
- The closer the center of gravity is to the base of support, the more stable the object will be.

- The closer the center of gravity is to the radius of rotation, the faster an object will move.
- The higher the center of gravity is upon landing of a vault, floor skill, or a dismount, the lighter and more controlled the landing will be.

Action and reaction. For every action there is a reaction. For example, in a handstand the body should be straight and tight and the head in neutral. If the gymnast lifts the head (causing segmentation), the back will arch. In contrast, if the gymnast tucks the head, the back will round.

Axis of rotation. An axis of the body is the line through the center of gravity around which rotation occurs. In a freely suspended, unsupported body, the axis of rotation passes through the center of gravity. In a supported body, the axis is at the contact point or in a nearby joint making contact.

Adjusting the body parts around the axis of rotation will speed up or slow down the rotation. When body parts are extended, the rotation slows down; when body parts are tucked, the rotation speeds up. There are three axes of rotation:

1. Longitudinal plane (twisting): A longitudinal line runs from head to toe. It divides the body in half symmetrically. Examples of movements in the longitudinal plane are log rolls, pirouettes, and jump full turns.

2. Horizontal/transverse plane (rotational): A transverse line runs parallel to the floor at any level from side to side. Examples of movements in the transverse plane are forward and backward rolls on floor and hip circles on bars.

3. Medial/sagittal plane (sideward): A sagittal line runs perpendicular to the body at any level and goes from back to front. An example of a movement in the medial/sagittal plane is a cartwheel.

Force and Center of Gravity

Gravity is a force that acts on all objects, the whole body, and parts of the body. Force from gravity is always in a downward vertical direction. In order for motion to occur, force must be applied to displace the center of gravity past the base of support. Gravity can be used to an advantage on some skills by displacing the center of gravity to move the body forward or backward with the pull of gravity. For example, if a gymnast is going to perform a front hips circle on the horizontal bar, she would begin in a front support position with weight over the hands. When the gymnast wants to go forward, she moves her shoulders forward, shifting her center of gravity and allowing the forward movement.

A force applied directly through the center of gravity will move the body in the direction of the force of the application, which is called linear motion. A force applied away from the center of gravity will cause rotation, which is called rotary motion. As a spotter, you must understand this concept in order to correctly apply force to assist gymnasts with skills.

Absorption of force. As a gymnast jumps higher or jumps down from an object, he or she must learn how to dissipate the force of the body. The "giving," or force absorption, occurs through the bending of the joints, which allows the body to keep moving and gradually slow down. For example, when the gymnast jumps from the balance beam, she will bend at the hips, knees, and ankles to absorb the force of the landing.

Force production. Force must be produced to counteract gravity in many gymnastics moves. For example, in a jump, there must be a coordinated effort of both the arms and the legs. The bending of the hips, knees, and ankles and the backward swing of the arms are followed by a pushing of the legs against the floor with an upward swing of the arms to full extension. This coordinated movement with the correct timing generates the force for the gymnast to leave the ground.

Know Your Students

Every child filters information in a different way (table 1.2). Preschool children are primarily either visual/spatial or auditory learners. Girls are primarily auditory learners and young boys are primarily visual/spatial learners. As children develop, so do different learning styles or preferences. Adults usually filter most information through two or three preferred learning styles, with one being dominant.

Historically, most education has been based on learning, teaching, and testing linguistically. This meant that if the verbal/linguistic style was not a person's strongest method of processing information, that person would have difficulty learning. If gymnastics were only taught linguistically, the information would primarily reach the auditory learners. With young children, that generally means that girls would process the information more effectively than boys. Certainly, in an area that has a kinesthetic basis and requires so much spatial activity, all available approaches should be utilized.

Gardner's concept of multiple intelligence encourages the instructor to offer a variety of cues to the learners, who may use different intelligences to process information. Programs should reflect the abilities, needs, interests, and learning styles of each person. Therefore, a wide range of teaching approaches and verbal cues should be used to meet the needs of all learners.

This expansive approach to teaching also helps people to understand relationships between ideas, concepts, people, and things in the world. The following are descriptions of the various types of learners. The following list was developed based on Gardner's theory.

Verbal/Linguistic Learners

Verbal/linguistic learners respond to auditory information and relate to terminology and language. This intelligence is used in listening, speaking, reading, and writing. These learners enjoy lengthy descriptions and the use of correct terms. Give vivid verbal instructions to these learners. Use proper gymnastics terms such as "extend," "flex," and "invert."

Logical/Mathematical Learners

This learning style deals with inductive and deductive reasoning, numbers, and relationships. Logical learners have the ability to recognize patterns and shapes and to make connections between pieces of information. These learners relate to analytical, concrete, and sequential descriptions. When teaching logical learners, list the sequence of steps and use percentages, degrees, angles, and mathematical concepts when giving instructions. The students will need to analyze and sequentially break down the skill or combination. They also may need to be led through a skill step by step. They respond well to lists of progressions or skill charts.

Bodily/Kinesthetic Learners

Kinesthetic learners process information primarily through bodily sensation. These learners relate to physical movement and inner physical knowledge. They have a finely attuned sense of touching, feeling, moving, and experiencing. They use full body movement and feel comfortable trying physical skills initially and repeatedly. Given the proper training, they usually have excellent gross and fine motor coordination. They feel their body parts making contact with other body parts, with the mat and apparatus, and with the teacher's hands during spotting. The kinesthetic sense can be isolated when the learners work quietly by closing the eyes to better feel the hand placement of the roll or cartwheel, the lunge to handstand, or whatever element of a skill the learners are acquiring. If body parts are manipulated or moved, learners get the "feel" of the skill. A small touch will tell learners to make a correction. The use of different textures in matting and in hand and foot spots can also be very helpful for tactile learners.

Interpersonal Learners

Interpersonal learners learn the best while in an interactive social setting. They enjoy working with partners, with the coach, or in small groups; they will be the most productive while working in one of these settings. Because they are peer-motivated and have strong sociological needs, they are great demonstrators. Involve them in every skill by having them work with partners who give feedback. Frequent interaction—such as cooperative games with partners; group work in practicing skills; and home projects with parents, siblings, or those in their peer groups—will help to keep these learners on track.

Intrapersonal Learners

Intrapersonal learners draw from previous experience and are good at linking concepts for greater understanding. They learn best by working independently and tend to be self-motivated. They need time to absorb information and explore skills on their own without too much input from the outside world. They use trial and error and prefer to figure out things on their own. Since intrapersonal learners are self-paced and self-directed, they respond well when given a project with a number or goal in mind, such as "Practice until your legs are straight," or "Perform 10 handstands that hit vertical." They also do well when placed slightly apart from the others (perhaps at the end of a line) so that they can learn in their own medium and have spaces of time in which they can learn on their own. Help interpersonal and intrapersonal learners feel comfortable by giving them challenges and choices. "Either by yourself, or with a partner, perform...."

Musical/Rhythmical Learners

Musical learners respond to auditory information and have the ability to recognize tonal patterns, rhythm, and the underlying beat. These learners learn best through the use of music or rhythm. They often sing the rhythm of a skill or skill combination to themselves or out loud. Young children love the use of poetry and rhyme and enjoy learning and saying phrases such as "knee scale, doggie tail" or "left side, right side, left side" when learning alternating chassés or skips. When working with musical learners, use a clap, snap the fingers, or use rhythmical phrases or one-word sequences that can be spoken to the beat of the skill. Always address the rhythm of the parts of the skill with these children (for example, "toe, ball, heel" while walking or landing). Because they also hear how the skill sounds as the hands, body, or feet come into contact with the floor or apparatus, they can usually tell if a skill has been performed properly by the way it sounds. They can sometimes identify a skill by the way it sounds even if they are not looking. Always speak with tonality, using lyrical speech where appropriate, because these children can "hear" texture.

Naturalist Learners

Naturalist learners deal with the shapes, objects, patterns, and tendencies that are found in nature—including human nature. This type of learning takes into account people's ability to understand and relate to natural phenomenon. These learners learn by watching, studying, and identifying with natural phenomenon. They enjoy patterns and shapes. As young children they are fascinated with the shapes of leaves, snowflakes, trees, and objects found in the sky. They are interested in animals and enjoy trying to replicate animals' movements.

Table 1.2 CHILDREN'S LEARNING STYLES

Learning style	Characteristics	Identifiable traits	Phrasing instructions
Verbal/Linguistic Word awareness	Processes information primarily on a verbal basis. Responds to written and auditory information and relates to terminology and language.	Focuses on face or mouth. Stays still while listening. Responds to speech Speaks and breathes in even rhythm.	"This is called a pike." "Say it with me." "Tell me what this is called."
Logical/Mathematical Number awareness	Processes information logically, concretely, sequentially. Recognizes patterns, shapes. Makes connections between pieces of information.	Stands with head straight, knees locked. Takes shallow breaths. Uses big words. Notices details. Likes precise instructions.	"Think about ..." "The order (or sequence) is..." "The arm was vertical." "Why...?" "How would you..."
Visual/Spatial Image awareness	Processes information by seeing. Thinks in images. Sees spatial relationships.	Looks observant. Will move to see demonstration Speaks rapidly in quick bursts of words. Uses large arm gestures to draw pictures.	"Look at..." "See the..." "Watch for.." "Lift your *legs* up to the bar." Use prepositions: on, off, around, through, up, down.
Bodily/Kinesthetic Body awareness	Processes information through bodily sensation. Excellent motor coordination. Needs to know how skill feels. Has good body and spatial awareness.	Stands centered. Stands relaxed. Breathes abdominally. Likes to touch people when talking, reaches out to people. Speaks at slow pace. Hands-on learner.	"Can you feel your muscles working?" "You should feel..." "Straighten..." "Put weight on the balls of your feet."
Interpersonal Social awareness	Processes by relating, working, and communicating with others. Understands people. Works well with others.	Uses outward gestures. Stands clustered with others. Likes to role play. Speaks emphatically. Speaks at rapid pace.	"Let's do rolls as a group." "Hold your partner's hand as he (she) balances." "Help the others in your group."
Intrapersonal Self awareness	Deep awareness of feelings and ideas. Reflective and analytical. Needs private space and time. Works best alone.	Stands with weight slightly back. Focuses down or on diagonal; little eye contact. Body is relaxed. Breathes in long, meditative breaths. Maintains personal space.	"Can you tell me..." "Work on..." "Think about and practice..." "Try to..." "See how many you can do."
Musical/Rhythmical Sound / tempo awareness	Thinks in sounds, rhythms, patterns. Feels the beat, tempo, or rhythm. Responds to music. Uses rhythmical phrases.	Stands and sits slightly forward, as if listening. Tilts head slightly. Always notices music. Claps, snaps, or drums rhythm of steady beat. Sways to music. Rhythmic gestures.	"It sounds like this..." "Listen for..." "Make a pop with your feet." "Hear the..." "The rhythm is, hand, hand, foot, foot—1, 2, 3, 4."
Naturalist Nature awareness	Relates to objects found in nature. Able to make connection between similarities and differences. Works best when given cues from nature.	Comparative thoughts. Outward, shifting focus. Good peripheral vision, very observant. Speaks excitedly. Breathes shallowly and rapidly in upper chest.	"What does this skill look like?" "Have you seen an animal move like this?" "Walk like a..." "Pull tuck in tight like a raindrop."

2

Exploratory Gymnastics

Exploratory Movement

SPATIAL AWARENESS

Directions		Areas	Patterns	Levels	Distances	Ranges	Planes
Forward	Downward	General	Straight	High	Near	Large	Horizontal
Backward	Diagonal	Personal	Curved	Medium	Away	Medium	Longitudinal
Left	Vertical		Zigzag	Low	Toward	Small	Sagittal
Right	Horizontal						
Upward							

BODY AWARENESS

Body parts		Body shapes		Body positions	Body surfaces
Head	Wrists	Small	Straight	Lying	Front
Eyes	Fingers	Large	Angular	Sitting	Back
Chin	Thighs	Wide	Round	Standing	Side
Neck	Legs	Narrow	Twisted	Prone	Top
Back	Hamstring	Tall	Symmetrical	Supine	Bottom
Chest	Buttocks	Short	Asymmetrical	Kneeling	
Rib cage	Knees			Inverted	
Abdomen	Shins				
Hips	Ankles				
Buttocks	Feet				
Torso	Heels				
Shoulders	Toes				
Elbows					

BODY AWARENESS (What the body can do)

Nonlocomotor	Locomotor		Maneuver weight
Parts of body can . . .	**Alternating feet**	**Exploring circular movements**	Receive force
Circle/roll	(walk, run, skip, slide, gallop)	Straight (pencil) roll	Apply force
Twist/turn/rotate	Landing on 2 feet (jump)	Side (egg) roll	Lift (raise)/lower
Round/curve/curl	Landing on 1 foot (hop, leap)	**Exploration and lead-ups**	Balance/support
Point/flex (bend)	**Exploration using feet**	**for apparatus**	Pull/push
Straighten (extend)	Elephant	Exploring mounts	Hang
Tighten (tense)	Monkey	Exploring beam	**Manipulate**
Relax/stretch	Horse	Exploring vault	Throw/catch

(continued)

Exploratory Movement (continued)

BODY AWARENESS (What the body can do)

Nonlocomotor	Locomotor		Maneuver weight
Parts of body can . . .	**Alternating feet**	**Exploring circular movements**	
Static (stillness)	Kangaroo	Approach	Strike/kick
Dynamic (moving)	**Exploring hands and feet**	Exploring bars	Roll/bounce/toss
Swing/sway	Alligator crawl	Exploring hangs	
Grasp/release	Puppy dog walk	Exploring suspended	
Exploring balance,	Camel walk	and swinging skills	
flexibility, and support	Crab walk		
Support on 1, 2, 3, 4	Bear walk		
body parts	Inchworm		
Bridge	Bunny rabbit jumps		
Cross-leg sit to stand	Frog jump		
Thread the needle	Seal walk		
	Mule (donkey) kick		
	Spider walk		
	Chimp with tail in air		

RELATIONSHIPS

Body parts, other people, apparatus, equipment, directions

Top/bottom	Inside/between/outside	Surrounding
Over/under	In front of/behind	Together/apart
Into/out of	Beside/across	Near/far
High/low	Toward/away from	Above/below
Meeting/parting	Horizontal/vertical	On top of/beneath
Up/down	Parallel/perpendicular	Around/through
On/off	Open/closed/square	Touching
Around/over	Turned in/turned out	Spread apart

EFFORT

Flow	Time	Force	Space
Even/uneven	Fast/slow	Firm/fine	Direct/indirect
Free/bound	Steady/irregular	Strong/weak	Straight/flexible
Controlled/changeable	Accelerating/decelerating	Heavy/light	
Smooth/rough	Sudden/sustained		
Flowing/irregular			

Before you begin to teach individual skills in gymnastics, you should present the concept of movement exploration to your students. Do not rush the self-discovery phase of development or try to move into formal gymnastics too early. Students will be more successful if they can discover on their own how parts of the body work. Then, when moving on to formal skills, they will be better prepared, have greater body awareness, and be able to transfer that learning to positions and skills.

Use the movement chart (above) to give students a wide variety of movement experiences. Use the categories and terms in the movement chart to ask open-ended questions for the students to solve. The movement chart in this chapter provides a list of movement concepts that every student should experience. The sample activities in this chapter are specific to gymnastics. However, the same techniques of using open-ended questions or challenges would be used to explore the other concepts listed in the chart.

The movement exploration activities in this chapter are educational in nature. Through a series of questions, challenges, and explorations, the students educate themselves about their own bodies. Therefore, the exploratory gymnastics technique is often called educational gymnastics, and it will help prepare beginning gymnasts for basic body positions and movements for basic gymnastics skills. The activities will also introduce many of the specific gymnastics terms that gymnasts will need to know later. The exploratory gymnastics challenges are phrased in the way you would talk to the gymnasts, and students' expected responses appear in parentheses; all other information is presented directly to you, the instructor. You can use these questioning techniques to provide students with exploration opportunities for other parts of the movement chart.

EXPLORING BODY AWARENESS

Developing body awareness by exploring and discovering the parts of the body, the movement of different body parts, and the positions that the body can make is the first step in the development of basic body positions. The five parts of the body that usually determine body and skill positions are the head and neck, the torso (trunk), the arms and shoulders, the wrists and hands, and the legs and feet.

Gymnasts must be aware of the locations of body parts and how they work alone and with other body parts. More importantly, gymnasts need to learn how the muscles feel when they work together and also to develop the ability to consciously control the muscles and joints of the body.

You will ask open-ended questions that function as exploratory challenges. These questions should cause the students to think about how the body or technique feels, looks, or sounds or how it is related to other body parts or apparatus. Continue to apply this concept to other exploration situations.

We'll cover an exercise for body awareness here. First, isolate the body part, muscle group, or skill so that the students can focus on one idea. Then, ask open-ended questions to allow the students to think about how their bodies work. Here are some examples: "What are the different ways that the part moves? How can it be used? How does it feel when moving? Is there tension or a feeling of tightness? Does it invert? Does tightening or contracting one muscle affect another muscle?" You may cover one or two concepts and challenges each day and gradually build the base of awareness and knowledge.

Head and Neck

• Stand with your body still and look straight ahead. When the head is in this position it is called the neutral or level head position and it is where your head is most of the time. Make your neck long (level position). What happens? (Shoulders are pressed down and head is level.)

• Bend your head forward and bring your chin toward the chest. This time, tilt your head back slightly until you are looking up at the ceiling. Now, back to neutral, then chin to chest.

• Try moving your head out of the neutral position and find the different ways you can move your head while keeping the rest of the body still.

• Put your head in the neutral position. What can you see while looking straight ahead? Now keep the head still, in neutral position, and try moving the eyes but not the head. What can you see now?

Torso

- Place your hands on your chest. Place your hands on your belly. Place your hands on your back. Show me your hips. Do you know another word for this section of your body? One name is the torso. The torso includes the chest, abdomen, back, and hips and is sometimes called the trunk of the body.

- Stand up straight and tall. When standing the body is like blocks stacked up, one on top of the other. The legs and feet support the torso and the torso supports the head. Most of the time, when you're in a standing position, the blocks are in one straight line. Put your body in a straight line. Now put your body in a position where one block (head, torso, or legs) is not in line with the other blocks. How does your body feel when one part of your body has moved?

- Try standing in one straight line again. Stand on both feet with your hips directly over your feet. The shoulders are directly over your hips (square) and the head is in neutral. When the blocks are all stacked in line, with the weight distributed over the bottom block (your feet), it is easier to balance.

- Tighten your abdominal muscles and pull your shoulders forward. What happens? (The upper back rounds.)

- Tighten the buttocks muscles. What happens to other parts of the torso? Keep your buttocks tight and try to bend forward. What happens? (You cannot bend forward if you keep your buttocks tight.)

- Round your back. While staying rounded, feel your spine, or bones, in your back. Those are called vertebrae. How do they feel?

- Stand tall in one straight line and try rounding your back one vertebra at a time. Now try to straighten one vertebra at a time.

- Stand in one straight line and place your right hand on the back of your left shoulder. Move the left arm and shoulder forward and backward. The bone moving toward the center of the back is called the shoulder blade, or scapula.

- Stand in one straight line and tighten the upper-back muscles and pull the shoulders back (try to bring the shoulder blades closer together). What happens to the back?

- Stand in a straight line with the shoulders above the hips (hips and shoulders square). Try moving (or shifting the blocks of the body) so that the shoulders are not over the hips. Try other ways to move so that the blocks are not in line.

- Sit on the floor with your legs together and straight in front of you. Keep your back straight and bend only at the hips. What shape or letter does the body make? The hips work like a door that opens and closes. What other things open and close? Try opening your door wider at your hips. Try closing your door almost shut at the hips. Open at the hips just a little. Open a lot.

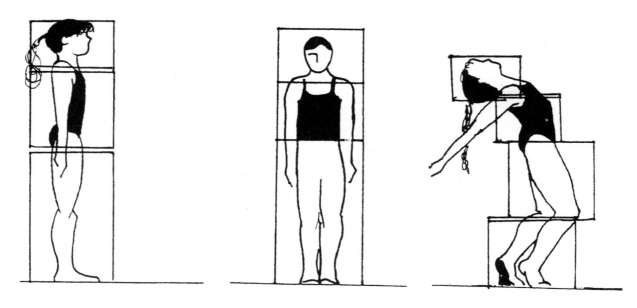

Arms and Shoulders

- The arms include the shoulders and elbows. The hands are connected at the wrist joint; we'll work with the wrists and hands later. For now, isolate the shoulder and elbow of one arm. Show me your elbows. Show me your shoulders.
- Rotate your shoulders forward and make circles. Rotate your shoulders backward. Draw small circles in the air with your elbows. Make circles by going the other direction. Draw big circles in the air with your arms. Draw circles the other way.
- Explore all the ways you can move your arms at the joint. In what positions can you move the arms?
- Bend your arms and try putting bent (flexed) arms at different levels (high, medium, low). Now try straightening the arms at different levels.
- Explore all the different patterns that can be made with the arms (straight, curved, zigzag). Bend the arms and let the elbows make different patterns in the air. Try writing your name with an elbow.
- Keep the body still and find all the places that the arms can go. Put your arms to the side at a medium level, in front at a medium level, behind, close together in front, apart in front, high over the head, low by the sides, and in front at a medium level.
- The arms are connected to the torso at the shoulders. Move only your shoulders and find out what the shoulders can do.
- Try to elevate your shoulders by bringing them up toward the ears. Try to lower your shoulders by pushing them down toward your hips.
- Push your shoulders backward. What happens to your upper back? (The upper back arches.)
- Push your shoulders forward. What happens to your back? (It rounds.) What happens to your chest? (It becomes hollow or sunken.)
- The arms swing from the shoulders. Find all the ways that your arms can swing.
- The arms also rotate from the shoulders. What does *rotate* mean? Find all the ways that your arms can rotate.

Hands and Fingers

- At the end of the arms are the hands. The hands move at the wrists. Move the wrists. What can they do? (Help support handstands, shift for skills on bars.)
- The hands are very important. What are some things that the hands do? (Hold, grasp, hang, support.)
- Explore all the ways that the hands and fingers can move. In what directions can they be placed? (On the floor underneath, on top of the head, beside each other, facing forward, facing backward, facing sideways, facing inward.)
- Move just the fingers and not the wrists. What can the fingers do? (Wiggle, help balance a handstand, grip the apparatus.)
- Humans walk on two feet. Many animals walk on four. What do the two front feet do for animals? (Help them balance; help them run faster.)
- Try supporting the weight of the body on hands and feet. Explore all the ways that you can support the weight of the body. Can the hands support the body better when the fingers are together or spread apart? (Apart.)

Legs and Feet

- The legs are usually the main support for the body and are the bottom block.
- Explore all the leg positions that support the body.
- Try putting the legs at different distances from each other and at different places on the floor.

- Bend and straighten the legs at the knees. Try to balance on one leg and bend and straighten the free leg. Try to bend and straighten the leg that you are balancing on (support leg). What muscles can you feel working? Are there any differences in the muscles when you stand on one leg and when you stand on two legs?

- Stand with your feet together. Bend the knees as far as you can, keeping the heels on the floor.

- While standing on both feet, try to point the toes. What happens? Now sit on the floor and try pointing and bending (flexing) the feet at the ankle. How is it different? What muscles are working?

- Sit on the floor and circle your feet at the ankles. Draw circles with your feet. Draw circles going the other direction. Point your toes (pencil points). Flex your feet as much as you can (hook). Try drawing the alphabet with your feet.

- While sitting on the floor, find all the positions of the legs. What parts can bend and straighten?

- Move straight legs and change the direction that the knee is pointing. Where does the rotation come from? (The hips.) When the legs are next to each other in straight lines, it is called parallel. When rotated out from the hips, it is called turned out. If rotated in from the hips it is called turned in.

EXPLORING BODY POSITIONS

- While sitting (standing or lying) on the floor, explore different ways that the body can bend or straighten.
- Become as small as you can. Become as large as you can.
- Become as wide as you can. Become as narrow as you can.
- Become as tall as you can. Become as short as you can.
- Bend as many body parts as you can. Straighten all the body parts.
- Get in a position where the legs are together. Get in a position where the legs are spread apart.
- Try a position bending only at the waist.
- Try a position bending only at the hips and have the nose close to the knees.
- Try a position where there is a bend at the waist, knees, and ankles.
- Try a position where the legs are spread apart and there is a bend at the waist.
- Try a position where the body is at a low level and the hands are at a high level.
- Try a position where the feet are at a high level and the hands are at a medium level.
- Try a position where the hands are supporting the body.
- Try a position where the body is in a straight line except for the head.
- If both sides of the body look the same, then the shape is called *symmetrical*. Make a symmetrical shape. Now change one side of your body. That is called *asymmetrical*. Make a different symmetrical shape. Now change one side to make it asymmetrical.

EXPLORING BALANCE AND FLEXIBILITY

The easiest standing balance position is on two feet approximately shoulder-width apart. Standing on one foot and maintaining balance is much more challenging. Enhance and develop balance in your gymnasts by allowing them to experience varying bases of support; raising, lowering, or changing the center of gravity; changing the number of body parts that provide the base; and extending different body parts to equalize the weight. Encourage gymnasts to move into balance positions slowly and with control. Then, have them try to hold a balance position in a static balance for a minimum of 3 seconds.

- Try to find a balanced position on two feet. Bend or change parts of the body until you almost lose balance. Pretend to be a statue or frozen and hold that position.
- Try to find a balanced position on one foot. Take the other foot and place it at a low level, medium level, then high level.
- Try to find a balanced position on one foot. Take the arms and place them in front at a low level, medium level, then high level. Now place them directly over the head. Now try placing them down by the side. Try behind you. Shake the arms. Can you still keep the balance? What can you do with other parts of your body to help you balance on one foot? (Hold arms steady to the side, tighten abdominal muscles.)
- Try to find other body parts to balance on. Try to balance on your buttocks. Try on your belly. Try to balance on two shins. Try to balance on a shin. Try to balance with one hand and one knee.
- Try to make a good base by balancing on your hands and knees in a wide bridge. Now bring the hands close to each other and the feet close to each other. If someone gently pushed, which bridge would fall over—the wide bridge or the narrow bridge? (The narrow bridge.)
- Explore other ways to balance.

Cross-Leg Sit to Stand

- Sit on the floor with legs and arms crossed.
- Try to stand up without using the hands to push off the mat.
- Now try to sit back down without using the hands.

Thread the Needle

- Start in a standing position with your hands clasped in front of you.
- Try to find a way to thread the needle by stepping through your hands without unclasping your hands.
- Try to reverse it and step back through.

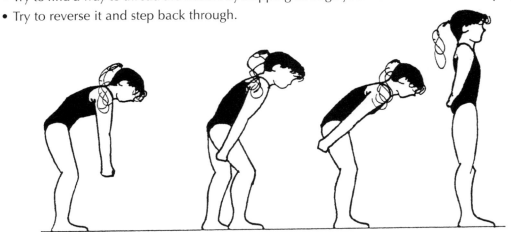

EXPLORING SUPPORT SKILLS

Gymnasts must develop upper-body strength because various types of arm support are used on floor, beam, bars, and vault. This section presents a variety of animal movements and other exploration challenges that can be used to develop upper-body strength, weight-transferring skills, balance, and other skills necessary in supporting body weight. Children especially love animal movements, so a wide variety of these movements are presented to keep the learners motivated and interested. When appropriate, formal gymnastics terminology is used so that you may start incorporating the vocabulary of positions into your lessons.

Many students will only be able to perform some of the skills because they lack the upper-body strength to support their own body weight. The easiest support positions are those in which the arms are extended straight and only part of the body weight is supported by their arms. Progressively add more of their body weight to strengthen muscle groups to maintain the balanced support position, and develop enough strength to keep straight arms.

Support on Three or Four Body Parts

- Try to support the body with four body parts. Try to make a support with three body parts.

- Try to support the body with three body parts, then lift one of the parts and see if you can still support the rest of the body.

- Try to make a support with the face to the ceiling (rear support). Try to make a support with the belly facing the floor (front support).

- Try to make a tall support. Try to make a support that is close to the floor. Try to make a wide overpass. Try to make a narrow tunnel.

- Try to support the body with one or two hands with your side to the floor (side support). Is it easier with one or two hands?

- Try to support the body with four body parts with your belly to the ceiling. Try to make an archway with three body parts.

- Try to support the body with three body parts with your belly to the ceiling and then lift one of the parts and see if you can still support the rest of the body.

- With your belly to the ceiling, try to make a support that is close to the floor. Try to make a wide overpass. Try to make a narrow tunnel.

- Move like a monkey, lion, puppy, snail, alligator, snake, bear, frog, and horse. What are some other animals that you can imitate?

- Show me how you would move across the floor with weight on the hands and feet. Move at a high level. Move at a low level. Move with the body wide. Move with the body narrow.

- Find a way to move just the hands and keep the feet in place. Find a way to move the feet and keep the arms in place.

- Move the hand and leg of the same side. Now the hand and leg of the other side.

- Find a way to travel across the floor while supported by three body parts. Change one of the body parts and still travel on three parts and put a body part at a medium level.

- Support the weight on the hands and lift the hips off the floor at a low level. Try to lift hips a little higher. Can you lift the feet slightly off the floor?

Arm Support

- Support the weight on the hands and lift the hips off the floor at a low level. Try to lift hips a little higher. Can you lift the feet slightly off the floor?

- Try to find a way to support your body in a sideways position by using the hand and foot of the same side. Stay sideways and try to have both feet on the floor and keep a straight support arm. Try to walk around in a circle with your feet while keeping your arm straight. Try your other arm (see figure below).

- Make a support with your belly facing the floor and your hands under your shoulders. Make your arms straight. Keeping the arms straight, pretend your hands are "glued" to the floor.

    - Slightly lift your legs off the floor and put them in a different position.

    - Now try a different position: one leg straight and the other leg bent.

    - Try a position with both legs bent.

    - Try a position with both legs straight. Now try to bring those straight legs closer to your "glued" hands.

    - Try a position with your legs far apart.

    - Explore all the other positions you could place your legs in without moving your hands.

Arm Support on Folded Mats

- Squat between two folded mats and place your hands on the mats on either side of you. Now lift your legs off the floor so that you are supporting your body weight just on two parts (your hands).

- Keep your body supported by the hands and bend both legs. Now try to bend at the hips and bring one leg out in front of you. Try to bring the other leg out in front of you. Keep your legs together. Now try to spread them apart.

- Keep your body supported by the hands and explore all the positions that you can put your legs in without swinging your body.

- Now move to the floor away from mats. Sit on the floor and place your hands on the floor beside your hips. Try to lift your body off the floor and support all your weight on just your hands.

    - Sit in tuck and try to find ways to lift your body off the floor.

    - Now sit in straddle and try different ways to lift all or part of the straddle off the floor.

    - Try a pike and try to lift part or all of the pike off the floor.

V-Sit Support

- Sit on the floor in tuck. Place your arms behind you by your hips for support. Try to lift one foot until your leg is straight and off the floor. Now put that leg down and try to lift the other leg.

- Keep your back straight (you might need to lean back a little) and try to lift one leg high so that your foot is as high as your head. Now put the first leg down and try to lift the other leg high. Now, try to lift both feet off the floor at the same time and still keep both legs straight and your back straight. Keep your abdominal muscles tight. Try to look like the letter V. Only your hands and your buttocks support your body.

  - Keep the V shape and try to bend one leg and keep one leg straight. Switch legs.

  - Try to flutter kick your legs as if you are swimming. Flutter them quickly. Now slowly. Which is easier? What muscles do you feel working?

  - Try to cross your legs one over the other (criss-cross).

  - Try to keep your back and legs straight and grab your ankles.

Animal Movements

Animal movements are not just support moves but also locomotor movements on three or four body parts. They are included in this section because they help develop the upper-body strength that is necessary for support skills.

Alligator Crawl

- Lie on the floor with your belly touching the floor.
- Crawl, staying low, using your arms and legs to move across the floor like an alligator.

Puppy Dog Walk

- Using your hands and feet, walk across the floor like a puppy dog.
- Try to keep your arms and legs almost straight.
- Now try to walk like the puppy and lift one leg and walk across floor.
- Walk again but lift a different leg.

Camel Walk

- Get on your hands and feet and round your back.
- Using your hands and feet, walk across the floor like a camel.

Crab Walk

- Sit on the floor.
- Reach back and place both hands on the floor.
- Lift your buttocks off the floor.
- Keep your arms straight in a crab position.
- Let your crab walk forward. Let your crab walk backward. Can your crab walk sideways?

Bear Walk

- Using only your hands and feet, walk across the floor like a bear: move the right arm and the right leg at the same time. Now the left arm and left leg at the same time.
- Keep arms and legs straight.
- Do the bear walk, but this time, walk way up on your toes.
- Now try the bear walk but keep your entire foot on floor to stretch the back of the legs.
- When bears run fast, they move their two front legs first, then their two back legs. Try that movement first slowly, then try running like a bear, moving your front legs, then your back legs.

Inchworm

- Place your hands and feet on the floor, keeping your arms and legs straight.
- Keep your feet still and walk your hands forward as far as you can, just like an inchworm.
- Now keep your hands still and walk your feet as close as you can to your hands.
- Walk your hands, then your feet. (Sequence in formal gymnastics: closed pike, walk hands to open pike, walk feet to closed pike.)

Bunny Rabbit Jump

- Squat on the floor with your hands and feet close together.
- Lift your hands and move them forward, placing them on the mat.
- Push off both feet and bring them close to the hands like a bunny rabbit.
- Take little bunny jumps. Take big bunny jumps.

Frog Jump

- Squat on the floor and place your hands on the floor.
- Push off with your hands and feet and jump up and forward.
- Try a small frog jump. Try a high frog jump. Try a jump that travels forward only a short distance. Now, try a big frog jump. What did you need to do to make a big jump?

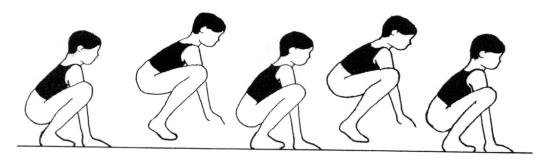

Seal Walk

- Lie on the floor on your belly and straighten your arms. Keep arms straight and look straight ahead.
- Use only your arms and walk forward, dragging the rest of your body behind you in a seal walk.
- Keep your legs together and straight with your feet pointed.

Switcheroo

- Place hands on floor, folded mat, bench, or carton. Keep arms straight.
- Kick one straight leg up off the ground, switch legs in the air, and land on the other foot.

Donkey Kick

- Squat down and place your hands on the floor.
- Keeping arms straight, lift your hips and kick both legs in a donkey kick behind you in an upward diagonal.

Spider Walk

- With your belly to the floor, place your hands on the floor.
- Put your feet up on a mat stack, spotting block, or medium balance beam.
- Keep your arms straight and your body tight to perform the spider walk.
- Walk your feet sideways around the mat or down the length of the beam.
- Switch, placing your hands on the mat and your feet on the floor.

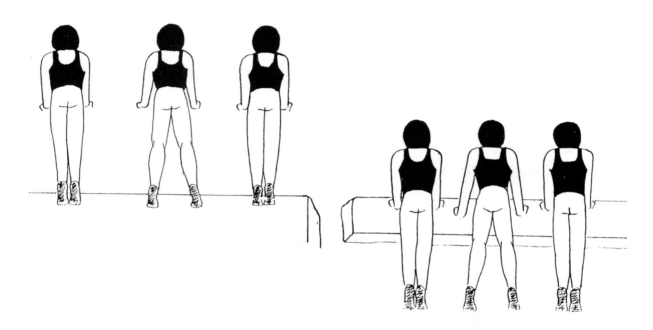

Chimp With Tail in the Air

- Place your hands and feet on the floor.
- Lift one foot and pretend it is a chimp's tail in the air.
- Move both hands forward, lifting your tail high in the air as you hop your other foot forward.

EXPLORING LOCOMOTOR SKILLS

Locomotor skills include walking, running, jumping, hopping, leaping, sliding, skipping, and galloping. These skills take place on the floor and beam, during approaches and landings on vault, and on jumps to mount and dismount from bars. This section presents the five basic patterns for locomotor skills on the feet. Learners will explore the foot patterns at different levels, directions, patterns, and forces. Included are the animal moves that creatively reinforce body positioning while students move in an upright locomotor pattern. Students also need to experience alternating foot patterns, jumps, one-leg landings, and turns.

Give gymnasts many opportunities to travel moving forward, backward, and sideward. Challenge them to use different movement patterns, speeds, forces, tempos, and foot patterns. Gymnasts need to explore and experience locomotor skills to prepare for the locomotor, dance skills, and variations of foot patterns found in gymnastics.

Foot Patterns

The type of landing, the amount of time in the air, the position of the legs in the air, and the force of the steps determine the name of the skill.

There are five basic foot patterns found in physical education:

- One foot to other foot (alternating). These include the walk, run, slide, chasse (gallop), skip, and leap.
- Two feet to two feet. This is a jump.
- Two feet to one foot. These include the hop and leap and the beginning step of a walk, run, slide, gallop, and skip.
- One foot to two feet. These include the jump and assemblé.
- One foot to same foot. This is a hop.

To make things easy at first, practice small, alternating foot patterns with a steady beat and slight force such as walking, marching, and running. Although the skip seems to be an alternating pattern, it is actually a combination skill of a step-hop on right, then a step-hop on left. The skip also has a syncopated rhythm, which means that the accent is on the up beat or the sound has an uneven rhythm. Some beginners will find the syncopation helpful, while others may find it more difficult to master. The gallop and slide are also syncopated. Begin teaching the skip, gallop, and slide with the syncopation, because if these steps are altered and performed to an even, steady beat, balance and rhythm become an issue.

Rhythm of the skip is:

Step-hop, step-hop, step-hop, step-hop.

And 1, and 2, and 3, and 4.

Rhythm of the slide and gallop is:

Step-close, step-close, step-close, step-close.

And 1, and 2, and 3, and 4.

Exploring Alternating Foot Patterns

- Explore all the ways, directions, and patterns that you can walk. Make your walk faster. Make it slower.
- Try walking on different parts of your feet. Try walking with your feet close together. Try far apart. Try taking small steps. Take big steps.
- Try running in a straight pattern. Try running in a curved pattern. Try running in a zigzag pattern. (You may use cones for the different patterns.) Run with your knees high in front. Now try to kick your buttocks with your heels.

- Try walking on relevé (balls of the feet). Run on relevé.
- Try walking as loudly as you can. Now as softly as you can. What did you need to do to walk quietly?
- Try jumping off of two feet and landing on two feet. Try different ways to position your feet when you land (together, apart, stride).
- Try skipping forward, now backward. While skipping forward, lift the knees as high as possible.
- Try sliding forward, now backward. Slide quickly, now slowly.
- Try taking off from one foot (hop) and landing on the same foot. Try taking off from one foot and landing on the other foot (leap). Try to go farther than you did the last time.
- Explore all the ways you can move or travel. Sometimes alternate the feet, sometimes use the same foot, sometimes land on both feet. Can you find some new ways to travel?

Exploring Jumps

Balance while moving is a big factor in the success of a locomotor skill. It becomes especially important as the foot pattern has more force and more time in the air. Therefore, when a gymnast leaves the floor with any force, he or she has a better chance of gaining a balanced position with a two-foot landing than with a one-foot landing. Initially, the feet need to be wide enough apart to give a good base of support. Remind the students to bend the knees (plié) to cushion the landings. As students become more experienced, they can narrow the base of support and begin landings on one foot.

Give the gymnasts many opportunities to leave their feet, become airborne, and land on two feet. Some variations include jumping over objects or onto targets, jumping from the mat up to a piece of equipment, or jumping down from a piece of equipment. Gradually increase the height that they jump to or from. Gymnasts can also practice jumps with a springboard. Remember that beginners should limit the heights they jump from.

- Jump off two feet and land on two feet as softly as you can.
- Jump off two feet and land with the legs in straddle.
- Jump as high off the floor as you can and still land softly. What did you need to do to land softly? (Bend the knees.)
- Jump off one foot and land on two with the feet next to each other.
- This time when you jump, bring the legs into a tuck position while in the air.
- Try to jump and turn to face the other wall while in the air.
- Jump over the hula-hoop. Jump with one foot inside the hula-hoop and the other foot outside the hoop. Jump over the hula-hoop.
- Jump up to the folded mat. Jump down from the folded mat. What did your legs need to do differently? (Bend more to jump up, push harder with feet to jump, bend more to land.)
- Try to jump from different heights. When you land, try to land in a safe landing position and keep your balance. Bend your knees on the landing, then quickly stand up tall and balance without moving the feet. That is called "sticking" the landing.

Exploring Landing on One Foot

Leaps and hops are the most difficult of all locomotor movements and it is hard to balance when landing on one foot. Make sure that students begin with small hops and leaps in the beginning.

- Try to balance on one foot. Now try to leave the floor and land on one foot.
- Try to take a few steps, leave the floor, and land on one foot. Try the other foot.
- Try to take a few steps, leave the floor, jump high in the air, and land on one foot.
- Try all the ways that you can move, leave the floor, and land on one foot.

Animal Movements

Elephant Walk

- Begin in a standing position.
- Make an elephant trunk by clasping your hands in front of you.
- Bend forward at the waist and round your back.
- Walk slowly like an elephant and swing the "trunk" from side to side.

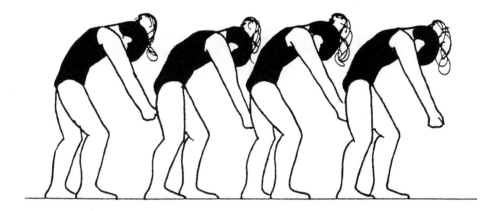

Horse

- Gallop like a horse.

Monkey

- Walk like a monkey with your arms hanging down by your side.

Kangaroo Jump

- Put arms in front like the front legs of a kangaroo.
- Jump in a straight pattern.
- Now zigzag.

EXPLORING TURNS

Turning with one or two feet helps the learner develop balance and kinesthetic awareness. Students will learn how to use their sight to help them with their turns.

- Try all the ways you can to turn on one foot. Try to find a way to turn on two feet. Keep the body in one straight line.
- While standing, lift up onto the toes. Try to find a way to turn without letting the toes leave the floor. Try at a high level, then a medium level, and then a low level.
- Show how you balance on one foot. Try turning on that one foot. Try turning on the other foot.
- Try turning with the body at different levels. Try turning with the arms extended out at different levels.
- Try lifting your rib cage and tightening your abdominal muscles as you turn.
- As you turn, try to look at something in back of you to help you turn.
- Try turning on one foot with the hands extended out. Now try turning with the hands in close. Which turn was faster? Which one was easier to keep your balance? What did you do to slow down?

EXPLORING TWISTING ROTATIONS

Beginning gymnasts enjoy exploring different rolls on the floor. They must become comfortable with the different sensations as they invert and change their orientation to the floor. This will help them later as they perform forward and backward rolls on the floor and eventual rotations in the air. They will have the spatial awareness necessary to know when to change their body positions to perform the skills and to land safely.

- Explore all the ways that you can rock, roll, and twist your body while staying on the floor.
- Find a way to roll like a pencil. Find a way to roll like an egg.
- Find a way to roll with your hands over your head.
- Start at a low level on knees and elbows and try rolling sideways.
- Rock and roll on the floor with your back curved.
- Explore other ways you might roll with your body.

Pencil Roll

- Try to roll with your arms straight over your head.
- At first, have a partner hold your hands together during the roll.

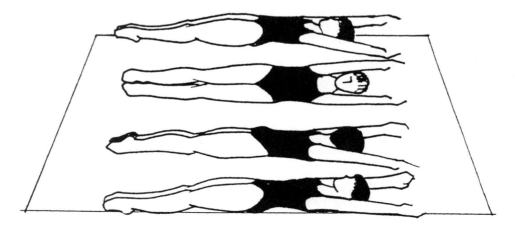

Other Challenges

- Place beanbags between the elbows and knees and squeeze the beanbags.
- Try to roll with your hands and feet lifted off the floor.
- Try to roll up the incline mat.
- Try a roll with beanbags between your knees and ankles.

Side Tuck (Egg) Roll

- Lie on the floor and bring your knees up in a tuck.
- Hold your shins tightly and roll sideways down the mat.
- For a challenge, open legs in a straddle while rolling onto the back and close legs back to tuck for the prone part of the roll.

EXPLORING SIDEWARD TUMBLING

The exploration for sideward tumbling covers activities that eventually lead to the cartwheel. Use stacked panel mats, benches, hula-hoops, or ropes to perform the following skills:

- Try to put two hands on the stacked mats and jump, bringing your legs to the other side. Turn around. Repeat the other way.
- Place hands on the stacked mats and try to lift your legs to the other side but land on one foot and then the other.
- Pretend the mat (or bench, rope, inside of hula-hoop) is a low wall that you want to get over. Explore the different ways you can use your hands and feet to cross over the wall. This time pretend that only your hands can go on the wall and only your feet can touch on either side of the wall.

EXPLORATION AND LEAD-UPS FOR APPARATUS

Providing lead-ups for apparatus is very important, but safety must be considered. Make sure that pathways are clear, that mats or soft areas are used, and that you begin with low surfaces.

Exploring Mounts

Use a beam, bench, or carton for this exploration.

- How many of you have ridden a horse or pony? When you got on the horse it was called "mounting the horse." The word *mount* means to get on.

- Try to get on the balance beam (bench, carton) the same way that you would get on a horse.
- Explore different ways to safely mount the beam (low beam with mats underneath) by using your hands to get on. (Caution: No jumping or running steps.)
- Explore different ways to safely mount the beam (low beam with mats underneath) without using your hands to get on.

These skills will be lead-ups for vault and beam mounts. Use folded mats for this exploration.

- Explore all the different ways that you can mount or land on the stacked mats. Approach from different sides of the folded mats.
- Can you find a way to mount just with your feet?
- Find a way to mount with hands and feet.
- Find a way to mount with one hand and one foot.
- Find a way to mount in which you start with your hands already on top of the folded mats.

Exploring Beam

The beam is one of the best tools to develop balance and motivate students to advance locomotor skills that they have learned on the ground. The beam can also be a valuable tool to help develop upper body strength.

Exploring Beam Balance

Begin with a line on the floor, then a line on a bench. Progress to a wide beam on the floor, then a slightly elevated beam.

- Explore all the ways that you can balance and hold a position like a statue on the beam. Keep your muscles tight and hold the statue position while you count to five.
- What makes balancing on a balance beam different than balancing on the floor? What do you need to do to keep your balance? Can you put your body in as many positions on the beam as you can on the floor?

Exploring Beam Support

On the beam, perform many of the same animal movements that you performed on the floor:

- Puppy dog walk
- Bear walk
- Inchworm
- Donkey kick
- Frog jump

Explore all the ways that you can support the body by using the hands on the beam. What makes a support on a balance beam different than a support on the floor?

Exploring Beam Locomotor Skills

Make sure gymnasts can perform all the locomotor movements on the floor first. Remember that the legs should be slightly turned out on beam for stability.

If you use manipulative objects such as balls, bean bags, or scarves, begin on the floor and then a low beam. Manipulatives are used to add motivation and excitement, but gymnasts must be developmentally ready and have the prerequisite locomotor and manipulative skills.

It is also a lot of fun for the students to perform activities such as the hokey pokey and the Macarena on the beam. These dances help develop balancing skills.

- Try to walk with a beanbag balanced on your head. Walk with the beanbag on your shoulder. Find another place to balance the beanbag as you walk.
- Try to find another way to move down the beam with a beanbag on your head. Try to walk backward. Walk at a medium level. Walk sideways.
- Try to throw a ball up and catch it, then take a step. Throw the ball up again, then take a step. As you feel confident, try to throw the ball higher.
- Try to walk and circle a ball around the waist. Walk and weave the ball through your legs.
- Try to throw a scarf up and catch it on your head, then on your shoulder, and on your elbow. Try to catch the scarf on different body parts.
- Try to walk while throwing and catching a scarf. Start with the scarf leaving your fingers only a few inches.
- Try to walk and balance a tennis ball on the strings of a racket. Try to walk and bounce a tennis ball on a racket.
- Step over beanbags while walking on the beam.
- Try different locomotor skills while moving forward on the beam. Start by moving slowly and with control.
- Try backward locomotor movements.

EXPLORING THE VAULT APPROACH

- Explore different ways you can run.
- Try running but hold your arms as still as you can. Hold your hands clasped in front of you and run. Run with your arms up in the air. Try running with your hands on your waist. Put your hands on your back and run. What happens to your run?
- Try swinging your arms or pumping them. What happens now?
- Run slowly. Then run faster. Run as fast as you can. What do you need to do to run fast?
- Try taking really big steps. Now take small steps.
- Try leaning backward when you run. Try leaning forward when you run.
- Try running at a high level, medium level, and low level.
- Run with your legs almost straight. Run by bringing your knees up high on each step. Run and try to kick up your feet behind you.
- Leave the floor and go as high as you can between each step. Now try to run by keeping your feet low to the floor.
- Try running on your toes. Try running while rolling down on your foot from the toes through the ball to the heel.
- Try running loudly. Now softly. Which way can you run faster, loudly or softly?
- Try running and jumping on a target (in a hoop) with both feet. Try running and jumping over a target and landing on both feet.
- Try running, land on a target with both feet, and jump in the air as high as you can and keep your hands on your waist. Try it again, but this time lift your arms up overhead as you jump. On which jump did you go higher?
- Try running, land on a target with both feet, and lightly slap your thighs with your hands when you jump as high as you can. Try to touch the ceiling.
- Try running, land on a target from a short distance away with both feet, then jump in the air as high as you can. This time, jump on the target from farther away. Remember to land on two feet.
- Run, land on a target, and perform a straddle jump. Jump upward and forward so that you land farther away on the landing from the straddle jump. Try different jumps after landing on the target.

EXPLORING BARS

It is very important for you to spot and support beginning students on bars. You must have "hands on" contact with the gymnasts even while they perform exploratory movements.

Exploring Hangs

• Keep both hands on the bar and try not to let your body swing as you lift your feet up off the floor.

• Explore all the positions you can make while holding the bar with both hands and not swinging the body. Find a position and try to hold it for 5 seconds, then find a different position.

Exploring Suspended and Swinging Skills

As the gymnasts become more successful, gradually add more activities in which they must support their weight in a dynamic (moving) position. These skills are still listed under "exploration," but you start to provide more instructions and feedback.

Run Under Bar

• Begin with the bar at shoulder height.
• Stand at arm's length behind the bar and place hands on bar.
• Keep arms extended.
• With head positioned between arms, run under bar.
• Release the bar.
• Turn around to face the bar and repeat.

Run Under Bar and Swing Back

• Run under bar.
• Fully extend legs and torso.
• Pull legs up to tuck and swing backward.
• Raise hips at the end of the back swing.
• Let go to stand up with arms extended.
• Slightly bend knees on landing, then stretch up in salute.
• Sequence: run, swing, tuck, back swing, release, stand, salute.

Other Challenges:

- Grip, run under bar, release, turn, grip, swing in tuck (or pike or straddle), release, stand.
- Grip, swing forward and back staying in tuck, pike, or straddle.
- Grip, swing in tuck, pike, straddle, let go at top of swing, stand.
- Grip, swing (in tuck, pike, or straddle), release at top of swing, stand, turn, grip, swing (tuck, pike, or straddle), release at top of swing, stand.

COMBINATIONS AND ROUTINES

As soon as you teach any new skills, introduce the idea of putting skills together to form combinations and routines. You may need to give examples at first, but as soon as possible, allow students the chance to problem solve and put the routines together. Guide the gymnasts by giving categories but not specifics of skill movements.

Here are some examples of skill challenges for combinations:

- Start in a balanced position on three body parts. Find a way to move forward on those three parts and finish with a sideward rolling movement.
- Find a way to travel at a low level, balance, change your direction, then move at a high level in a zigzag pattern.
- Perform three consecutive jumps. Each jump must look different.
- Start in a position that is symmetrical, travel in an alternating locomotor pattern that is asymmetrical, then perform a symmetrical jump and land in a balanced symmetrical shape.

On their own, students will start understanding transitions and how some movements more naturally flow to other types of movement. When given a choice, students *will always* perform movements and skills that are developmentally appropriate for them and their level of skill development.

3

Foundational Positions and Movements

Body Positions and Movements

Squat/tuck	Pike	Straddle	Standing straight body (stretched)	Other body positions	Leg positions	Arm positions
Sitting tuck	Sitting pike	Sitting straddle	Straight body	Stride	Stride	Oblique
Squat stand	Standing pike	Standing straddle	Stretched body	Gymnastics point	Straddle	Straight overhead
Supported tuck	Supported pike	Straddle stand	Hollow stand	Initiation lunge	Parallel	Crown
Supine tuck	Supine pike	Supported straddle	Arch stand	Finish lunge (salute)	Turnout	Side middle
Inverted tuck	Inverted pike	Supine straddle		Safe landing	Plié	Front middle
		Inverted straddle				Front low
						Opposition

Nonlocomotor		Locomotor	
Standing balances (straight line from supporting foot to head)	**Nonstanding balances**	**Alternating foot patterns**	**Twisting rotation (turns)**
Relevé hold	Stride split	Forward walking	Squat turn
Coupé and passé	Straddle split	Backward walking	Relevé turn
Front attitude	Inverted shoulder stand	Lateral walks	**Horizontal circular rotation**
Battement	**Support on 3 or 4 body parts**	Relevé walk	Back rocker
Standing balances (straight line from nonsupported foot to head)	Front support	Step-hop (skipping)	
Arabesque	Rear support	Chassé	
Scale	Side support	**Landing on 2 feet**	
Lever	**Front support on floor series**	Stretch jump	
Nonstanding balances (knee balance)	Bridge	Tuck jump	
Knee stand	**V-sit progression**	Pike straddle jump	
Knee lunge	**Supports (holds) with arms folded on mats**	Pike jump	
Half split	Tuck support	Stride jump	
Knee scale	L or pike support	Jump half turn	
Balance in knee scale	Straddle L support	**Landing on 1 foot**	
		Stride leap	

In his book *Teaching Developmental Gymnastics,* Garland O'Quinn compares the movements of the body to music: He uses the terms *motor notes, motor chords,* and *motor patterns.* The basic element in music is the note. Notes are put together to form chords. Chords are put together to develop the musical phrase. In gymnastics a motor note is one single position or basic movement in isolation. A motor chord is two or more motor notes put together. A motor phrase is the complete skill or motor pattern. This model can be used quite successfully and facilitates the use of the part–whole method of teaching.

An example of a motor phrase is the forward roll. The sequence of a forward roll is straight-body stand, standing pike support, tuck head, push off feet, roll to inverted tuck, tuck stand, straight-body stand, salute. Before learning the forward roll, gymnasts should experience all of the individual motor notes, or parts, of the skill. Gymnasts would learn the straight-body stand, standing pike support, inverted tuck, tuck stand, and all of the other parts of the forward roll in isolation. The next step is to perform a motor chord by combining two or more pieces. For example, gymnasts attempt to roll from an inverted tuck position to a standing position. To complete an entire motor pattern, gymnasts combine all of the motor notes to perform a forward roll.

These motor notes are the building blocks of gymnastics. In this chapter the motor notes are called foundational positions and movements. Gymnasts must learn the foundational skills before they move on to formal gymnastics skills. Gymnasts should already have experience in exploration and problem-solving activities in exploratory gymnastics. Now they are ready to learn and practice skills by using the correct terminology and perform the motor notes in formal gymnastics positions and movements. Gymnasts must spend time practicing the positions and movements to build strength, flexibility, kinesthetic and spatial awareness, balance, basic coordination, correct weight placement, and positioning that will be utilized in future skill development. Gymnasts will then be ready to move to the next level of related floor and apparatus skills.

The learning cues, which are different cues for different learning styles, are presented in the words that the instructor would say to the gymnasts. All other information is presented directly to the instructor.

BODY AWARENESS TERMINOLOGY

Some terminology may have been introduced during the movement exploration phase in chapter 2. After you explore the body parts, the next step is to teach the technical names. Give specific words in instructions and look for precise movements. A good drill is to name a body part by using specific terminology. Give the learners an action for that part that they can respond to and perform. This will help the learners be aware of the body parts, the movements the body parts can make, and the proper technical terms used in gymnastics. You can then use terminology to increase the students' understanding of the skill.

Some terminology is too advanced for beginners. Therefore, you can introduce technical terms slowly by using the words while describing the positions and skills so that the learners will become familiar with the terminology.

BASIC BODY POSITIONS

There are six major body positions: tuck, pike, arch, hollow, straddle, and straight body. All other body positions are variations and can be performed from a sit, stand, or lying position. Arm and leg positions vary and are used to assist the body in balance, momentum, delivery, and style.

In chapter 2, "Exploratory Gymnastics," the body parts were first isolated. First the gymnasts need to explore the different positions that the body can make. The students do so by responding to challenges that they can solve in different ways through exploratory

Important Terms to Know: Head and Neck Positions

- Head neutral (level), back, forward, turned (chin over shoulder), parallel to ceiling
- Head beside, between, on top of, down
- Neck long, chin lifted, chin tucked

Torso

- Torso (back) rounded, hollow, straight, arched
- Torso twisted (shoulders not in line with hips)
- Hips flexed or straight
- Hips square, open, or closed

Arms and Shoulders

- Arms at high, medium, or low level
- Arms straight, bent, rounded, curved
- Arms swing forward, backward, and sideward
- Arms rotate forward and backward
- Arms close together, shoulder-width apart, greater than shoulder-width apart
- Arms in front, in back, beside, above, below
- Shoulders pressed down, elevated (pushed upward), pushed forward, or pushed backward

Hands and Fingers

- Wrists flexed, extended, or straight
- Wrist circles
- Hands beneath or on top of
- Hands supporting or grasping
- Fingers pointing away or toward
- Fingers facing forward or backward
- Fingers together or spread apart
- Fingers straight or flexed
- Thumbs together (touching)

Legs and Feet

- Knees straight or bent
- Legs apart or together
- Legs turned out, parallel, turned in
- Feet flexed or pointed
- Ankle circles

gymnastics. The next step is to combine body parts and work with the body as a whole by using specific terminology for precise body positions as well as arm and foot positions the gymnasts must learn and experience. Understanding the skill and variations and being able to perform and have a working knowledge of terminology are the nuts and bolts, or the foundation, of future skills. This foundation terminology will give the teacher and the gymnast a common language that can be used to describe gymnastics skills. Students will learn and combine skills more easily if they are familiar with the technical names and can immediately associate the positions with the names.

FOUNDATIONAL BODY POSITIONS

As you teach each position, have the gymnasts say the name while in that position. Teach one position, repeat the name, then teach another position and repeat the new name. Check gymnasts' positions for correctness because this will be important later. Continue to add to the positions and check for correctness until the students learn all the positions.

Young children enjoy fun phrases that allow them to use their imaginations to visualize a movement. To assist the teacher, "kinder cues" or phrases will be used as learning cues for many of the beginning skills. The teacher can experiment with creating additional kinder cues.

Here is a good formal gymnastics drill: Say the formal gymnastics name and have the gymnasts get in the proper position as quickly as possible. Make it a game. For example, you can say, "Sitting tuck…sitting pike…squat stand…straight-body stand…lying straddle…inverted pike…lying tuck," while watching gymnasts quickly get into each position.

Tuck

The tuck is a basic position that involves hip and knee flexion. The knees are bent to maximum range and pulled toward the chest. A tuck position is used in many skills such as forward rolls, squat-ons, and tuck jumps.

Sitting Tuck

The sitting tuck is a foundational skill and the easiest tuck to perform.
- Sit on floor with the torso vertical and the rib cage and abdomen lifted.
- Bend the knees to maximum range and point the feet.
- Tighten the tuck by grasping the shins and pulling them to the chest.

Squat and Squat Stand

A tuck position in which the body weight is supported evenly on two feet with the chest close to the knees is called a squat. If the torso is vertical, it is called a squat stand.
- Support the body weight evenly on two feet.
- For the squat, bend hips and knees until thighs are touching chest.

Supported Tuck

- Support the tucked body with the hands slightly in front of the feet and the weight shifted to the hands.
- Challenge: Raise the body *slightly* so that there are a few inches between the heels and the buttocks. You will feel the tension in your thigh muscles.

Supine Tuck

- Lying on the floor in a supine position, bend legs at knees and hips.
- You may grasp the shins.

Inverted Tuck

- In a supine position, bend legs at knees and hips.
- Point the feet.
- Round the spine as you lift the hips off the floor above the shoulders.
- Contract abdominal muscles and keep them tight.

Learning Cues for Sitting Tuck

Verbal/Linguistic
- Sit on the floor with the torso vertical and the rib cage and abdominal muscles lifted.
- Keep the spine vertical.
- Bend at the hips.
- Bend the knees to maximum range and point the feet.
- Pull the knees to the chest and keep the upper back straight.
- Help by grasping shins and pulling to them to the chest.

Logical/Mathematical
- Keep knees and hips bent at least 90 degrees.
- Keep body position symmetrical.

Visual/Spatial
- See bent knees together, close to the chest.
- Tuck the body in tight like a ball.

Bodily/Kinesthetic
- Feel the feet and knees together.
- Feel thighs touching the chest.
- Feel shoulders pressed forward and down.
- Feel abdomen tighten.

Naturalist
- Make the shape of a raindrop.

(continued)

(continued)

Common Errors

- Tuck is insufficient.
- Legs are apart.
- Buttocks are touching heels and chest is down.

Pike

The pike is a basic position that involves hip flexion and straight legs. If the angle is 90 degrees or greater, it is called an open pike. If the angle is less than 90 degrees, it is called a closed pike. The pike position is used in many skills such as an L support, pike jump, and front hip circle.

Sitting Pike

The sitting pike is a foundational skill and the easiest to perform.

- Sit on floor with legs straight and together and feet pointed.
- Keep the torso vertical and hips flexed.
- Lift the rib cage and abdominal muscles.

Standing Pike

- Stand in pike with legs straight and hips flexed so that torso is horizontal.
- Keep weight forward on the front of the feet.

Standing Supported Pike

- Stand in supported pike with the hands on the floor slightly in front of the feet, which are shoulder-width apart.
- Shift the weight partially to the hands.

Supine Pike

- Lie on the floor with body in a supine position.
- Bend at the hips, lifting legs perpendicular to the floor.

Inverted Pike

- In a supine position, pike at the hips.
- Lift the hips off the floor and above the shoulders.

Learning Cues for Sitting Pike

Verbal/Linguistic
- Sit on the floor with legs extended to the front.
- Keep legs together and straight with feet pointed.
- Keep back straight and the rib cage and abdomen lifted.

Logical/Mathematical
- Keep legs straight and the flexion at torso 90 degrees (more than 90 degrees for closed pike).
- Make one line from the top of the head to the bottom of the spine.
- Keep torso vertical and legs perpendicular at 90 degrees.
- Make a symmetrical body position.

Visual/Spatial
- Make the shape of an L for an open pike.
- Make the shape of a V for a closed pike.
- See the legs and feet together and straight.
- Make a straight line with the legs.
- Make a straight line with the spine from the head through the hips.
- Kinder cue: Make a pike sandwich and close the sandwich tight.

Bodily/Kinesthetic
- Feel the muscles above knees squeezed tight.
- Feel the abdomen lifted and tight.
- Feel the insides of legs together.
- Press the shoulders down and feel the neck elongate.
- Feel the tops of the feet stretching to a point.

Common Errors
- Knees are bent.
- Bend is coming from the upper back instead of the hips.
- Chest is dropped.

Straddle

The straddle is a basic position in which the legs are straight, opened sideward (possibly to maximum range), and sometimes turned outward. Most of the time the hips are flexed and the angle is 90 degrees or more. When the angle of hip flexion is less than 90 degrees it is called a pike straddle, sometimes referred to as a pancake. The straddle is used in many skills such as a straddle forward roll, straddle jump, straddle handstands on floor and beam, and sole circles on bars.

Sitting Straddle

The sitting straddle is a foundational skill and the easiest straddle to perform.

- Sit on floor with the legs straight and apart and extended sideways with legs turned outward, feet pointed.
- Keep the torso vertical and hips flexed at 90 degrees or more.
- Keep the rib cage and abdominal muscles lifted.

Standing Straddle

- Stand with weight on two feet in a straight-body position with hips square and legs shoulder-width apart.
- Keep the torso vertical with back straight, abdominal muscles tight, and chest lifted.

Piked Straddle Stand

- Stand with weight on two feet and legs straight and apart with hips flexed.
- Keep the legs straight and the torso bent forward at the hips.

Piked Supported Straddle

- Stand in supported straddle with the body in pike and the legs apart in straddle position.
- Place the hands slightly in front of the feet on the floor, shoulder-width apart, with the weight shifted partially to the hands.

Piked Supine Straddle

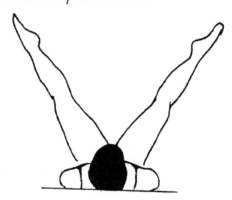

- Lie on the floor in a supine position.
- Lift legs, rotate them outward, and open them to maximum range with the hips flexed.

Piked Inverted Straddle

- Lie on the floor in a supine position with legs rotated outward in a pike straddle.
- Continue to lift spine until hips are above shoulders.

Learning Cues for Sitting Straddle

Verbal/Linguistic
- Sit on the floor with legs opened sideward to maximum range.
- Keep the torso vertical with hip flexion of 90 degrees or more.
- Keep the rib cage and abdomen lifted.
- Keep the legs straight and slightly turned out with the knees facing upward.
- Point the feet.

Logical/Mathematical
- Create maximum angle between legs.
- Maintain vertical torso with a straight back.

(continued)

(continued)

- Make one line from the top of the head to the bottom of the spine.
- Keep back vertical and legs horizontal.
- Make a symmetrical body position.

Visual/Spatial

- Keep chest and torso lifted.
- Knees face the ceiling.
- The legs make the letter V.
- Open the legs away from each other.
- Kinder cue: Make the points of a star with the feet, hands, and head.

Bodily/Kinesthetic

- Feel the muscles above the knees squeezing tight.
- Reach out to the walls with the fingers and toes.
- Feel the backs of the knees touching the floor.
- Point the feet until you feel the heels leave the floor.
- Feel the chest lifted and abdomen tight.

Naturalist

- Kinder cue: Stretch the points out like a snowflake.

Common Errors

- Knees are bent.
- Legs are turned in.
- Abdomen is loose.
- Back is rounded.
- Chest is dropped.

Straight Body

The straight body is a basic position in which there is no flexion at the hips or knees. Feet may be parallel or turned out to 45 degrees. It is called a stretched body when the body is straight and the arms are over the head. The straight-body position may also be called a layout. In the straight-body position there is one straight line from head to feet and in the stretched-body position there is one straight line from fingers to feet.

The straight-body position may be found in the start, middle, or end position of a skill. It is one of the most important positions to learn and it is very important to train gymnasts to maintain a tight, straight body; also stress that the abdomen and buttocks should be tight and the chest lifted. Build gymnasts' awareness of this position by having them stand straight; then ask them to bend over in a pike. Then have them stand back up in a straight body again, tighten all of the abdominal and buttocks muscles, and try to pike again. If gymnasts' muscles stay tight, they cannot pike. This tightness is very important in a lot of skills.

Variations with a straight line or a slight curve in the body include the hollow and arch. Gymnasts must develop and practice good body awareness of the straight, hollow, and arch positions.

Straight Body

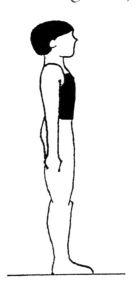

- Stand with legs straight and together.
- Keep the abdomen tight and the rib cage lifted.

Stretched Body

The stretch position is the same as the straight body with the arms overhead. There is one straight line from fingers to feet.

- Stand with legs straight and together.
- Stretch arms overhead by the ears.
- Keep abdomen tight and rib cage lifted.

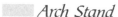 Hollow Stand

- Stand in a stretched-body position.
- Contract the chest and abdomen inward with a pelvic tilt.
- Bring shoulders forward, which will create a rounded upper back.
- Naturalist: Get in the rainbow position.

One way to get experience with a hollow body is to lie on the back. Place the hands on top of the thighs and contract the abdomen by lifting the shoulders approximately 6 inches off the floor. Slightly bend the legs, keep the lower back on the floor, and reach the hands toward the knees.

Arch Stand

- Stand in a stretched-body position.
- Pull arms backward by the back of the ears, which will cause an arch to occur naturally.

In the arch, the upper and lower portions of the back are stretched backward in a curve. However, for beginners the term *arch* should not be used because most people will incorrectly overemphasize the arch. Use the term *curve* to describe the arch. Perform small "supermans" to gain experience with the proper arch. Lie on the floor in a prone, stretched-body position. Keep head neutral and lift the arms up slightly off the floor, bringing the arms overhead past the ears. This also brings the shoulders off the floor and forms the arch in the upper back.

Learning Cues for Straight Body

Verbal/Linguistic

- Stand with legs together and straight.
- Keep the abdomen tight and the rib cage lifted.
- Keep the weight forward on the front of the feet.
- Keep all muscles engaged (feel them working).

Logical/Mathematical

- Make a straight line with the body perpendicular to the floor.
- Keep hips and shoulders square.

Visual/Spatial

- Make a straight line from head to feet.
- Position the pelvic bones directly over the balls of the feet.
- Keep a neutral head position.

Bodily/Kinesthetic

- Feel weight forward on the front of the feet.
- Feel abdomen and buttocks muscles tighten.
- Feel feet and legs together.
- Feel torso tighten in front and in back with rib cage lifted.
- Feel center line of the body going from the head through the feet.

Naturalist

- Make the shape of a strong tree trunk.

Common Errors

- Body is loose and saggy.
- Weight is back on the heels.
- Legs are apart.
- Lower and middle back are arched.
- Head is not in line with the body.
- Abdominal and buttocks muscles are loose.

Other Body Positions

Other body positions include the stride, gymnastics point, initiation lunge, finish lunge, and safe landing position. In these positions, one or both knees are flexed or the legs are straight but separated with one foot in front of the other. A salute is not considered a body position. It is used to present or finish a skill. In the salute the arms are overhead and the body position is usually a finishing lunge or an arch (but be careful not to arch in middle or lower back). The shoulders are pressed back and down and are oblique (arms are in a backward diagonal line).

Stride

- Stand on the floor with one leg in front of other leg as if standing on a line.
- Keep one foot approximately 8 to 12 inches in front of the other with legs slightly turned out.
- Keep the torso vertical.
- Keep the chest, rib cage, and abdomen lifted.
- Make the body shape of torso and legs look like an upside-down Y if viewed from the side.

Gymnastics Point (Tendu)

The gymnastics point is used mainly as a preparatory position and is derived from a ballet skill known as the tendu.

- Begin in standing stretched-body position.
- Place one leg in front, keeping that leg straight and the foot pointed. Touch the toe lightly to the floor.
- Place arms overhead and in line with the body, making a vertical line from fingers to the foot of the support leg.
- Keep hips square by keeping a straight horizontal line across the front of the pelvis.
- Keep support leg straight and supporting body weight.
- Keep head neutral.
- Feel the tightness in the thigh (quadriceps) of back support leg.
- Keep abdomen and buttocks tight with rib cage lifted.

Initiation Lunge

There are two types of lunge positions. One is a lunge that is used to initiate a skill (preparatory movement) and the other is a finishing lunge used to stabilize and present the end of a skill. The lunge to initiate a skill is one of the most important tumbling positions to master. In this lunge the weight is forward over the flexed knee. This position gets the weight forward and ready to begin a skill.

Finish Lunge

Many times the finish of a skill segues from the initiation lunge to the finish lunge.

- Begin in a lunge position.
- Pull the arms back in oblique (lifted upward and backward in an upward diagonal).
- Shift the weight to evenly distribute it between both feet but also keep the front leg bent.
- Keep back leg straight and tight.
- Feel a counter pull: arms pull up and back while torso is forward over front leg.
- Keep hips square by keeping a straight horizontal line across the front of the pelvis.
- Feel hips centered.
- Make a vertical line from foot to knee of the front leg.
- Keep chin lifted.
- Keep torso vertical with rib cage lifted.
- Keep abdominal and buttocks muscles tight.

Learning Cues for Initiation Lunge

Verbal/Linguistic

- Begin in standing stride position with straight arms overhead by the ears.
- Keep head neutral.
- Flex the front knee.
- Keep back leg straight.

(continued)

(continued)

Logical/Mathematical

- Keep arms overhead and in line with body. Make a diagonal line from fingers to the foot of the back leg.
- Keep hips square by keeping a straight horizontal line across the front of the pelvis.

Visual/Spatial

- Keep front leg bent with knee over front foot.
- Keep head neutral.

Bodily/Kinesthetic

- Feel body weight shifted forward over the front support foot.
- Push hips forward.
- Feel arms touching ears.
- Feel back leg straight and tight.
- Feel tight abdominal and buttocks muscles.
- Feel rib cage lifted.
- Feel the tightness in the thigh (quadriceps) of front leg.

Interpersonal

A good test for the lunge is to feel the tightness in the thigh of the front leg. A partner should be able to feel the performer's tight muscle working.

Common Errors

- Weight is over the back leg.
- Hips are not square.
- Front leg is bent too much or not enough.
- Line from fingers to foot of back leg is crooked.
- Arms are not by ears.

Safe Landing Position

Gymnasts should learn this "still" balanced position and be able to quickly position the body on cue. Have gymnasts "hold" the position and then say, "Finish" or "Salute" to learn how to end a skill.

- From a standing position, softly bend knees to demi-plié position.
- Align knees directly over the center of the feet.
- Keep abdominal muscles tight and the upper body vertical.
- Arms are in front low diagonal. Hold 5 seconds, then salute.

FOUNDATIONAL POSITIONS FOR LEGS AND ARMS

Most gymnastics leg and arm positions have their origins in ballet and modern dance and are optional in gymnastics. However, some students already have experience with dance and will use the terminology.

It is important to learn how the legs and arms work to initiate, execute, enhance, or end a skill. Leg and arm positions are a part of technique and assist the body in balance, momentum, delivery, and style. Gymnasts should practice positions separately in standing and then in walking patterns before combining the arms and legs or utilizing them with the gymnastics skills.

Leg Positions

The straddle, stride, parallel, and plié are leg positions. All but the parallel position require a certain amount of turnout initiated from the hips. The ability to turn out the legs is important for correct positioning in many skills, and if performed properly, turnout will greatly enhance the aesthetic appearance of gymnasts' skills. However, the turnout required in gymnastics is less than the turnout required in dance and should never be forced. It must happen in the hip socket and not in the ankle joint. If gymnasts turn out their feet and not their legs, pronation (fallen arches) and knee problems can occur.

Parallel

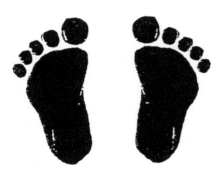

Place one foot beside the other with toes of both feet facing forward. Feet may be apart or touching each other. This is a symmetrical body position.

Turnout

The feet may be beside each other with the heels touching, or the feet can be in "train" position with one foot behind the other. The toes of each foot are in a slight diagonal from the midline of the body.

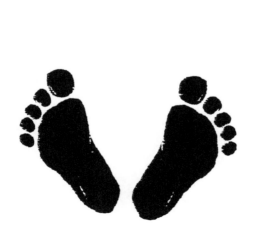

Plié

Plié *(plee-AY)* is the bending of the legs and is done in any of the leg positions. A demi-plié is a small bend in the legs, which helps the body absorb the shock of landings by "giving," or bending, the legs. The plié is essential to safe landings. Gymnasts must control the muscles to react and change the amount of knee bend in response to the height of the jump. On a landing, gymnasts must bend the legs and bring the heels to the floor while maintaining good body alignment. This leg position may be symmetrical or asymmetrical.

Arm Positions

The shoulder girdle is pressed down and the sternum is lifted in all arm positions. In most gymnastics arm positions the arms are straight. Arm positions are either relational or directional. *Relational* refers to a position in relation to another body part: over the head, in front of the body, below the hips, and so on. *Directional* refers to a general direction that the arm moves: forward diagonal, backward diagonal, front middle, side middle, and so on.

Arms in Oblique

Oblique is a position essential to the stabilization of the body in lunges and in finishing turns. The arms are lifted to an upper diagonal position behind the body. This arm position keeps the chest lifted and keeps the torso vertical. This is a symmetrical body position that could be described as a V with the arms.

Straight Arms Overhead

The straight arms overhead position is used frequently, especially in starting positions and in inverted support positions. The hands are over the head in line with the body and the insides of the arms are touching the ears.

Rounded Arms Overhead ("Crown")

- Curve both arms overhead.
- Curve fingers inward toward each other.

Arms in Side Middle

- Extend arms out to the sides, parallel with the floor, palms down. Make the letter T with the arms.

Arms in Front Middle

- Extend arms in front of the body, parallel with the floor, palms down or rounded.

Arms in Front Low

- Extend arms in front of the body, 45 degrees lower than front middle with the palms down.

Arms in Opposition

One arm is in front of the body opposite the lead leg, which is what gives this position its name. If the right foot is forward, then the left arm is in front middle. The right arm might be in various positions except front middle. The other arm is usually at side middle; it might also be overhead.

FOUNDATIONAL BALANCES

Before beginning foundational balances, allow learners to discover how the size of the base and shifting body weight changes their balance (see "Exploring Balance and Flexibility" in chapter 2, page 30). The formal gymnastics balances include a variety of positions on one foot as well as the stride split, straddle split, V-sit, and shoulder stand.

A person is in a balanced position when the center of gravity is over a good base of support. When the center of gravity is shifted or the size of the base of support changes, then the person must compensate by making adjustments in other parts of the body. This can be done by extending other body parts to equalize the weight distribution or by contracting muscles and exercising muscle control.

Standing Balance Skills (Straight Line From Supporting Foot to Head)

The relevé, coupé, passé, front attitude, and battement are positions that form a straight line from the supporting foot or feet to head.

 *Relevé Hold*

The relevé *(REL-uh-VAY)* hold is a straight-body position in which the gymnast lifts up on the balls of the feet to the highest possible position and balances.

Learning Cues for Relevé Hold

Verbal/Linguistic

- Stand in a straight-body position.
- Step forward, lifting onto the toes of both feet.
- Bring the back foot to the front foot until ankles are together. Keep the legs slightly turned out and the weight on both feet.
- Continue lifting up to the balls of the feet to the highest relevé possible as arms lift overhead.
- In ballet, arms begin in side middle and lift to a rounded overhead position (crown) during the lift of the feet.

Logical/Mathematical

- Keep body vertical.

Visual/Spatial

- Focus straight ahead.
- Lift chin, press shoulders down, and make neck long.
- Make the body in the shape of a pencil (toes come together in a point at the bottom).
- Keep entire body still while balancing.

Bodily/Kinesthetic

- Feel the floor with the balls of the feet.
- Feel ankles and inner legs squeezing together.
- Squeeze muscles tight in abdomen and buttocks.

Musical/Rhythmical

- Move upward into a balance position at an even pace.

Assist

- Stand behind and hold gymnast's hips to assist in balance.

Common Errors

- Balance is not maintained.
- Knees are bent.
- Body is not in a straight line.
- Abdomen and buttocks are loose.
- Head is out of neutral position.

Coupé

Coupé *(koo-PAY)* means to cut. As a step it has many forms. Here is a simple version of the skill.

- Stand on one leg with weight over the front of the foot.
- Flex the free leg with the toes pointed and resting at the ankle of the support leg.
- Point foot sharply to cut under the leg.
- Face knee forward or sideward; practice both positions.
- Place arms in a crown.

Passé

Passé *(pah-SAY)* is the same basic body position as coupé, but the toes of the lifted leg are placed at the knee instead of the ankle of the supporting leg. Lift passé up until upper leg is horizontal.

Front Attitude

- Balance on one leg.
- Feel weight on the front of the foot.
- Lift the other leg up in front so that the thigh is parallel with the floor.
- Turn out the lifted leg and flex the knee.
- Tighten muscles of standing leg.

Battement Forward

The battement *(bat-MAH)* is a large swinging motion of the leg. The swing can be forward, backward, or sideways.

- Begin with weight on back foot (left) with front foot (right) in point (gymnastics point).
- Lift right leg up to horizontal or above in front of body.
- Keep both legs equally turned out.
- Feel weight as far back as possible on the foot of left leg.
- Keep hips square and right leg parallel to floor.
- Tighten quads of left leg.
- Keep back vertical.
- Stand tall with chest lifted.

- Keep chin up and eyes focused forward.
- Lower left leg slowly and repeat on other side.

Standing Balance Skills (Straight or Curved Line From Nonsupported Foot to Head)

The arabesque, scale, and lever form a straight or curved (arched) line from the nonsupported foot to the head. In an arabesque the back is vertical. A scale is an arabesque with the torso tilted slightly forward from the hip socket to allow the leg to lift higher. In a lever, continue the forward tilt, keeping a straight line until hands touch the floor. The scale and lever have a seesaw movement: the lifting of the back leg causes the torso to tip forward. In the lever, it is important to keep a straight line from the head and torso to the toes of the raised leg. There must be no break (bending) at the hip or dropping of the chest.

Arabesque *(air-uh-BESK)*

- Stand in a stride body position.
- Extend the back leg with pointed foot as high as possible while keeping the torso vertical.
- Keep the back vertical and the back leg lifted between 6 inches and 90 degrees off the floor.
- The arabesque may have a slightly flexed support leg when used for landings out of a skill.

Scale

- Stand in a stride body position.
- Extend the back leg with pointed foot as high as possible by tilting the torso slightly forward from the hip socket to allow the leg to lift higher and perform the scale.
- Keep a straight line from the head to the toes of the raised leg.
- Make a lever with body so that the chest lowers proportionately with the lift of the scale leg. Back leg is 90 degrees or higher.

Lever

In this position there is a straight line from the fingers through the head, hips, and support leg, which should be maintained throughout. The fulcrum of the lever is the hips. The body works like a seesaw with the support leg as the base.

- Start in a lunge.
- Lean torso forward, keeping support leg straight.
- Lift the back leg while still maintaining the straight line going through the T, or lever, position.
- Lever the body forward at the hip. Keep support on one leg until hands touch the floor.
- Return to T position.
- Continue bringing torso up until back leg touches the floor.
- Finish in lunge.
- Arms remain overhead and in line with body, making a diagonal line from fingers to the foot of the back leg as hands touch the floor.
- Keep hips square by keeping a straight horizontal line across the front of the pelvis.
- Keep head neutral.

Learning Cues for Arabesque, Scale, and Lever

Verbal/Linguistic

- Stand with one foot in front of the other, slightly turned out and approximately 8 to 10 inches apart for children and 12 to 15 inches for adults. The weight is forward on front foot. For lever, begin in gymnastics point and step forward.
- Extend the back leg with pointed foot as high as possible.
- Keep the torso vertical for arabesque.
- Maintain balance on straight support leg.
- Keep both legs straight, hips square, ankle and toes of free leg extended.
- Hold head and chest high with torso in front of support leg.
- Keep the arms in side middle to keep chest lifted for arabesque and scale.
- Keep arms overhead in lever.

Visual/Spatial

- Shift pelvic bones forward over ball of support foot.
- Keep shoulders back and chest up.
- Face heel inward, not upward, to make a longer line.
- Keep head neutral.
- Safety issue: To keep pressure off the lower back and to raise the height of lifted leg, remember to keep the torso in front of the standing leg.
- Kinder cue: Make an airplane.

Bodily/Kinesthetic

- Feel weight as far forward on standing leg as possible.
- Feel chest lifted in the beginning of the movement with tight torso.
- Keep both legs slightly turned out.
- Feel the tightness in the thighs (quads) of both legs with a straight knee on the standing leg.

Assist

- Place one hand on belly and other hand under free leg.

Common Errors

- Knees or hips are bent.
- Hips are not square.
- Muscles are loose, which causes loss of balance.
- Lower back is overarched.
- Shoulders are not pulled back.
- Line from fingers to foot of lifted back leg is bent.
- Arms are not by ears in lever.
- T position in scale and lever is lost when back leg or chest drops.

Nonstanding Balance Skills: Knee Balances

Knee Stand

- Kneel on both knees with legs together.
- Square the hips and lift the chest.
- Arm position may vary.
- Create a straight line from knees to head.

Knee Lunge

- Begin in a knee stand.
- Place one foot forward on floor until leg is bent at 90 degrees and slightly turned out.
- Keep the shin of the back leg on the floor with the top of back foot resting on the floor.
- Keep the weight placement primarily on the front foot.
- Keep the arms in oblique and chest lifted.

Half Split

- Begin in push-up position from knees.
- Bring one leg forward and under hips until knee and lower leg rest on floor.
- Keep back leg straight with the top of foot on floor.
- Point both feet.
- Push arms off the floor and raise torso to a vertical position.
- Lift arms out to the side for balance.

Knee Scale

- Begin in push-up position with hands shoulder-width apart and fingers facing forward.
- Bring one leg forward and under hips until knee and lower leg rest on floor.
- Lift other leg off the floor and raise to horizontal or above while in a straight, balanced position.
- Make a line parallel to the floor from head to toe, then lift leg up higher if possible.
- Focus straight in front.

Balance in Knee Scale

Gymnast performs, without hand support, an arabesque on the shin.
- Begin in a knee scale.
- Lifts arms out to a slight oblique.
- Kinder cue: Fly your airplane steady in the sky.

Nonstanding Balance Skills: Splits

The splits are a skill that cannot be pushed, but they are achievable over time. Static holds in the split position will enhance the skill for even the most inflexible person. These are good skills to assign as "homework" after you review and stress correct procedure. Put procedures in writing: "Use a static hold—NO bouncing! Go only to the point of tension, NOT pain, and hold 60 seconds or more." Splits require no special apparatus for the students to practice and the students can benefit from practicing the skill daily.

Stride Split

- From a kneeling lunge position, slide the front leg forward to a stride split position.

Straddle Split

Beginning in a standing straddle position, slide the legs apart into a straddle split. Beginners may start in a supported straddle so that the hands can be used for support while the legs slide apart. You may want to try going from hand support to forearm support.

Learning Cues for Stride or Straddle Split

Verbal/Linguistic

- Begin in a kneeling lunge position for stride split and slide front leg forward to maximum stretch and straighten back leg.
- Begin in straddle position for straddle split and slide legs apart.
- Keep weight centered, hips square, and knees straight.
- Keep trunk straight.

Logical/Mathematical

- Try to attain a 180-degree line with the legs.
- Try to make a straight line with legs from foot to foot.
- Keep hips and shoulders square.
- Keep shoulders and hips at right angles to legs.

Visual/Spatial

- For stride split, place hands on either side of front leg (hands to one side will cause improper rotation of the hips).
- Keep back knee on floor for stride split.
- Keep back foot tucked under with top of foot touching floor in stride split.
- Kinder cue: Make a tent; take the tent down to the floor. Make a triangle, then squish the triangle.

Bodily/Kinesthetic

- Feel both legs completely straight.
- Feel the legs slide apart until you are sitting on the floor with straight legs.
- Feel weight on the back leg for stride split. (Students will naturally and unconsciously shift over to the front leg to avoid stretching the large quadriceps muscle in the back leg.)
- Feel back knee on the floor in stride split, not out to the side.

Common Errors

- Weight is not centered over both legs in stride split (student sits to the side of the front leg).
- Back leg is bent in stride split.
- Legs are turned out in stride split.
- Abdominal muscles are loose.
- Two hands are on one side of leg.

Inverted Balance Skills

Some students who are overweight or have neck problems might not be able to do the shoulder stand. Make sure body weight is supported by the shoulders and upper back and not on the head and neck.

Inverted Shoulder Stand (Candle)

The tight, straight body is a very important position in advanced skills. To prepare gymnasts for the feeling of a straight body in inverted skills, have them try straight-body lifts first and then inverted shoulder stands (see figure below). This is a lead-up skill for handstands, cartwheels, and round-offs. To help prepare gymnasts for this skill, first have them try the following drills.

Straight-Body Lift From Supine Straight Body

- Begin in a supine straight-body position.
- Tighten all the muscles in the abdomen, back, and legs.
- Instructor or partner will lift the legs about 12 inches off the floor to see if body can be lifted in one straight line.
- If body starts to sag or pike, squeeze buttocks muscles tighter.
- For a challenge, keep arms above the head.

Straight-Body Lift From Front or Rear Support

For another challenge, begin in front or rear support and have partner lift body until horizontal.

Learning Cues for Shoulder Stand

Verbal/Linguistic

- Begin in seated tuck.
- Push through feet to roll onto back.
- In the roll backward, extend the hips and legs directly above the shoulders to candlestick position.
- Maintain a straight line from shoulders to toes.
- Place arms beside the hips on the floor to provide a stronger base of support.

Logical/Mathematical

- Sequence is seated tuck, roll to inverted tuck, extend to shoulder stand.
- Open the angles in the inverted tuck.
- Create a vertical line from shoulders to toes.

Visual/Spatial

- Look straight ahead on the way to inverted tuck; watch the toes on the way up to candle.
- See knees and feet together on the way up to candle.
- See body fully extended in a straight line from shoulders to toes.
- Point the feet.
- Kinder cue: Make a giant birthday candle.

Bodily/Kinesthetic

- Squeeze the buttocks and tighten abdomen as hips rise.
- Feel knees and feet together throughout.
- Feel feet above shoulders at the end of candle.
- Feel hands and upper back touching the floor when at the top of candle.

Musical/Rhythmical

- Count three beats down and three beats up. The movement can be fluid, or you can hold the candle position before coming down.

Assist

- Support by holding gymnast's feet. Assist gymnast into a foot and leg position in line with and above shoulders.

Common Errors

- Body straightens out too soon and loses momentum.
- Mid and lower back touch floor with feet up in the air.
- Legs straighten, but not the body (piking).
- Buttocks and abdominal muscles are loose.

FOUNDATIONAL SUPPORT

The term *support* refers to any position in which the body is supported partially or totally by the arms or hands. In most cases the body is above a piece of apparatus such as a folded mat, a balance beam, or a bar. Foundational positions include positions on folded mats or on the floor.

Support With Three or Four Body Parts

A front support is any support position in which the arms are extended and in front of the body. A rear support is any support position in which the arms are extended and behind the body. A side support is any support position in which one arm or both arms are extended to the side of the body.

Front Support

The front support is also called the push-up position. Many gymnasts will need to begin with a modified push-up from the knees before going to a full front support. The front support is an important position used in more advanced skills. Gymnasts must be able to keep the arms straight. Have gymnasts get in a front support position with straight arms and try to hold the position for 1 minute. Then have gymnasts get in a front support but bend the arms and try to hold for 1 minute. Gymnasts will find that they can hold the support longer with straight arms.

Learning Cues for Front Support

Verbal/Linguistic
- Begin in a prone straight-body position.
- Place hands under shoulders and push down on floor.
- Push body upward from feet until arms are straight and weight is evenly distributed on both hands.
- Support a tight body with arms straight.
- Maintain a straight-body position by keeping back straight, not rounded or arched.

Logical/Mathematical
- Maintain a downward diagonal line from head to toes.
- Keep a vertical line from hands through shoulders with arms at right angle to floor.
- Keep feet at right angle to floor.
- Make the body symmetrical.

Visual/Spatial
- Keep head in line with body.
- Look at floor directly beneath head.
- Keep heels right above balls of feet.
- Keep fingers facing forward.
- Kinder cue: Make a ramp for the cars.

Bodily/Kinesthetic
- Feel the floor as you push with hands until arms straighten.
- Feel abdominal muscles tighten to keep lower back straight.
- Feel back and buttocks muscles tighten to keep from piking.
- Squeeze legs and heels together.
- Keep muscles above knees tight.

(continued)

(continued)

Musical/Rhythmical

- Push down equally and at the same time with both arms.

Assist

- Place one hand under belly and lift at waist. Place one hand under thighs.

Common Errors

- Body leans too far to one side.
- Body weight is not distributed between the hands and feet.
- Body is not in a straight line.
- Back is arched or rounded.
- Arms are bent.
- Torso is loose.
- Legs are apart and bent.

Rear Support

- Begin in sitting tuck position with hands beneath shoulders and fingers toward feet.
- Push hands on floor until arms straighten.
- Push hips up and tighten buttocks.
- Extend the legs and squeeze straight legs together.
- Support body on hands and feet.
- Create an upper diagonal line from toes to head.
- Keep arms perpendicular to floor.
- Keep torso straight in a downward diagonal in front of you.
- If necessary, begin with a crab, or table, position before progressing to a rear support.
- Challenge: Begin in a front support. Keeping arms and body straight, turn 180 degrees to rear support, and continue to turn another 180 degrees to front support.

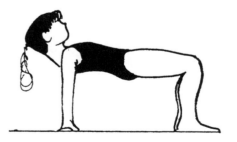

Side Support

- Squat on floor with hands placed to one side of the body.
- Maintain balance and direct the feet away from the hands.
- With feet together on floor, extend arm to execute a side support in a straight-body position with the other arm extended outward and upward to a vertical position for balance.
- Body is straight and tight and forms a downward diagonal from head to feet.
- Body forms a T position that has fallen over and is balancing on the base and on one side of the T.
- Challenge: Perform the side support with only one foot on floor. Change position of top leg to coupé, passé, or straddle.

Front Support on Floor Series

Developing upper-body strength to support the entire body and shifting the body weight to the hands is an important foundational skill for floor, bars, beam, and vault skills. The purpose of the front support is to develop body awareness in the shifting of body weight. In the front support series, begin in a front support on floor with arms extended and abdomen lifted. Push off feet and shift weight forward so that arms support weight. Perform a supported tuck, straddle stand, and open pike stand in a series, returning to front support in between each position. Stay symmetrical throughout.

Front Support to Supported Tuck

- Begin in a front support.
- Push with the feet, shifting the weight to the hands, and raise the hips as the legs are lifted. Pull legs in to a squat position with feet between the hands.
- Use abdominal muscles to help tuck.
- Hold in momentary supported tuck.
- Return to front support position.
- Sequence is front support, push and shift weight, lift hips, supported tuck, push, front support.

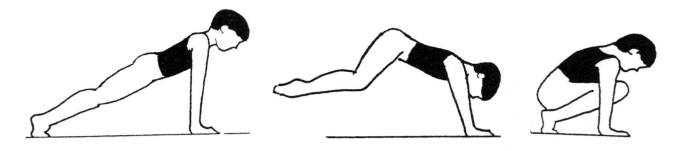

Front Support to Supported Pike Straddle Stand

- Begin in a front support.
- Push with the feet, shifting the weight to the hands, and raise the hips as the legs come forward.
- Place the feet outside of the hands in a supported pike straddle position.
- Keep the hips over the hands in straddle.
- Keep the upper back rounded and head inside the arms.
- Hold in momentary supported pike straddle.
- Return to front support position.
- Sequence is front support, push and shift weight, lift hips, supported pike straddle stand, push, front support.

Front Support to Supported Pike Stand

- Begin in a front support.
- Push with the feet, shifting the weight to the hands.
- Raise the hips, keeping legs together, to place feet close to the hands in supported open standing pike stand.
- Keep chest round and head in.
- Hold in momentary supported pike.
- Return to front support position.
- Sequence is front support, push and shift weight, lift hips, supported pike stand, push, front support.

Supported Tuck, Push, Lift Hips in Tuck, Return to Squat

- Begin in a supported tuck position with hands shoulder-width apart and fingers facing forward and slightly open.
- Keeping legs together, shift weight to hands and push off with feet.
- Lift hips upward, bring the tuck up *off the floor,* and point the feet.
- Return to land in supported tuck.
- Sequence is supported tuck, push and shift weight, lift hips in tuck, supported tuck.
- Purpose: To totally support the body on the hands (similar to chimp with tail in the air).
- Assist: Assist by supporting upper arm and lifting on shin.
- Caution: Shoulders will shift forward slightly over hands, but if the shoulders move too far forward, the gymnast will collapse forward onto face.

Bridge

The bridge is a more advanced foundational skill than the support skills covered up to this point. It is an arched position with hands and feet flat on the floor and abdomen raised. This position is used in walkovers and limbers. The most important component of the bridge is range of motion, particularly the flexibility in the upper back and shoulders. These are the two areas that will require the most attention.

Safety issue: This skill may not be recommended for some people. For the health of the spine, bridges must begin in the shoulders and follow an even curve in the spine. The shoulders must be directly over the hands. Many beginning gymnasts incorrectly arch at the lumbar spine where the abdominal muscles are weak and the spine is the most vulnerable. Practice bridges that emphasize upper-back and shoulder flexibility with the shoulders over the hands. Avoid overarching the lumbar spine. Never let students "walk" their hands closer to their feet. This puts additional stress and arch on the lower back. Instead, they should try to straighten their legs to shift the range of motion to their shoulders.

To begin practicing the bridge start on the floor. An elevated mat may be used once gymnasts are able to support a bridge with straight arms. The elevation will place the weight of the upper body over the hands so that the stress is off the lumbar spine.

Learning Cues for Bridge

Verbal/Linguistic
- Begin supine on the mat with legs bent, feet together, and hands directly under shoulders.
- Push down on the hands and feet while pushing the hips and spine up off the mat until the arms are straight.
- Form an arch with the back, which is supported more by the hands than the feet.
- Push into the shoulder and upper-back area, not into the lumbar spine.
- Lower the back by rounding down to floor.

Logical/Mathematical
- Try to create a straight line from hands through shoulders.

Visual/Spatial
- Place hands under the shoulders, palms on floor, fingers pointing toward feet.
- Keep the shoulders over the hands.
- Think of pushing the spine upward and forward.
- Push up to see the wall behind you.
- Lift until the shoulders are directly above the hands.

(continued)

(continued)

Bodily/Kinesthetic

- Push until arms are straight, keeping muscles tight.
- Feel the muscles push into upper back, not lower back.
- Feel weight equally on hands and feet.
- Feel a stretch in the upper back and shoulders, but no pain in the lower spine.

Interpersonal

- Work with a partner and check to see that the shoulders are directly above the hands.
- Place hand on upper back to help the partner feel where the arch should be. (This is feedback from one student to another student. This is not meant to be a substitute for assistance from the teacher.)

Musical/Rhythmical

- Arms and legs straighten at the same time.

Assist

- Place one hand on upper back and one on middle back to help the gymnast avoid pushing into the lower back (lumbar area).

Common Errors

- A long, low bridge is created from not pushing into shoulders.
- Arms are bent.
- Chin is tucked in.
- Back is straight.
- Only the lower back is pushed upward.

V-Sit

The V-sit is considered a support when the hands are placed behind the hips on the floor. A V-sit without hands is considered a balance. Gymnasts must have strong abdominal muscles to perform the V-sit. There are many types of skills that gymnasts can perform while in the basic V-sit position; these skills can add variety and provide the muscle strength necessary to perform the skill.

The following are some variations for V-sit skills: Sit in tuck and support upper body by placing hands behind hips on floor. Lean back so that the hands and buttocks support the weight. Lift one or both legs off the floor in many different ways to build abdominal strength. Keep the abdominal muscles tight and lifted but not pushed out. Here are some more specific variations for V-sit positions:

- Perform V-stag.
- Perform V-sit flutter kick.
- Perform V-sit criss-cross.
- Perform V-sit while grasping ankles.

The V-sit hold, a more advanced hold covered in chapter 4, is considered a support because the V is lifted off the floor and totally supported by the hands and arms. Therefore, the V-sit with hands to the V-sit without hands are part of the progression leading to the more advanced hold.

V-Sit Variations

Learning Cues for V-Sit

Verbal/Linguistic

- Sit in tuck.
- Support upper body by placing hands behind hips on floor.
- Extend legs to a 45-degree angle so that legs and body are both in a V position.
- To perform the V-sit without arms (which is a balance and strength activity), pull straight arms to side middle or up and back to an upper diagonal in oblique.

Logical/Mathematical

- Tilt the pike backward so that the legs and torso are on upper diagonals.
- Make a closed pike with the body.
- For V-sit without arms, reach arms up and behind head on a diagonal.
- Make a huge V with entire body.
- Be symmetrical.

Visual/Spatial

- Abdomen is tight and lifted but not pushed out.
- See knees and feet together in front of you.
- See muscles above knees working.
- See pointed feet in front of you.
- Keep sternum and upper back open and wide.
- Focus on an upper diagonal where the ceiling meets the wall.

Bodily/Kinesthetic

- Feel chest and sternum lifted, back straight.
- Feel abdomen tight.
- For a V-sit without hands, pull arms upward and backward.

Naturalist

- Sea anemones open and close (moving from tuck to V).

Assist

- Place one hand under thighs. Place one hand on back.

Common Errors

- Knees are bent.
- Chest is rounded.
- Back is arched.
- Weight is not balanced.
- Toes are not pointed.
- Legs can't stay up because of weak abdominal muscles.

Support With Arms on Folded Mats

There are many body positions in which the body weight is supported only by the hands and arms. The handstand is one of the skills in which all the body weight is supported on two body parts and is inverted. This skill will be discussed in chapter 4. Other positions in which the body is supported on two body parts, whether on the floor or on stacked mats, are often called holds.

The hold positions are easier to perform initially on folded mats, benches, or chairs. Hold positions require a lot of upper-body and abdominal strength. In the beginning stages even a momentary lift of the legs to these positions will help develop gymnasts' strength. However, make sure gymnasts do not arch the back or swing the legs for momentum; instead, gymnasts should use abdominal strength for control and balance in these positions.

Tuck Hold

This skill develops the upper-body strength that is necessary for future skills such as the straddle L and L.
- Begin in seated tuck between stacked mats with hands shoulder-width apart.
- Place hands on the folded mats with fingers facing forward.
- Extend arms by pushing down and straightening the elbows.
- "Roll" shoulders back for balance as tuck is elevated.
- Keep shoulders directly above hands. Keep head up and feet pointed.

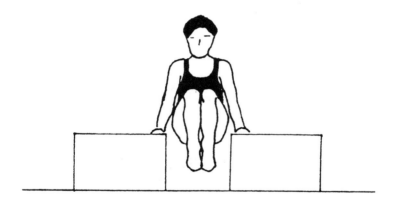

L Hold

Same as tuck hold except for the following:
- "Roll" shoulders backward for balance as the abdominal muscles contract and the feet elevate to a pike.

If you are unable to perform the L, work on abdominal strength by lifting legs a few inches off the floor. If lift cannot be maintained, lower the legs to the floor and lift the legs again and lower as necessary. Try to control legs and not let them drop to the floor.

Straddle L Hold

Same as L hold except for the following:

- Start in seated straddle between stacked mats.
- "Roll" shoulders backward for balance as straddle is elevated.
- Assist: Place one hand under thighs. Place one hand on back.

LOCOMOTOR SKILLS: ALTERNATING FOOT PATTERNS

Locomotor skills are used on the floor and beam, on approaches and landings on vault, and on jumps to mount and dismount bars. The basic foot patterns in physical education skills transfer into patterns that are stylized for gymnastics and dance. Variations of walking forward, backward, and sideward while alternating feet utilize different parts of the foot, leg positions in between each step, speeds or tempos of the movement, and levels of the body.

Forward Walking

- Stand on floor with weight forward on standing leg and other foot pointed in front.
- Slightly turn out the legs.
- Shift weight to pointed foot, articulating through the toes, the ball of the foot, and the heel.
- Point the back foot and bring it through a turned-out coupé to transfer it to the front.
- Keeps hips square as you step.
- Keep repeating process to execute a walk across the floor.
- Sequence is toe, ball, heel; toe, ball, heel. Back foot leaves the floor heel, ball, toe.
- Length of the step is the length of a gymnastics point (straight leg extended with foot pointed in front). Steps should be so smooth that from the waist up, it looks like you're on wheels.

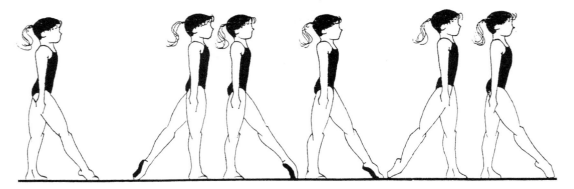

Backward Walking

- Stand on one foot with the other foot turned out and pointed to the back so that the big toe is touching the floor.
- Shift weight backward onto the pointed foot as the front foot points and transfers through a turned-out coupé to the back.
- Keep repeating process, each time reaching back and locating the floor with the big toe before stepping.
- Extend a straight and slightly turned-out leg backward, transfer weight onto it as you straighten the front leg, bring it through coupé, and then extend it behind you.
- Extend leg at a low diagonal from floor to hip socket.
- Sequence is coupé, extend, transfer, coupé, extend, transfer.
- Kinder cue: Say, "Touch, step, touch, step, touch, step" as you walk
- Other challenges: Quickly touch the floor with the big toe, lift the leg slightly, then step. (Tap, step, tap, step.)

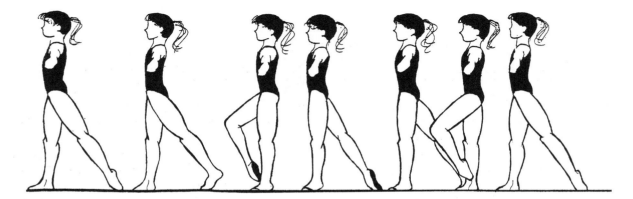

Lateral Walks

- Stand on floor.
- Walk by stepping side, together, side, together.
- Keep steps shoulder-width apart or smaller.
- Fully point foot between each step.
- If in relevé, keep heels directly above balls of feet.
- Keep arms out in side middle.
- Sequence is side, close, side, close, side, close.

Relevé Walk

The relevé walk is walking forward, backward, or sideward in relevé with heels directly above the balls of the feet.

Learning Cues for Relevé Walk

Verbal/Linguistic
- Stand on floor in relevé with heels directly above balls of the feet.
- Point the back foot through the toes while completely transferring the weight to the front foot.
- Pass the back leg to the front, keeping it straight and fully pointed.
- For a challenge, try backward and lateral walking.

Logical/Mathematical
- Keep steps small, measuring only the length of the extended leg.
- Keep a space between the pointed foot and the floor before each step.
- Keep rib cage lifted.
- Keep hips and shoulders square.
- Keep top of head parallel to the ceiling.

Visual/Spatial
- Walk only on the balls of the feet.
- Keep legs slightly turned out.
- Extend leg all the way through to a pointed foot between each step.
- Focus straight ahead.
- Keep heel directly above ball of foot.

Bodily/Kinesthetic
- Feel space between pointed foot and floor before each step.
- Feel shoulders pushed down.
- Feel chin, chest, and rib cage lifted.

(continued)

(continued)

Musical/Rhythmical

- Keep steps evenly paced.

Common Errors

- Weight is too far back, creating a low relevé.
- Toes are not pointed in between each step.

Other Challenges

- Try to kick to 45 degrees between each step.

Step-Hop (Skipping)

- Step, bending and extending the knee and foot, which lifts the knee of that leg with a hop.
- Step with other foot and hop.
- Continue step-hop sequence, which is a skip.

Chassé

The chassé *(sha-SAY)* is a springing type of movement (step-together or gallop motion) that can be performed forward or sideward. It is generally used as a preparatory movement landing with the front leg raised in preparation for the next skill.

Chassé means to chase—one leg chases the other. The chassé is similar to the hurdle used in approaches for vault and tumbling.

Learning Cues for Chassé

Verbal/Linguistic

- Begin in straight-body position.
- Step forward and spring slightly off floor.
- Bring legs together momentarily in the air.
- As back leg reaches front leg, slide front leg forward again (back leg chases front leg).
- Land in plié on the back leg with the front leg lifted slightly in preparation for the next movement (similar to a gallop).

Logical/Mathematical

- Sequence is step, together, slide; step, together, slide; rhythm is similar to a gallop.
- Push off front leg, come together in air, land on back leg.
- Cross legs slightly so that they move up and forward along a thin horizontal line.
- Keep torso vertical.
- Keep arms in opposition and parallel to the floor.

Visual/Spatial

- Focus straight ahead.
- Step on the ball of the foot.
- Kinder cue: Be a pencil in the air. Really show the sharp pencil point with your toes.

Bodily/Kinesthetic

- Feel legs turned out.
- Squeeze ankles together in the air.
- Feel the balls of the feet touch the floor.
- Squeeze knees straight at the top of each chassé.

Musical/Rhythmical

- Spend more time in the air than on the floor.
- Make a quick transfer of weight.
- Rhythm is:

  Push, squeeze.

  1-2, and 1-2.

Common Errors

- Takeoff step is too large so that legs barely come together in the air.
- Feet don't push through until they point.

LOCOMOTOR SKILLS: LANDING ON TWO FEET

Jumping is a locomotor skill and is used on floor and all apparatus. In most cases a jump is from two feet in the takeoff to two feet in the landing. However, many physical educators agree that any time the body is airborne and the landing is on two feet, technically it is a jump. The shape or action of the body while in the air distinguishes most jumps.

A jump may initiate a skill, be the punch or rebound of a skill, occur in flight as a set in the middle of a skill combination, or it could be the dismount or landing. Jumps should initially be practiced landing on a flat mat. Arm positions vary on landings. When practicing safety falls, a gymnast should place arms overhead to protect the head and neck. When safely landing and completing a skill, the gymnast may place the arms overhead, out to side middle, at front lower diagonal, at front middle, down by the sides, or place the hands on the knees at the finish. At the initial landing the arms are used to assist the gymnast in balancing, or "sticking," the landing. After gymnast sticks the landing safely, arms should finish in a salute.

Be sure to prepare the feet and ankles with warm-up and stretching activities such as pliés, relevés, arch lifts, and ankle circles before training jumps and landings. Before teaching jumps, review the information about falling safely and the safe landing position in chapter 1.

The most frequently used jump is the stretch jump; all other jumps have an initial stretch jump as a take-off. Refer to the learning cues of the stretch jump, which apply to other jumps.

Stretch Jump

The stretch jump is a takeoff from two feet into a stretched-body position and a landing on two feet.

Learning Cues for Stretch Jump

Verbal/Linguistic

- Start in a straight-body position with arms overhead or down by sides.
- If arms are overhead, bring the arms down and bend knees. Arms are used to gain momentum in the jump.
- Then swing arms forward and upward overhead.
- Push through the feet to extend the entire body into the air in a vertical stretched-body position.
- Land on both feet in plié to cushion the landing, keeping the chest up.
- Upon landing, lower the arms sideward, then to a forward low diagonal. Stick the landing and extend arms to balance with salute for a minimum of 3 seconds.

Logical/Mathematical

- Sequence is jump, stretch tall, bend knees, balance, salute.
- Jump equally from both feet.
- Send a vertical line up.
- Keep legs parallel throughout.
- Keep head neutral and parallel with ceiling.
- Kinder cue: Blast off like a rocket!

Visual/Spatial

- Focus straight ahead.
- See your arms come up in front of you.
- Kinder cue: Keep the body straight like a pencil (pointed feet are the sharp pencil tips).

Bodily/Kinesthetic

- As you feel the arms brush past the legs, push off the floor and point toes.
- Feel the arm swing overhead and pull you up into the air.
- At height of arm swing, feel the arms next to the ear.
- Feel the muscles above the knees tighten in the air.

Interpersonal

- Stand behind a partner and hold at waist to help boost the jump while keeping partner's back vertical.

Musical/Rhythmical

- Time the jump so that arms swing forward and overhead for momentum as legs straighten.
- Tempo of the arm swing is fast—as fast as you can lift the arms.

Assist

- Stand behind gymnast and hold gymnast at waist to support and stabilize torso.

Common Errors

- Arms are not in front as feet land.
- Arms are too slow or are not used for momentum.
- Push through legs and feet is insufficient.
- Chest is too far forward (piking).
- Body does not stretch in jump.
- Knees do not bend to absorb landing and help maintain balance.

Tuck Jump

- Start in a stretched-body position.
- Do a stretch jump, swinging the arms down, then forward and overhead for momentum.
- Immediately lift knees to chest in tuck position.
- Bring arms to chest height to touch the knees or shins.
- Keep chin and chest up.
- Point feet.
- Stretch body back out to a vertical straight-body position before landing.
- Upon landing, lower the arms sideward, then to a forward low diagonal.
- Stick the landing and extend arms to balance with salute.
- Sequence is jump, tuck knees to chest, open, bend knees, salute.
- Kinder cue: Put a high tuck in the sky.

Pike Straddle Jump

- Start in a stretched-body position.
- Do a stretch jump, swinging the arms down, then forward and overhead for momentum.
- Immediately lift legs sideward to a straddle position with torso vertical and knees facing upward.
- Keep torso vertical as you jump, lifting legs turned out and sideward to 180 degrees.
- Feel the legs push away from the floor, then pull legs up toward ears.
- In straddle, legs are parallel to floor.
- Bring legs together before landing.
- Legs must move quickly, especially when bringing them together on the way down.
- Land on both feet in safe landing position.
- Keep chest up by pressing arms down and pushing sternum up.
- Lift arms overhead, sideward, or in front in jump.
- Straddle jumps vary with the gymnast's ability to straddle legs.
- Sequence is jump, straddle, legs together, bend knees, salute.

Pike Jump

This will be a difficult skill for many beginning gymnasts who lack flexibility.

- Start in a stretched-body position.
- Do a stretch jump up, swinging the arms down, then forward and overhead for momentum.
- Immediately pull straight legs up in front to pike at hips with torso vertical and legs together, knees facing upward, feet pointed.
- Keep the chest vertical as legs lift straight up to 90 degrees.
- Stretch body back out to a vertical straight-body position before landing.
- Upon landing, lower the arms sideward, then to a forward low diagonal.
- Stick the landing and extend arms to balance with salute.
- Pike jumps will vary with the gymnast's ability to pike legs.
- Pike angles vary from 45 to 90 degrees.
- Sequence is jump, pike, open, bend knees, salute.

Note: This skill requires good abdominal strength to lift both legs up quickly, and it requires hip flexibility to form the pike position in the air. Gymnasts who have problems with this skill may benefit from extra work on strength and flexibility. Share this information with students to encourage them to work on strength and flexibility on their own time.

Stride Jump

- Begin in a straight-body position.
- Do a stretch jump up, swinging the arms down, then upward and sideward or to opposition for momentum.
- Immediately lift legs and open to stride position.
- Keep torso vertical and split legs in stride approximately 90 degrees.
- Keep an equal angle of split (from 45 to 180 degrees) in each leg.
- Push with back leg and pull with front leg.
- Keep hips and shoulders square.
- To help keep hips square, bring arms to opposition.
- Keep chest up by pressing shoulders down and pushing sternum up.
- Bring legs together before landing.
- Upon landing, lower the arms sideward, then to a forward low diagonal.
- Stick the landing and extend arms to balance with salute.
- Sequence is jump, stride, legs together, bend knees, salute.

Note: The most common error is uneven legs. Usually front leg is lifted too high for the gymnast's ability so the back leg drags and bends.

Jump Half Turn

This skill is also considered a rotation skill because of the longitudinal turn of 180 degrees. The twisting motion that occurs in jumps is defined directionally by whatever shoulder goes back first. Both shoulders are important because the opposite shoulder assists the turn by pulling the shoulder in the direction of the turn. For example, when a gymnast turns to the left in a jump, it is the left shoulder that leads the turn but it is the pulling forward of the right shoulder that controls the force of the turn. Gymnasts should practice turning in both directions.

- Stand in a straight-body position.
- Jump, swinging the arms forward and overhead for momentum.
- Keep arms rounded overhead (crown) with chin lifted.
- At height of jump turn the head in the direction of the rotation (spot or look at the destination), pull with the opposite shoulder and hips and legs to execute a 180-degree turn in the air.
- Keep a vertical line from fingers to toes.
- Turn at the height (top) of the jump.
- Keep legs parallel throughout.
- Keep head parallel with ceiling.
- Upon landing, lower the arms sideward, then to a forward low diagonal.
- Stick the landing and extend arms to balance with salute.
- Sequence is stretch jump, look, turn, bend knees, salute.

Jump Drill

Once students learn a variety of jumps, they can practice them in many different ways. For vault and beam dismounts and for a little practice with proper body positioning during safe landings, try jumps that take you upward and forward. But remember that most floor and beam jumps, turning jumps, and many of the other jumps do not move forward or backward. So practice jumps vertically as well as upward and forward.

- Practice jumps from floor, folded mats, beam, or vault box.
- Practice vertical jumps with an emphasis on gaining height.
- Jump up onto a mat stack.
- Jump down from a mat stack.
- Jump from mat to mat or board to mat.
- Run, rebound on target with two feet, and perform a jump.

Jump and Rebound Practice

A rebound is a quick upward jump or punch using very little flexion of the hips, knees, or ankles. It is performed immediately upon landing on the target to accelerate into the jump off the floor. The punch is what creates power and momentum to perform more advanced skills.

Perform a sequence of jumps without stopping. For example, perform three stretch jumps; or a stretch jump, then tuck jump; or a stretch jump, tuck jump, then straddle jump.

Jump from mat to mat to practice different jumps (stretch, tuck, straddle, pike) as well as experience a rebound.

- In a rebound, the landing is the takeoff.
- Return to the air as quickly as possible using the quickest and smallest bend and extension of the knees.
- Look at the board and mats without dropping the head.
- Sequence is jump, rebound, jump, rebound, jump, land.
- Try to stick each landing by using correct technique and no movement of the feet.

LOCOMOTOR SKILLS: LANDING ON ONE FOOT

Landing on one foot is the most difficult skill of all. Gymnasts should have a lot of experience with hops and small leaps before attempting stride leaps.

Stride Leap

- Take off from one foot, perform a stride in flight, then land on the other foot.

Learning Cues for Stride Leap

Verbal/Linguistic

- Take one or more steps.
- Push off with one leg.
- Perform a stride leap in the air.
- Land on the other foot.
- Arms begin in a downward curve touching the thighs and rise up to opposition.

Logical/Mathematical

- Sequence is run, run, stride leap, land on one foot.
- Push off one leg, make a 45- to 180-degree stride high above the floor.
- With the arms, make a right angle parallel to the floor.

Visual/Spatial

- See straight and turned-out front leg.
- See arms frame front leg.
- Keep head lifted; look down with eyes, not by dropping head.

Bodily/Kinesthetic

- Feel the push off the back leg.
- Swing front leg up.
- Squeeze quadriceps muscles tight and point feet.

Musical/Rhythmical

- Push off the floor with the back leg while it is still in front of the front leg. (This is to avoid rocking horse effect.)
- Rhythm is:

  Run, run, leap; run, run, leap.

  1, 2, 3; 1, 2, 3.

  Use this pattern to practice both right and left leaps. Clap this pattern for the student as you say, "Run, run, right, run, run, left."

Naturalist

- Kinder cue: It's been raining, so you need to leap over puddles.

Common Errors

Most children will try to initiate this skill with the front leg when the back leg really begins the skill. If the students' leaps have the rocking-horse look, tell them to push with their back legs sooner and harder. Uneven separation of legs occurs because the front leg is lifted too high while the back leg drags, which occurs because back, buttocks, and quadriceps muscles are not contracted strongly.

ROTATIONAL MOVEMENTS: TWISTING ROTATIONS (TURNS)

Squat Turn

- Do a squat stand with one foot in front of the other.
- Execute a 180-degree turn while looking to opposite wall.
- Keep chest up and don't lean forward.
- Keep calves next to backs of thighs throughout.

- Stay on balls of feet.
- Keep turn smooth and even in tempo; open arms sharply to finish.
- Assist: Stand on floor next to side of gymnast away from the turning motion. Hold hands on gymnast's hips to help maneuver the half turn.
- Sequence is tuck stand, half turn, tuck stand.
- Arm sequence is side middle, overhead, oblique.

Relevé Turn

A relevé turn is a half turn performed on the balls of the feet.

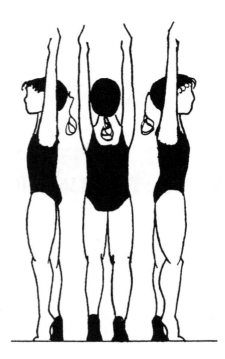

Learning Cues for Relevé Turn

Verbal/Linguistic

- Stand in a straight-body position with one foot in front of the other foot.
- Lift up on the balls of feet (relevé position) and close back foot to front foot in relevé.
- Keeping heels high, look directly behind you to turn 180 degrees (half turn) toward the back foot.
- Keep weight on the balls of the feet.
- Finish by opening arms to oblique and lowering heels.
- Curve the arms over the head during the turn.

Logical/Mathematical

- Sequence is lift, pivot, open arms.
- Execute a 180-degree turn.
- Perform half turn by squaring hips and shoulders to the opposite wall.
- Stop momentum by opening arms back on a high diagonal.
- Keep neck long and top of head parallel with ceiling.

Visual/Spatial

- Rise up high on toes and quickly look to the opposite wall so that the spot can lead you in the half turn.
- Keep heels elevated directly above the balls of the feet.
- Open the arms on an upper diagonal behind you to finish.
- Kinder cue: Take the elevator up to the top floor, turn, go out the back door.

Bodily/Kinesthetic

- Feel the weight on the balls and toes of feet.
- Feel inner thighs squeezing together at the end of the turn.
- Feel tight muscles in abdomen and buttocks.
- Feel the weight completely centered between the feet; do not let it shift from foot to foot.
- Feel the arms rounded high above the head with fingers facing each other.
- Feel the arms open sharply up and behind you.

Musical/Rhythmical

- Rhythm is:

  Turn, open.

  1, 2.

Assist

- Place hands on hips. Regrasp at end of turn to assist in balance.

Common Errors

- Shoulders are not on top of hips.
- Heels drop before turn is complete.
- Turn is not "spotted" (head does not lead turn to spot a point on opposite wall).
- Shoulders lift during turn.

ROTATIONAL MOVEMENTS: HORIZONTAL CIRCULAR ROTATION

Back Rocker

- Lie in tuck, keeping a firm grip on knees.
- Rock back and forth sequentially through the spine, keeping the back rounded.

Floor Exercise

4

Floor Skills

NONLOCOMOTOR SKILLS ON FLOOR		LOCOMOTOR SKILLS
Balance	**Support**	**Using feet**
Italicized skills are introduced in this chapter.	**Animal movements**	**Alternating foot patterns**
	Donkey kick	Forward walks
Standing balances (straight line from supporting foot to head)	Puppy dog (lift back leg)	Backward walks
	Switcheroo	Lateral walks
Relevé hold	**Support on 3 or 4 body parts**	Relevé walks
Coupé and passé	Front support	Step-hop (skipping)
Front attitude	Rear support	Chassé
Battement	Side support	*Battement walks*
Standing balances (straight line from nonsupported foot to head)	**Front support on floor series**	*Passé walks*
	Bridge	*Grapevine*
Arabesque	**V-sit progression**	*Waltz step*
Scale	**Supports with arms on folded mats**	*Front chassé*
Lever	Tuck support	*Back chassé*
New standing balances	L or pike support	*Side chassé*
Side scale	Straddle L support	**Jumps landing on two feet**
Y scale	**Supports (hold) with arms (no mats)**	Safe landing position
Nonstanding balances (knee balances)	*Tuck support*	Stretch jump
	L or pike support	Tuck jump
Knee stand	*V-sit support*	Pike straddle jump
Knee lunge	**Handstand progression**	Pike jump
Half split	*Runner's lunge, kick up one leg*	Stride jump
Knee scale	*Lunge, lever, single leg up, lever, lunge*	Jump half turn
Balance in knee scale	*Lunge, lever, single leg up, feet together, lever, lunge*	*Assemblé*
Nonstanding balances (splits)	*Lunge, lever, handstand, lever, lunge*	*Stride split jump (120–180 degrees)*
Stride split	*Handstand*	*Front stag jump*
Straddle split	*Handstand stride split (90–180 degrees)*	*Jump full turn*
Inverted shoulder stand		**Landing on one foot**
		Stride leap
		Stride split leap (120 and 180 degrees)

(continued)

LOCOMOTOR SKILLS ON FLOOR
ROTATIONAL MOVEMENTS

Twisting rotations	Sideward rotations	Horizontal circular rotations	
Turns in place	**Cartwheel progression**	Back rocker	**Back walkover progression**
Squat turn	*Mini-cartwheels*	*Back rocker progression*	*Rocking bridge*
Relevé turn	*Lunge, cartwheel, lunge*	**Forward rolls**	*Jumping bridge*
Coupé or passé	*Hurdle cartwheel*	*Tuck forward roll*	*One-leg hopping bridge*
pirouette	*One-arm cartwheel*	*Straddle to tuck*	*Bridge kickover*
Moving turns	*Dive cartwheel*	*Pike to tuck*	*Wall touch from a kneel*
Side tuck roll	**Exploring sideward tumbling**	*Straddle forward roll*	*Backbend*
Straight roll	Handstand	*Tuck to straddle*	*Backbend to kickover*
	Handstand, stride split	*Pike to straddle*	*Back walkover*
	Lunge cartwheel	*Pike forward roll*	**Front walkover progression**
	Running hurdle cartwheel	*Tuck to pike*	Handstand
	Round-off progression	*Straddle to pike*	Bridge
	Handstand, snapdown	**Backward rolls**	Rocking bridge
	Round-off	*Backward tuck roll*	Backbend to stand
	Round-off, rebound	*Tuck to straddle*	Handstand to bridge
		Tuck to pike	Front limber
		Backward straddle roll	Handstand split to one-leg bridge
		Straddle to tuck	Front walkover
		Straddle to pike	**Front handspring progressions**
		Backward pike roll	*Hurdle cartwheel*
		Pike to tuck	*Round-off*
		Pike to straddle	*Blocking*
		Back extension roll lead-ups	*Handstand to flatback*
		Back extension roll	*Block to flatback*
			Front handspring
			Back handspring progressions
			Stretch jump
			Shift back
			Shift back, jumping to flatback
			Back handspring

Floor exercise contains many of the basic skills for all events in both men's and women's gymnastics and is the basis for all gymnastics. Therefore, floor activities should be included in every gymnastics class.

Equipment: A mat or a spring floor is the basic activity area for floor exercise skills. The wedge (incline mat), octagon mats, trapezoid mats, folded mats, and other teaching aids may be used.

Spotting and safety: As gymnasts progress to more complex skills, their chances of falling also increase. Proper mats are a necessity and falling techniques must be reviewed frequently (see "Landing and Falling" in chapter 1, page 9).

School: In the school setting of gymnastics, floor and tumbling skills make up the majority of gymnastics units.

This chapter covers many of the basic skills that are performed on the floor. Review chapters 2 and 3, "Exploratory Gymnastics" and "Foundational Positions and Movements," because they form the foundation for this chapter. This chapter allows gymnasts to master basic floor skills that allow them to progress to more complex movements. The "motor notes" introduced earlier are listed in the movement sequence for each skill. Also included in this chapter are many lead-ups that break down the skills into smaller, more manageable parts that can then be put together to form whole skills. Another function of a lead-up is to enhance a skill once the basic skill is learned. Unlike exploratory gymnastics, foundation skills, floor skills, and lead-ups are specific and correctness is expected.

BALANCE SKILLS

Review the biomechanics related to balance (page 20) in chapter 1. Basic balance is a skill that gymnasts must have before they move to other pieces of apparatus. The following skills are a continuation of the balance skills in chapter 2 (page 30). These skills require more balance and flexibility than the basic skills in chapter 2 require.

Review	
Standing Balances *(Straight line from supporting foot to head)* Relevé hold Coupé and passé Front attitude Battement	***Standing Balances*** *(Straight line from nonsupported foot to head)* Arabesque Scale Lever **New Skill** ***Standing Balances*** Side scale Y scale

Side Scale

- Stand in straight-body position.
- Lift one leg sideward at or above horizontal.
- Keep hips square.
- Keep arms out to the side.
- Keep torso vertical and make a horizontal line from fingers through toes of scale leg.
- Keep both legs equally turned out.
- Return to straight-body position.

Y Scale

- Stand in straight-body position.
- Keep standing leg straight and lift one leg sideward with hand supporting inside of heel and knee facing ceiling.
- Make a giant letter Y.
- Return to straight-body position.

SUPPORT SKILLS

Review	
V-sit Progression *Supports With Arms on Folded Mats*	**New Skill** *Supports (Hold) With Arms (No Mats)*
Tuck support L (pike) support Straddle L support	Tuck support L (pike) support V-sit support

Support skills prepare gymnasts for other skills that require the support of body weight such as forward rolls, backward rolls, handstands, cartwheels, round-offs, limbers, walkovers, and handsprings. These skills appear in their own sections in this chapter.

Review all of the previous support skills in chapter 3, page 78. All of the skills listed in this section are advanced because they require gymnasts to lift all of their body weight from the floor. This requires much more upper-body and abdominal strength and is much more difficult to perform than the basic support skills presented earlier. However, even lifting the body momentarily will help develop muscles and prepare the body for future apparatus work.

Tuck Support

- Sit in tuck with hands shoulder-width apart, fingers pointing forward on the floor on either side of torso.
- Roll shoulders back and extend arms by pushing down and straightening elbows. Keep knees at chest height as tuck is lifted off the floor.
- Keep shoulders directly above hands, head up, and feet pointed.
- Try to hold for 3 seconds.
- Return to sit in tuck.

L Support

- Start in seated pike with hands on the floor shoulder-width apart, fingers pointing forward.
- Extend arms by pushing down and straightening elbows. Bring shoulders back for balance as pike is elevated.
- Try to hold for 3 seconds.
- Keep shoulders directly above hands.
- Keep head up and feet pointed.
- Return to seated pike.

V-Sit Support

- Begin in a V-sit with hands on either side of hips and fingers pointing forward on the floor.
- Extend arms by pushing down and straightening elbows until V is lifted off the floor.
- Try to hold for 3 seconds.
- Keep shoulders directly above hands.
- Keep head up and feet pointed.
- Return to V-sit on floor.

INVERTED SUPPORTS

Review

Animal Movements
Donkey kick
Puppy dog (lift back leg)
Switcheroo

Supports on Three or Four Body Parts
Front support
Rear support
Bridge
Side support

Front support on floor series

Two inverted support skills on the floor are headstands and handstands. The purpose of the headstand is to give gymnasts inverted body awareness of the straight-body position. The headstand is controversial because many instructors think that there are other ways for gymnasts to experience inversion without risk (for example, the handstand and inverted candle).

To ensure the safety of your students, you may choose not to teach the headstand. If a person is overweight or lacks upper-body strength or body awareness, the headstand may place too much pressure on his or her head and neck, which could result in injury.

The handstand is one of the most important skills to master because so many skills depend on a solid handstand. It is considered the basis of gymnastics and is found in the cartwheel, round-off, handspring, walkover, and limber.

New Skill

Handstand Progression	Handstand
Runner's lunge, kick up one leg	Handstand forward roll
Lunge, lever, single leg up, lever, lunge	Handstand stride split (90-180 degrees)
Lunge, lever, single leg up, feet together, lever lunge	

The following is the progression for the handstand:

1. Review exploration of handstand supports in chapter 2, including the front support, donkey kick, monkey with tail in the air, and switcheroo. These skills lead up to the handstand.
2. Beginning skills: These are a progression of lead-ups that involve bringing the legs together near vertical in handstand position and lunging out.
3. Intermediate skills: This involves hitting vertical in handstand.
4. Advanced skills: These include holding the handstand position in vertical, the handstand stride split (90 to 180 degrees), and the handstand forward roll.

The handstand lead-up skill that follows—runner's lunge to kick up one leg—begins with the arms already on the floor to ensure that gymnasts have enough body strength to perform a beginning handstand. Some instructors teach the handstand from a gymnastics point to horizontal kick to a lever into the handstand. The progression used in this text builds the shoulder and arm strength and ensures proper hand placement (fingers pointing forward, not turned out) for performing a successful handstand and preventing injury. Therefore, the lead-up drills have the gymnasts place the hands on the floor first before initiating the kick. This progression gives gymnasts the feeling of inversion without putting force from the momentum onto the arms. Otherwise, momentum of the body weight moving forward could be too much for the arms to handle and gymnasts could injure the wrists, elbows, or shoulders or fall face forward onto the floor. Also, if you teach the handstand with a lunge first, gymnasts will apply the lunge skill to other floor or tumbling skills such as the cartwheel and round-off. Once gymnasts can successfully perform a lunge into a handstand, then they move to the next skill progression: leg lift to horizontal, to gymnastics point, then lunge and lever.

Runner's Lunge, Kick Up One Leg

- Begin with one leg in a tuck and the other leg extended behind the body (runner's lunge) with the hands shoulder-width apart about 12 inches in front of the foot and arms straight.
- Keep head neutral and arms by ears.
- Push with the tucked leg and kick the straight back leg upward until tucked leg is lifted off the floor.
- Keep extended leg and torso in one straight line.
- Return to tuck support with one leg extended.
- Sequence is tuck support with one leg extended, push and shift weight, lift hips, kick up one leg, tuck support with one leg extended.

Lunge, Lever, Single Leg Up, Lever, Lunge

The purpose of this skill is to attain a partial handstand by combining the lever, proper weight support, and body alignment from feet to the hands without reaching vertical. This skill also teaches control of the landing.

- Lunge, lever.
- Lift the back leg and push off the front leg as you place the hands shoulder-width apart on floor.
- Push against the floor to elevate the shoulder girdle.
- Bring the back leg to vertical as the hips align directly above the shoulders.
- Leave the front leg in horizontal.
- Center the weight over the hands in an inverted straight line from hands to toes of back foot.
- Return to floor in lever, then lunge.
- Sequence is lunge, lever, push with foot and shift weight to hands, lift up one leg, lever, lunge.

Lunge, Lever, Single Leg Up, Feet Together, Lever, Lunge

The purpose of this skill is to close the legs quickly (without attaining vertical) and to open them back up for the landing.

- Lunge, lever.
- Lift back leg almost to vertical.
- Lift and close front leg to top leg, bringing feet and legs together (feet and legs "kiss").
- Keep both legs straight and vertical when making contact.
- Separate legs in stride.
- When first foot touches floor, lift hands to maintain lever.
- Return to lunge.
- Sequence is lunge, lever, push and shift weight, lift hips, kick up one leg, bring legs together, stride, lever, lunge.

Handstand

The handstand is considered an intermediate skill. The handstand will now proceed from a gymnastics point to horizontal kick to a lever into the handstand. Remember that the handstand is an essential skill that gymnasts must develop to prepare for more advanced skills. Eventually gymnasts must be able to attain a vertical handstand and hold that position for 3 to 5 seconds.

Learning Cues for Handstand

Verbal/Linguistic

- Begin in gymnastics point.
- Kick front leg to horizontal.
- Step through lunge into lever.
- Kick the back leg and push off the front leg as you place the hands shoulder-width apart on floor.
- Push against the floor to elevate the shoulder girdle.
- Bring the back leg to vertical as the hips align directly above the shoulders.
- Bring front leg to vertical to complete the handstand with the weight centered over the hands in an inverted straight-body position.
- Return to floor in lever, then lunge.
- Sequence is lunge, lever, push and shift weight, lift hips, handstand, lever, lunge, finish lunge.

Visual/Spatial

- Keep upper arms by ears throughout entire skill.
- Keep fingers open, elbows straight.
- See fingers by looking with eyes but not lifting head out of line.
- Keep shoulder girdle elevated throughout.
- Keep hips open in front; do not pike.
- Kinder cues: No turtle heads—turtles don't do good handstands. No banana backs.

Bodily/Kinesthetic

- Feel shoulders lifted in lunge, stretched forward in lever, and pushed out in handstand.
- Kick back leg as hard as you can.
- Tighten abdominal and buttocks muscles to keep torso straight.
- Feel weight over knuckles, not on the heels of hands.
- Push entire body up and away from the floor.
- Push tailbone forward to keep from piking.

Musical/Rhythmical

- Rhythm is:

  Lunge, handstand, lunge.

  1, 2, 3.

Assist

Whenever spotting a handstand, hold only the leg closest to you, *never* both legs. When spotted correctly, the gymnast will put down the free leg to stand up when he or she wishes or needs to get out of the handstand. If the spotter holds both legs, the gymnast will probably fall onto the head when he or she loses balance or tires. If the spotter makes contact with the near leg as the gymnast lifts it off the ground, the spotter can control that leg on the way up to prevent being kicked in the face while spotting.

Common Errors

- Arms drop in the lever; arms and legs bend.
- Momentum is too strong and kick is too hard.
- Body lands on a flat back.
- Chin is not tucked.
- Hands are too close to feet, which causes segmentation.
- Line from head to toe breaks.
- Abdomen and buttocks are loose.
- Arms are not by ears.
- Handstand collapses.
- Kick happens too late after hands touch.

Handstand Forward Roll

A good handstand, which can be maintained in proper position and alignment for 3 to 5 seconds, must be mastered before gymnasts attempt the handstand forward roll. Sequence is lunge, lever, handstand, round shoulders (hollow), tuck chin and bend arms, forward roll, straight-body stand.

Handstand Stride Split

- Perform a handstand.
- Keep the hips square.
- Separate legs into inverted stride.
- Return to floor in lever, then lunge.
- Sequence is lever, handstand to stride split, lever, lunge.

LOCOMOTOR SKILLS: ALTERNATING FOOT PATTERNS

Review	New Skill
Exploring Using Feet Alternating feet (walk, run, skip, slide, gallop) ***Alternating Foot Patterns*** Forward walks Backward walks Lateral walks Relevé walks Step-hop (skipping) Chassé	***Alternating Foot Patterns*** Battement walks Passé walks Grapevine Waltz step Front chassé Back chassé Side chassé

This chapter is a continuation of the locomotor skills in chapter 3. Review locomotor skills with alternating foot patterns (page 88).

Battement Walks

- Stand on floor in gymnastics point.
- Step and quickly brush the back leg forward with a slight turnout to 90 degrees or higher, then slowly lower to gymnastics point.
- Point the back foot and brush forward to transfer it to the front and lift quickly to 90 degrees or higher.
- Lower slowly with control.
- Lead with the heel on the brush through.
- Keep hips square as you step.
- Keep chest lifted and do not let back round during kick.
- Keep body erect, abdomen lifted.
- Keep repeating process to execute a walk across the floor.
- Keep arms at side middle and slightly oblique to keep chest up.
- Sequence is lift, lower, step, lift, lower, step.

Passé Walks

- Stand on floor in gymnastics point.
- Step onto pointed foot and lift back leg to passé with knee in front of body.
- Extend slightly turned-out leg and step forward, shifting weight to that foot.
- Point the back foot and bring it through to transfer it to the front, lift to passé, then extend and step forward, shifting weight to that foot.
- Knee leads to passé.
- Turn out supporting leg slightly.
- Passé leg can be turned out or parallel with other leg.
- Keep hips square as you step.
- Keep body erect and abdomen lifted.
- Keep repeating process to execute a walk across the floor. Arms remain in side middle.
- Sequence is lift to passé, extend, step, lift to passé, extend, step.

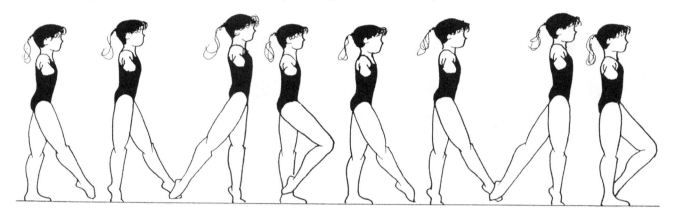

Grapevine

- Stand on floor with legs slightly turned out.
- Step to the side with right foot.
- Cross and step with left leg over right.
- Step to the side right.
- Cross and step with left leg behind.
- Keep hips square throughout the sequence.
- Sequence is step to side, cross in front, step to side, cross in back.

Waltz Step

There are three steps (beats) to a waltz step: (1) Low step in demi-plié, (2) high step in relevé, and (3) high step in relevé.

- Stand on one slightly turned-out leg with the free leg extended in gymnastics point.
- Step forward onto the free leg in plié (down).
- Step to relevé with second leg (up).
- Then follow with relevé with the first leg (up).
- Travel along on a line no wider than the width of a beam.
- Keep torso upright; don't lean forward.
- Keep body forward on balls of feet.
- If you can see the feet, the weight is too far back on heels.
- Keep legs slightly turned out.
- Sequence is step in plié, step in relevé, step in relevé; step in plié, step in relevé, step in relevé (down, up, up; down, up, up).
- Footsteps are not equidistant apart (the first step will be slightly larger than the second and third steps).
- Footsteps are as small as they can be while still being smooth.
- Hips and shoulders remain parallel to the floor.

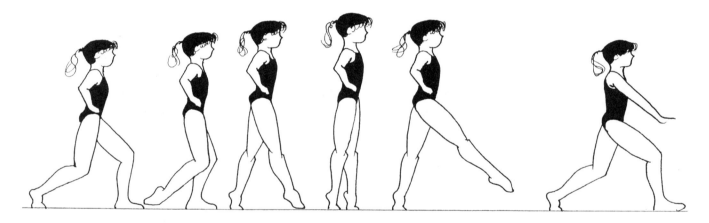

Front Chassé

Review the forward chassé (chapter 3, page 91). The chassé is very important as a preparatory movement for other skills.

Back Chassé

- Begin in gymnastics point with point in back.
- Step back on a slightly turned-out foot, touching only the ball of the foot to the floor.
- Immediately push off that foot to lift the entire body into the air.
- Legs come together in soussus (ankles together) in the air and continue to travel backward.
- Land on the front leg, similar to a backward gallop.

Side Chassé

- Begin in gymnastics point with point to the side and leg turned out.
- Bend standing leg and slide other leg to the side along the floor.
- Push off the leading leg and draw legs together, bringing heels together in the air.
- Land on back leg in a small demi-plié with leading leg slightly ahead of back leg.
- Keep arms in side middle throughout.
- Sequence is plié-slide, land; plié-slide, land.

LOCOMOTOR SKILLS: LANDING ON TWO FEET

Review	New Skill
Exploring Using Feet	***Jumps Landing on Two Feet***
Landing on two feet (jump)	Assemblé
	Stride split jump (120–180 degrees)
Jumps Landing on Two Feet	Front stag jump
Safe landing position	Jump full turn
Stretch jump	
Tuck jump	
Pike straddle jump	
Pike jump	
Stride jump	
Jump half turn	

Review locomotor skills with landings on two feet (chapter 3, page 92).

Jump Warm-Up

Review all of the jumps in chapter 3. Because quick vertical jumps off the balls of the feet are essential for attaining flight in tumbling, they should be a part of every floor warm-up.

- Stand in a stretched-body position on floor.
- Bend legs slightly as the arms come down.
- Swing arms overhead as the feet push off.
- Land in plié.
- Repeat, keeping arms overhead.
- Jumps should be high yet quick. Heels touch only briefly. Extend completely through legs and feet. Go up and forward on each jump.
- Kinder cues: Jump as if you are on a pogo stick across the floor. Jump like popcorn across the floor.

Assemblé

The assemblé *(ah-sahm-BLAY)* is a skill that moves from one foot to both feet. It is an important skill to learn because it is used on the approach for springboard and vault skills and for many tumbling skills.

Learning Cues for Assemblé

Verbal/Linguistic

- Begin in stretched-body position; step forward onto front foot.
- Brush the back foot forward past the support leg and up to at least 45 degrees.
- Push off support leg and travel upward until support leg meets the other leg in the air.
- Bring the feet together in the air before landing.
- Land on both feet, bending knees slightly.
- Keep the arms out to the side for balance throughout.

Logical/Mathematical

- Sequence is step, brush, assemblé, land.
- Back leg joins the front leg in the air.
- Back leg meets the front at 45 degrees.
- Torso stays vertical; arms stay parallel to floor.

Visual/Spatial

- Brush first leg at waist height.
- Keep legs on the same line.
- Keep the legs turned out in order to get the heels together.
- See legs assemble before landing.
- Kinder cues: Kick legs together in front of you. Make your back leg "hurry up" and catch your front leg before you land.

Bodily/Kinesthetic

- Feel ankles assemble in the air.
- Press shoulders and chest down; press sternum up.

Musical/Rhythmical

- Step, brush, assemblé, land.
- Allow enough time for first leg to get waist high before lifting second leg.

Common Errors

- Bottom leg kicks too early before the top leg has reached sufficient height.
- Chest drops and causes body to pike, which hinders the height of the legs.
- Legs don't assemble in the air.

Other Challenges

- Kick the top leg above horizontal.
- Perform an immediate relevé in soussus on landing.

Stride Split Jump

Review stride jump (chapter 3, page 98). Try to split legs to approximately 120 degrees for an intermediate jump, or split the legs to 180 degrees for an advanced jump. Sequence is jump, stride split, legs together, bend knees, balance, salute.

Front Stag Jump

- Begin in a straight-body position.
- Do a stretch jump up, swinging the arms upward to opposition.
- Immediately lift legs and do a split jump, bending the front leg to stag (bend the knee of front leg toward the back of the thigh).
- Thighs should be in even split, with bent leg at 90 degrees.
- Bring legs together before landing.
- Upon landing, lower the arms sideward, downward, then to a forward low diagonal.
- Stick the landing and extend arms to balance with salute.
- Challenges: Try to perform a back stag jump (do a split jump with back leg in stag). Try to perform a double stag jump (split jump with both legs bent in stag).

Jump Full Turn

Refer to jump half turn (chapter 3, page 99). This time, at the height of the jump, gymnasts pull harder and turn 360 degrees in the air. Have students practice jump turns in both directions. Sequence is jump, look, turn, bend knees, salute. Think *Look, look* for 360-degree turn.

LOCOMOTOR SKILLS: LANDING ON ONE FOOT

Review

Exploring Using Feet
Landing on one foot (hop, leap)

Landing on One Foot
Stride leap

New Skill

Landing on One Foot
Stride split leap (120 and 180 degrees)

Review locomotor skills with a one-foot landing (chapter 3, page 100).

Stride Split Leap (120 degrees)

The stride split leap (land on one foot) is similar to the stride split jump (land on both feet).

- Take one or two steps.
- Push off with one leg as the other leg simultaneously lifts up to waist height, creating a stride split in the air.
- Land on one foot and bend the knee on landing.
- Arms begin in a downward curve, touching the thighs, and rise up to opposition (front and side middle).
- Sequence is run, run, stride split, land on one foot.

Most split leaps are taught with a lifting of the front leg. However, you will have more success by teaching the push off of the back leg and brush forward of the front leg. If the students' leaps have the rocking-horse look, tell them to push with their back legs sooner and harder. As gymnasts become more advanced, the stride split should open to 180 degrees.

ROTATIONAL MOVEMENTS

Rotational movements include movements that rotate the body around a central axis. Review the rotational skills in chapters 2 and 3.

Twisting Rotations

Review

Turns in Place
Squat turn
Relevé turn

New Skill

Turns in Place
Coupé or passé pirouette

Pivot Turns and Pirouettes

A pivot is a turn around a single point of support from a standing position. A pirouette *(peer-ooh-WET)* is a turn on relevé with one foot, a turn in a handstand position, or a turn in the air while executing a jump.

Gaining the spatial and kinesthetic awareness of where the body is turning is crucial for gymnastics skills. The development of this upright awareness will happen through proper practice of turns.

It is important to remember that there are three main forces that turn the body:

1. The force of the turned-out leg when turning on one leg
2. The force of the arms
3. The force of the changing focus (termed the "spot" in dance disciplines)

In some twisting rotations the body turns in place on one foot or pivots on both feet. Review the squat turn and relevé turn in chapter 3, pages 101–103. Other turns move in a straight path.

Passé or Coupé Pirouette

The pirouette can be performed with the free leg in passé or coupé.

Learning Cues for Passé and Coupe Pirouette

Verbal/Linguistic

- Start in lunge.
- Initiate the pirouette with a push of the back foot as weight shifts to forward foot in relevé.
- Raise back foot so that the toe touches the ankle or knee of support leg.
- Pull with the shoulder opposite the back foot and spot a point on the wall, turning head quickly to find the spot.
- Curve the front arm in front middle with the other arm at side middle, then bring both arms to side middle or overhead (crown) to turn.
- Bring the free foot to its position at the same time that the relevé happens and at the same time that the arms arrive at their final turning position.
- Turn to desired destination by spotting a place on the wall.
- Open both arms in oblique to stop turn. (Lengthening the radius stops rotation.)
- Finish by placing free foot down in front of support foot.

(continued)

(continued)

Logical/Mathematical

- Foot sequence is step, relevé, shift weight, turn, open, finish.
- Arm sequence: Prepare arms by curving the same arm as front foot. Place the other arm to side middle, turn with arms centered in front or overhead. Open arms in high diagonal to finish.
- Body is erect and in a straight vertical line from the bottom of the rib cage through the ball of the support foot.
- Execute a 180-degree pirouette on one foot in relevé.
- Keep passé leg at least at 90 degrees to support leg. Keep coupé foot at ankle.
- Keep top of head parallel with ceiling.
- Open arms on a high diagonal behind you to stop.

Visual/Spatial

- Turn out the pointed foot so that the heel can turn you.
- Stay on relevé of foot for duration of turn, placing back leg at ankle or knee of support leg.
- Head leads the turn by focusing on a spot directly behind for a 180-degree turn and directly in front for a 360-degree turn.
- Go up before you turn; think, *Up, turn.*
- Try to open out and finish the turn on relevé rather than rocking back on the heel.
- Kinder cue: Turn like a tall top that spins.

Bodily/Kinesthetic

- Feel the weight on the turned-out foot and keep shifting or "cranking" the heel around.
- Keep pulling the passé up as you turn (it will be pushed down by the angular momentum of the turn).
- Keep chest up by pressing shoulders down and lifting sternum up.
- Feel the inner thigh muscle working to turn the leg out as you rotate.
- Feel the weight centered on the ball of the support foot.
- Keep pushing weight forward on the ball of the foot by tightening buttocks muscles so that you can end the turn on the ball of the foot.

Musical/Rhythmical

- Rhythm is:

  Turn, open.

  1, 2.

Assist

- Place hands lightly on gymnast's hips. Regrasp at end of turn to assist in balance.

Common Errors

- Turn is incomplete because of insufficient throw of outside arm outward and upward.
- Shoulders do not stay on top of hips.
- Spotting of turn is insufficient; spot is usually too slow and inaccurate.

Other Challenges

- Try turns with different leg positions (arabesque, attitude, stag).
- End in relevé and hold. (This is a timer for more difficult turns.)
- See how long you can hold in relevé. (This is a good balance drill.)
- Finish in various positions including lunge and scale.
- Turns may be half, full, one and a half, double, and so on.

HORIZONTAL CIRCULAR ROTATIONS: ROLLS

In general, lead-ups for the horizontal (transverse) circular movements should utilize an incline mat. The incline will assist gymnasts in shifting the center of gravity forward and utilizing momentum in the performance of the skill or changing the angle of the performance required for success.

Roll Lead-Ups

Review	New Skill
Back rocker	**Roll Lead-Ups**
	Back rocker progression
	Back rocker with backward roll hand position

Back Rocker Progression

Gymnasts should have had the opportunity to explore the log roll and the egg roll. Gymnasts should feel comfortable with the back rocker, which was introduced in chapter 3, page 104.

The purpose of this skill is to add one component of the roll at a time to standing position in preparation for forward and backward rolls.

Seated Tuck, Back Rocker, Seated Tuck or Squat

- Begin in seated tuck, grasping knees.
- Perform a back rocker.
- Return to finish in seated tuck or squat.
- Kinder cue: Make baby bear's rocking chair.

Seated Tuck, Back Rocker to Tuck Stand

- Begin in seated tuck, grasping knees.
- Perform a back rocker.
- Return to finish in a tuck stand with the arms lifted overhead.
- Try not to put hands down on mat; instead, lift up with arms.
- Kinder cue: Make mama bear's rocking chair.

Seated Tuck, Back Rocker, Tuck Stand, Stand

- Begin in seated tuck with arms overhead.
- Perform a back rocker, rocking farther back into inverted tuck.
- Roll up through tuck stand.
- Come to standing straight body with the arms lifted overhead.
- Sequence is sitting tuck, back rocker to inverted tuck, rock forward, tuck stand, finish in a stand.
- Kinder cue: Make papa bear's rocking chair.

Back Rocker With Backward Roll Hand Position

Review the back rocker progression. Here is the variation to prepare for the backward roll:

- Begin sitting in tuck with arms bent so that tops of hands are touching the shoulders (pizza hands).
- Roll backward, staying in tuck until entire back and palms of hands are touching the floor.
- Push with hands against floor and rock back up to sit in tuck again.
- Continue through the progression using the pizza hands placement.
- Most of the backward roll success will come from the hand placement.
- Finish by building momentum to a stand.

FORWARD AND BACKWARD ROLLS

The forward and backward roll consists of a beginning position, a roll, and a finish. All the variations will not be described or illustrated; however, you will soon notice that there are many combinations to try. Some possible choices follow.

- Starting positions include tuck, pike support, straddle support, scales, lunges, kneeling positions, and handstand.
- Rolls include the tuck, pike, or straddle.
- Finish positions include supine lying, seated (tuck, pike, straddle), tuck stand, pike support stand, straddle support stand, stand on one knee, V-sit, stand on one leg, scales, balances, and jumps.
- A roll can be performed on an incline mat (wedge), on level floor, on top of folded mats, or on beam. Start with an incline mat with each new roll.

Forward Rolls

New Skills

Forward Roll Variations

Tuck forward roll	Pike to straddle
Straddle to tuck	Pike forward roll
Pike to tuck	Tuck to pike
Straddle forward roll	Straddle to pike
Tuck to straddle	

Each skill should first be taught on an incline mat, then performed on the floor. When first teaching the forward roll, use the easier finishes such as supine and seated. The gymnasts may progress to more difficult finishes when they are able. When gymnasts first learn the forward roll, the emphasis should be on these elements:

- Bring the chin to the chest, which rounds the spine.
- Use the hands to support the body.
- Make floor contact with the back of the head, not the top.
- Roll progressively through the spine.

Tuck Forward Roll

A tuck forward roll is performed with the body in tuck for the entry and exit out of the roll.

Learning Cues for Tuck Forward Roll

Verbal/Linguistic

- Begin in a straight-body stand with arms straight overhead.
- Keep arms up and pike and round the spine slightly.
- Bend the knees into supported tuck, placing hands shoulder-width apart in front on floor.
- Tuck head, bringing the chin to the chest and keeping the back rounded.
- Lift hips and put back of neck and shoulders on mat behind hands, not in front.
- Push off the feet to initiate roll, transferring weight to the hands and back of upper shoulders into back rocker position.
- During the roll, tuck the legs, bringing heels close to buttocks.
- Maintain tuck position throughout the roll.
- Place the feet on the floor and lean forward to arrive in tuck stand.
- Immediately straighten legs to finish in a stretched stand.

Logical/Mathematical

- Sequence is stretched-body stand, supported tuck, tuck head, push off feet, roll to inverted tuck, tuck stand, stretched-body stand, salute.
- From vertical, reach to floor and close angles of tuck, push off floor, and rise up to standing with vertical arms and torso.

Visual/Spatial

- Place hands out in front of feet to make room for head and shoulders.
- Bring nose close to knees.

Bodily/Kinesthetic

- Feel knees together throughout.
- Feel upper arms touch head throughout.
- Feel chin touch chest.
- Feel back of head and upper back, not top of head, touch the floor.

Musical/Rhythmical

- Stretch stand, pike, reach, tuck head, push, roll, finish.
- Kinder cues: Hands touch only once. Hands up, stand up! Hands up high, hands down low, tuck your chin, and over you go! Get your head out of the way as you go to a back rocker position. Magic hands, tuck, elevator up!

Assist

- Touch back of head as a reminder to roll on back of head and upper shoulders.
- Place both hands on hips to assist hip lift and to control pressure on head and neck.

Common Errors

- Hands are too close to feet on mat, which leaves no room to put head down on mat between hands and feet. If head is placed down past hands it will not be tucked properly.
- Roll occurs on top of head.
- Spine is not rounded enough; hips are not lifted; chin is not tucked.
- Body opens out of tuck and lands flat.
- Hands reach to floor before the stand.

Tuck Finish: Forward Roll Variations

Finishing in tuck provides the easiest finish to stand up after the forward roll. Providing different start positions will keep the gymnast more motivated while still practicing a forward roll.

Straddle to Tuck

- Begin in a standing straddle.
- Reach forward and pike until hands touch the floor.
- Push off the feet and extend when the hips are above shoulders.
- Tuck, then roll onto back.
- Finish in a straight-body stand.
- Sequence is straddle stand, straddle pike support, tuck head, push off feet, roll to inverted tuck, tuck stand, straight-body stand, salute.
- Kinder cue: Stretch out in a snowflake (straddle) that is slowly and softly falling down to the floor. When you land on the floor, you melt into a raindrop (tuck).

Pike to Tuck

- Begin in a straight-body stand with arms straight overhead.
- Keeping arms by ears, reach forward, piking until hands touch the floor in closed pike support.
- Push off the feet and extend when the hips are above shoulders.
- Tuck, then roll onto back.
- Finish in a straight-body stand.
- Sequence is straight-body stand, pike support, tuck head, push off feet, roll from inverted pike to tuck, tuck stand, straight-body stand, salute.

Straddle Forward Roll

A straddle forward roll is performed with the body in straddle for the entry and exit out of the roll.

Learning Cues for Straddle Forward Roll

Verbal/Linguistic

- Begin in a standing straddle.
- Reach forward and pike the body, closing the angle until hands touch the mat in standing pike straddle support.
- Tuck head and push off the feet when the hips are above shoulders.
- Continue momentum of roll, maintaining the straddle.
- Push with straight arms to a straddle stand.

Logical/Mathematical

- Sequence is standing straddle, standing pike straddle support, tuck head, push off feet, roll to inverted straddle, seated straddle or push with hands to straddle stand.
- Reach forward half of your body length to perform roll.

Visual/Spatial

- Stand with legs shoulder-width apart.
- Place hands shoulder-width apart on floor.
- Keep piking and tucking head until you can see through your straddle, then push off your toes.
- Look through straight legs, then look at your belly, which will pull you over into roll.
- Keep looking through straddle until you see the floor again.

Bodily/Kinesthetic

- Feel chin close to chest.
- When you feel the push off the floor, bend arms slowly to roll.
- Feel tight, straight legs in straddle; don't bend legs at all.
- Feel back of head and upper back, not top of head, touch the floor.

Musical/Rhythmical

- Straddle stand, pike, reach, tuck head, push, roll, finish.

Naturalist

- Kinder cue: Stretch out in a snowflake (in straddle) that is slowly and softly falling down to the floor. When you touch the floor, tuck your head and roll.

Assist

- Touch back of gymnast's head as a reminder to roll on back of head and upper shoulders.
- Place both hands on hips to assist hip lift and to control pressure on head and neck.

Common Errors

- Legs are bent; chin is not near chest.
- Roll occurs on top of head; spine is not rounded enough.
- Body opens out of straddle too quickly.
- Support and push of hands are not even; weight is too far back.
- Hands are not placed inside straddle; push happens too late to continue or to come up to straddle support or stand.

Straddle Finish: Forward Roll Variations

The success to the straddle finish is the timing of the push from the floor. Providing different start positions with a straddle finish will give the gymnast an opportunity to perfect that timing.

Tuck to Straddle

- Sequence is straight-body stand, supported tuck, tuck head, roll to inverted straddle, push, straddle stand.

Pike to Straddle

- Sequence is straight-body stand, standing pike support, tuck head, push with feet, roll to inverted straddle, push with arms, straddle stand.

Pike Forward Roll

A pike forward roll is performed with the body in pike for the entry and exit out of the roll.

Learning Cues for Pike Forward Roll

Verbal/Linguistic

- Begin in a straight-body stand with arms straight overhead.
- Keeping arms by ears, pike and reach to closed standing pike until the hands touch the floor.
- Push off the feet and round the spine, transferring the weight to the hands and back of the head.
- Roll onto the back, remaining in pike.
- Finish in a straight-body stand.

Logical/Mathematical

- Sequence is straight-body stand, standing pike support, tuck head, push with hands, roll to inverted pike, straight-body stand, salute.
- Keep angle of pike as closed as possible.

Visual/Spatial

- See lower legs close to head throughout roll.
- Keep a closed pike shape throughout.
- Kinder cue: Make a sandwich, close it tight, put it in the toaster, and up it pops (with arms overhead)!

Bodily/Kinesthetic

- Feel chest on shins and rib cage on thighs.
- Push hard against the floor to stand up in pike.

Musical/Rhythmical

- Stand, pike, reach, push, tuck head, roll, finish.

Assist

- Touch back of gymnast's head as a reminder to roll on back of head and upper shoulders.
- Place both hands on hips to assist hip lift and to control pressure on head and neck.

(continued)

(continued)

Common Errors

- Spine is not rounded enough.
- Hands are down on floor before the stand.
- Momentum is not strong enough to come to stand while keeping legs straight.

Pike Finish: Forward Roll Variations

The pike finish is often the most difficult finish. The gymnast must have good flexibility and body control to maintain the closed pike position.

Tuck to Pike

- Sequence is straight-body stand, tuck support, tuck head, push with feet, roll to inverted pike, push, straight-body stand.

Straddle to Pike

- Sequence is straddle stand, standing straddle pike support, tuck head, push with feet, roll to inverted pike, push, straight-body stand.

Backward Rolls

New Skill	
Backward Roll Variations	Straddle to pike
Backward tuck roll	Backward pike roll
Tuck to straddle	Pike to tuck
Tuck to pike	Pike to straddle
Backward straddle roll	Back extension roll lead-ups
Straddle to tuck	Back extension roll

Each skill should first be taught on an incline mat if available. At first, concentrate on the technique of the starting position, hand placement, and the roll. The progression for the backward roll finish is a tuck to a squat to tuck stand, and then to a straight-body or straddle stand. Emphasize these elements when gymnasts first learn the backward roll:

- Bring the chin to the chest.
- Use the hands to support the body.
- Position the hands correctly to protect the head and assist with the roll.

The most common reason gymnasts are unsuccessful in this skill is ineffective hand placement. If the hands are not correct, then there is no leverage to push and bring the legs over in the roll and to take the stress off the neck. Keep in mind that some children lack the proper strength-to-weight for the backward roll. Be able to identify these children early on and unobtrusively give them the extra physical and moral support they need. These children may be limited to trying a backward roll down the incline mat with a spot, and then move on to other skills more suited to their physical condition. Gymnastics has so much to offer all children, but not if they decide that they are hopeless or that they hate or fear it.

Backward Tuck Roll

A backward tuck roll is performed with the body in tuck for the entry and exit out of the roll. The hand positioning is very important in the support and push phases of the skill. In the "ready" position, the tops of the fingers are placed near the ears ("pizza" position) with elbows pointing forward, not to the side.

Learning Cues for Backward Tuck Roll

Verbal/Linguistic

- Begin in a stretched-body stand with arms overhead.
- Bring hands to ears as you bend knees and descend through tuck stand to seated tuck (if on wedge, sit back on wedge).
- Begin rolling backward with the head tucked and the chin to the chest.
- Place hands on the floor by the shoulders with palms down and fingers pointing toward shoulders.
- Stay in tuck, lifting the hips and pushing with the hands against the mat.
- Extend arms to take weight off the head and neck while maintaining tuck position throughout.
- When the feet touch the floor, extend the legs and stand up to stretched-body stand.

Logical/Mathematical

- Sequence is stretched-body stand, tuck stand, seated tuck, inverted tuck, push with hands to complete backward roll, tuck stand, stretched-body stand.
- From a vertical stand, sit back in tuck stand, closing angles of arms and tuck to roll backward.
- Open angle of arms by pushing against mat; stand up through tuck stand to vertical.

Visual/Spatial

- Focus forward through tuck stand.
- Stay in tuck, keeping the back rounded.
- See your feet (not your knees) touch the mat.
- Focus forward to finish.
- Kinder cue: You are the baker or the pizza maker. Hold your pies (or pizzas) up. Now smash them on the mat. Don't get your knees messy. Put your feet down on the other side of the pizzas.

(continued)

(continued)

Make big elephant ears with your arms. Now make your elephant roll backward on the mat.

Bodily/Kinesthetic

- Sit back and push with your hands as hard as you can.
- Feel knees and feet together throughout; feel tops of fingers on shoulders.
- Point feet over the top, then feel them flex just in time to get the soles of the feet on the floor instead of landing on shins and knees.
- Push hands hard against mat until arms straighten.

Musical/Rhythmical

- Stand, tuck stand, roll, stand.

  And 1, 2, 3, 4.

Assist

- Hold gymnast at hips to lift weight up off shoulders and neck. Never pull on the legs.

Common Errors

- Hands don't get back into correct position.
- Hands don't push evenly or hard enough.
- Tuck opens, which causes loss of momentum; legs separate.
- Elbows drop in hand placement, which causes side rolling.

Backward Roll Variations in Tuck Starting Position

Tuck to Straddle

- Sequence is stretched-body stand, tuck stand, seated tuck, inverted tuck, push with hands to complete backward roll into straddle, straddle stand.

Tuck to Pike

- Sequence is stretched-body stand, tuck stand, seated tuck, inverted tuck, push with hands to complete backward roll into pike, stretched-body stand.

Backward Straddle Roll

A backward straddle roll is performed with the body in straddle for the entry and exit out of the roll.

- Begin in a wide straddle stand on the floor or with the backs of legs touching the wedge.
- Sit back, piking the straddle onto mat.
- Reach the arms down inside the straddle to cushion the landing momentarily, if necessary.
- Round the spine and bring arms to back roll position.
- Push off the hands until the arms straighten.
- Roll onto back, maintaining the straddle throughout.
- When feet touch the floor, stand up in straddle.
- Sequence is standing straddle, seated straddle, inverted straddle, push with hands to complete backward roll into standing straddle.

Backward Roll Variations in Straddle Starting Position

Straddle to Tuck

- Sequence is standing straddle, seated straddle, inverted straddle, push with hands to complete backward roll to tuck stand, stretched-body stand.

Straddle to Pike

- Sequence is standing straddle, pike straddle, seated straddle, inverted straddle, push with hands to complete backward roll to pike, stretched-body stand.

Backward Pike Roll

A backward pike roll is performed with the body in pike for the entry and exit out of the roll. A backward roll from a pike is much more difficult than the backward tuck roll; gymnasts should first perform this skill down an incline.

- Begin in a straight-body stand.
- Pike torso and lean backward.
- If necessary, place hands down on either side of legs to cushion the descent in pike.
- Quickly assume the backward roll arm position.
- Roll backward, pushing on the floor with the hands to straighten arms.
- Stand up through pike.
- Sequence is straight-body stand, standing pike, seated pike, inverted pike, push with hands to complete backward roll into pike, straight-body stand.
- Kinder cue: Roll backward, make a tent (or teepee) on the floor, stand up.

Backward Roll Variations in Pike Starting Position

Pike to Tuck

- Sequence is straight-body stand, standing pike, seated pike, inverted pike, push with hands to complete backward roll to tuck stand, straight-body stand.

Pike to Straddle

- Sequence is straight-body stand, standing pike, seated pike, inverted pike, push with hands to complete backward roll to standing straddle.

Back Extension Roll Progression

The backward roll skills are lead-ups to a back extension roll, which is an advanced skill. The back extension roll progression is as follows:

- Do bent-arm backward roll down wedge.
- Do bent-arm backward roll on floor.
- Roll backward to shoulder stand (candle).
- Roll backward down incline and pike over stacked mat or trapezoid.
- Do straight-arm tuck backward roll to pike down wedge.
- Do straight-arm tuck backward roll to pike on floor.
- Do straight-arm pike backward roll.

Shoulder Stand (Candle) Practice

The candle, or inverted shoulder stand, was introduced in chapter 3, page 77, and is important in the development of many skills on the floor and beam. Spend time with drills and variations of drills to develop this skill. The following is the progression:

- Do straight-body lift.
- Do seated tuck, roll to inverted tuck, extend to shoulder stand.
- Roll backward to candle from tuck stand, return to tuck stand.
- Roll backward to candle from stand, return to stand.
- Perform three candlesticks in a row from stand.
- Perform three candlesticks to straight jumps (increase the number each time).

Roll Backward to Candle From Stand, Return to Stand

- Begin in a straight stand.
- Bend the knees, shifting weight back to arrive in a tuck sit with the feet on the floor.
- Begin rolling backward to a back rocker, lifting the legs from tuck through pike.
- Extend the hips and legs to straight, creating a vertical line from shoulders.
- Position yourself high on the shoulders, with toes pointed to the ceiling and hip angle straight.
- Bring legs down and roll to tuck stand. Return to stand.
- Sequence is straight-body stand, tuck stand, back rocker to shoulder stand, roll to tuck stand, stand.
- For a challenge, try the following sequence: stand, candle, stand, stretch jump.

Backward Pike Roll Over Stacked Mat

- Begin in a straight-body stand with arms overhead.
- Sit back, piking torso.
- Roll backward, pushing on the floor with the hands to straighten arms (practice first with bent arms).
- Lift the legs over a stacked mat or trapezoid. Stand up through pike.
- Sequence is straight-body stand, standing pike, seated pike, inverted pike, push, backward roll into pike, straight-body stand.

Tuck With Straight Arms to Pike

- Begin in a straight-body stand with backs of legs touching the incline mat.
- Perform a backward roll, keeping straight arms in line with torso throughout.
- Hands are turned inward; fingers are pointed toward each other with palms facing away from the body.
- Once secure on incline mat, perform on floor.
- Sequence is straight-body stand, tuck stand, seated tuck with arms up and straight, backward roll with straight arms, tuck stand, straight-body stand.

Pike Backward Roll With Straight Arms

- Perform the backward pike roll, keeping the arms straight.
- Keep fingers pointing toward each other.

Back Extension Roll

- Gymnasts must have a solid handstand before attempting the back extension roll.

Learning Cues for Back Extension Roll

Verbal/Linguistic

- Begin in a straight-body stand.
- Sit back through tuck stand to roll with arms and legs extended until body hits handstand.
- Return to floor in lever, then do a finishing lunge.

Logical/Mathematical

- Sequence is straight-body stand, tuck stand, seated tuck, backward roll, extend to handstand, lever, lunge, finish lunge.
- From a vertical stand, roll backward to an inverted stand.
- Keep straight lines as long as possible in both positions.

Visual/Spatial

- Arms will not be visible until hands push off floor.
- Keep spine slightly rounded on the way up to handstand, but keep head in line with body.
- Watch toes on the way up to handstand; look at hands when body extends in handstand.

Bodily/Kinesthetic

- Feel straight arms touching sides of head.
- Feel the push backward off floor with feet.
- Push through straight arms until shoulders are extended in handstand.
- Lift the toes up toward the ceiling.
- Feel legs squeezed tight and together on the way up to handstand.
- Keep torso (abdominals and buttocks) tight and rib cage in so the back does not arch in handstand.

Musical/Rhythmical

- Stand, sit, push, handstand, lunge.

  1, 2, and 3, 4.

Assist

- Hold gymnast at hips to lift weight up off shoulders and neck.
- Move hands to support closest leg during handstand.

Common Errors

- Arms don't extend because of lack of strength or timing.
- Tuck opens up too early.
- Body is piked.
- Candle position isn't achieved before arm push.

Challenges

- Go through pike, not tuck.
- Try a straight-arm back extension roll.

SIDEWARD ROTATIONS

Review	New Skill
Exploring sideward tumbling Front support to supported squat Front support to supported pike Runner's lunge, kick up one leg Lunge, lever, single leg up, feet together, lever, lunge Traveling jumps on and off/over mats	*Cartwheel progression* Mini (half) cartwheel Weight transfers Lunge, cartwheel, lunge Hurdle cartwheel One-arm cartwheel Dive cartwheel

Mini-Cartwheels

A cartwheel is an inverted sideward tumbling skill that is a variation of the straight-body handstand position, which means that the lead-ups for the handstand are also the lead-ups for the cartwheel. Before moving into the beginning skills of mini-cartwheels (see figure below), gymnasts should have explored sideward tumbling skills (chapter 2, page 43). After students do the exploratory sideward tumbling movements, they will do the beginning skills for a cartwheel, which include a progression of lead-ups with an emphasis on transferring weight. The gymnasts will then progress to mini-cartwheels using stacked mats and a low rope; then they will progress to the lunge, cartwheel, lunge. The following are basic steps leading up to the cartwheel.

- Know how to place the hands.
- Be able to transfer weight by moving both hands, then both feet.
- Be able to transfer weight by moving both hands, then foot, foot.
- Be able to get the feet higher in the weight transfer.
- Be able to go hand, hand, foot, foot in the weight transfer.
- Perform the cartwheel.

Practice of Weight Transfers

Performing weight transfers and mini-cartwheels using stacked mats and over a low rope will increase the force of the kick. Hand and foot markers will assist correct placement in the development of the cartwheel. Break down the elements of the weight transfer by isolating the hands and the feet. In the beginning, gymnasts need to explore how weight transfers feel and try to isolate the different parts of the body to perform the skill.

Hand placement. The direction of the fingers is very important and a big safety issue in the performance of the cartwheel. To help gymnasts learn where to place the hands, use hand spots on a straight line made with chalk or tape.

Weight transfers. Have gymnasts place both hands on the floor and "jump" both feet to the side (perform side donkey kicks from one side to the other side). You can also use a stacked mat and have gymnasts jump the feet from one side to the other side of the mat (see "Exploring Sideward Tumbling," page 43).

Hands to Feet

- Stand to the side of stacked mat or low bench.
- Place hands shoulder-width apart on mat stack; face fingers sideways.
- Keep hands in place while jumping with both feet, leaving the floor simultaneously, to the other side of the mat or bench.
- Keep hands in place and jump back to original position.
- Kinder cue: Do a sideward donkey kick over the mat.

Gymnasts may have difficulty in the transition from a two-foot takeoff and two-foot landing to a foot, foot takeoff and foot, foot landing. First, perform the mini-cartwheel with weight transfer of both hands to both feet and then emphasize the change to foot, foot.

Hands, Foot, Foot

- Stand in a lunge with the mat stack in front.
- Place hands on the mat stack shoulder-width apart, one in front of the other, with fingers facing sideward.
- Kick the back leg first, then push with the front (lunge) leg into a modified handstand with legs in straddle. (Legs should not go to vertical in handstand.)
- Land foot, foot to finish in lunge.
- Kinder cue: Put your straddle in the sky.
- Sequence is stand, lunge, inverted straddle, lunge.

Get feet higher in weight transfer. Once gymnasts are able to transfer weight from one side to the other, they should try to get their feet higher. Once they can support their weight at this stage, they are ready go from foot to foot.

Hand, hand, foot, foot. Gymnasts may also have difficulty in the transition from placing two hands on the floor simultaneously to placing hand, hand in sequence. Repeat the mini-cartwheel with the emphasis on placing hand, hand instead of both hands simultaneously. Use ropes and handspots that show the start in lunge. Look for the second hand in line with the first and make sure the direction of the fingers is correct.

Lunge, Cartwheel, Lunge

The cartwheel emphasizes these elements:

- Moving through a lunge
- Timing and force of the kick (must kick early)
- Straight sideward handstand with inverted straddle
- Keeping the arms next to ears and not dropping them
- Rhythm and sequence of hand, hand, foot, foot

Learning Cues for Lunge, Cartwheel, Lunge

Verbal/Linguistic

- Lunge, then lever, placing hands (hand, hand) parallel and sideward on the same forward line as feet.
- Kick to inverted straddle handstand.
- When vertical execute a quarter turn.
- Land (foot, foot) on the opposite side in lunge. End facing in the direction in which the skill originated.

Logical/Mathematical

- Sequence is stretch stand, lunge, lever, quarter turn, straddle handstand, quarter turn, lever, lunge, finishing lunge.
- After lunge, body will make a quarter turn inside (body position like side cartwheel) and to end in lunge, body will make a quarter turn out.
- Keep a vertical line from fingers to toes, lunge at 60 degrees, kick to straddle handstand while executing a 180 degree turn, and land on opposite side in 60-degree lunge.
- Square shoulders and hips in lunge so that they are parallel to the wall.

- Keep one line from fingers to feet throughout skill.
- Keep equal space between hand and foot placement.
- Pass the arms and legs through the same plane.

Visual/Spatial

- Keep your arms by your ears.
- See your parallel hand placement on the floor, then your foot land in line with hand placement.
- If the right foot is the forward leg on the lunge, the pattern will be right hand, left hand, left foot, right foot.

Bodily/Kinesthetic

- Feel the push through your hands to lift your shoulders in handstand.
- Press hip socket of back leg forward to square in lunge.

Note: Always stand two arms' lengths apart so that there is no chance of kicking your partner.

Musical/Rhythmical

- Stand up quickly so that you don't pike.
- Rhythm is:

    Hand, hand, foot, foot.

    1, 2, 3, 4.

Assist

Stand behind gymnast as he or she becomes inverted and place near hand at near hip bone on the entry and the other hand over the back and on far hip as the gymnast turns the cartwheel.

Common Errors

- Arms drop on approach.
- Hands are placed too close to feet and feet too close to hands.
- Body is piked.
- Legs are bent.
- Legs don't remain straddled.
- Legs don't turn over the top.
- Turn is not complete.

Challenge

Here is a skill to challenge both you (the spotter) and the gymnast. The gymnast performs the cartwheel to handstand on low beam, which makes hand placement easy. Stand behind the gymnast (gymnast's back is toward you in the handstand) and place one hand on each hip to support the gymnast, then guide the gymnast to lower both feet to the floor away from you when gymnast is ready to come down. This can also be done on a line on the floor or close to a wall with fingertips touching the wall. Introducing the cartwheel to handstand on low beam allows you to practice the spot, and it helps the gymnast experience the side hand placement. Spotting this cartwheel prepares you to spot an aerial cartwheel. Both skills require the same spot but you need to move in more quickly to support the first hip earlier in the aerial cartwheel.

Hurdle Cartwheel Progression

The jump-hurdle is a preparatory move with a long, low, powerful chassé into a lunge. The chest must be over the takeoff foot in the lunge position. When the chest is in front of the takeoff foot, it causes the gymnast to push off forward and down instead of blocking. In the correct position, when chest is over the takeoff foot, the takeoff lifts the chest and makes it the axis (center of gravity) around which the movement rotates. This high center of gravity is also important in the dive and aerial cartwheels. One or more running steps can precede the hurdle.

- Practice the jump-hurdle in isolation.
- Practice a jump-hurdle cartwheel.
- Put it all together with a run, jump-hurdle, cartwheel.

Learning Cues for Jump-Hurdle Cartwheel

Verbal/Linguistic

- Begin in a standing position with arms down by the side and head neutral.
- Lean forward until you start to lose balance.
- Jump (block) from two feet, bringing arms overhead by ears, and land on nondominant foot with dominant leg slightly behind the nondominant leg.
- Immediately bring the dominant leg through to the front lunge entry of the cartwheel. (Bringing leg forward quickly is what gives power to hurdle.) Syncopate and step.
- Bring arms toward floor for tumbling pass.

Logical/Mathematical

- Sequence is jump, hurdle (chassé), lunge, cartwheel, lunge.
- Bring legs together in air until back leg passes through to the front and lands in lunge to initiate the cartwheel.

Visual/Spatial

- In the hurdle, as soon as front foot pushes off floor, see arms swing up to vertical.
- Once arms arrive outside head, they stay there. If you can see them, they have dropped out of place.

Bodily/Kinesthetic

- Feel legs come together in air and then back leg passes to the front in lunge.
- Feel body turn above hands.
- Turn torso by pushing through shoulders.

Musical/Rhythmical

- Arms reach top of their swing at the high point of the hurdle.
- Rhythm is:

    Chassé, lunge, cartwheel.

    1 and 2 and 3.

Assist

Place near hand at near hip bone on the entry and the other hand over the lower back and on far hip as the gymnast turns the cartwheel. (This spot is good practice for spotting an aerial cartwheel.)

Common Errors

- Arms drop as they enter the cartwheel.
- Hips turn too soon.
- Second arm comes across face (it should be behind ear).

One-Arm Cartwheel (Near Arm)

Safety precaution: Do not allow gymnasts to place the free hand behind the back because the hand must be accessible if needed.

- Proceed through the lunge, placing the dominant hand down as for the cartwheel but keeping the nondominant arm at the thigh, hip, or side.
- Kick both legs and take them through vertical.
- Land in lunge.
- Challenge: Perform far-arm cartwheel, which involves placing nondominant arm on floor and touching dominant arm to the side.

A variation is to let the gymnast begin with both arms overhead and swing the nondominant hand through (in a circle) instead of making contact with the floor. This will allow gymnast to place that hand down if necessary. The swing will also help with momentum and is a lead-up for an aerial.

Dive Cartwheel

The dive cartwheel is an advanced skill. A gymnast must have a good jump-hurdle and be able to gain flight before performing the dive cartwheel.

The dive cartwheel utilizes an arm circle. When the arms are lifted to vertical at the height of the hurdle, gymnast continues the arms upward and backward to create an arm circle that reaches horizontally outward at the same time that the lunge leg pushes off.

Learning Cues for Dive Cartwheel

Verbal/Linguistic

- Run, then hurdle with a very strong push off the forward foot and a stronger lift of the chest.
- Use an arm circle to gain momentum.
- Achieve flight as you kick and reach upward and forward, gaining an aerial straddle before placing hands on floor for cartwheel.
- Make the kick when the chest is over the thigh.
- When vertically inverted, immediately execute a quarter turn.

Logical/Mathematical

- Sequence is run, step-hurdle with arm circle, lunge, kick legs and torso over, land on hands, turn, lunge.
- Kick, reaching into a straight-body inverted straddle.
- Make the angle of the torso at takeoff no less than 120 degrees.
- Try to rotate around the highest center that you can.

Visual/Spatial

- Achieve flight before hands touch floor in cartwheel.
- Look straight ahead in hurdle.
- Reach horizontally in front of you, not to the floor. (Instructor: Put a focal point on wall or stand in front of gymnast and extend your hand as gymnast reaches for it.)
- Reach out, not down.
- Stop chest over thigh in landing to keep from falling backward and to enable you to land in arabesque.
- Land in arabesque if possible before lunge.
- Land in lunge.

Bodily/Kinesthetic

- Push off front leg as hard as you can, then forcefully kick back leg.
- Feel weight over front leg on landing (to enable landing in arabesque).

Musical/Rhythmical

- Circle arms as quickly as you possibly can.
- Push off front leg as quickly as you can.
- Reach and kick at the same time.
- Kick so early that you create flight before hands touch the floor.

Assist

- Place near hand at near hip bone on the entry and the other hand over the back and on far hip as the gymnast turns the cartwheel.

Common Errors

- Kick happens too late: chest is too far ahead of the legs to lift it into the air.

HORIZONTAL CIRCULAR ROTATIONS: ROUND-OFF

Review	New Skill
Exploring Sideward Tumbling	***Round-off progression***
Handstand	Handstand, snapdown
Handstand, stride split	Round-off
Lunge cartwheel	Round-off, rebound
Running hurdle cartwheel	

Here is the progression for the round-off:

1. Beginning skills: Lead-ups beginning with the hand placement for the round-off, a cartwheel with round-off hand placement, a cartwheel to handstand (with round-off hand placement), the round-off from stacked mats, the handstand snapdown, then the round-off.

2. Intermediate skills: Round-off, rebound and the running round-off, rebound.

3. Advanced skills: Round-off to back handspring.

Hand Placement for Round-Off

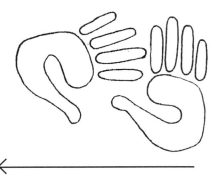

The hand placement is essential to the success of the round-off. The first hand is placed in the usual spot for the cartwheel but the second hand will turn so that the fingertips are facing the first hand (away from the direction of the round-off).

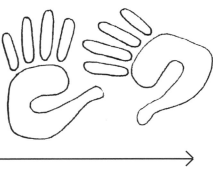

Cartwheel With Round-Off Hand Placement

Have students perform a lunge cartwheel but turn the second hand and place in round-off hand position. (Many teachers teach the round-off hand placement for both the cartwheel and round-off.)

This skill allows students to focus on the hand placement in a familiar skill—the cartwheel—and then make the one change—the hands. This is a good transition from the cartwheel to the round-off.

Cartwheel to Handstand With Round-Off Hand Placement

Perform a lunge to handstand (as if beginning the cartwheel) using round-off hand placement. In a round-off the feet come together slightly before vertical. Performing a cartwheel with round-off hands and bringing the legs together right before a handstand will help gymnasts learn to get the feet together as soon as possible.

Round-Off From Mat Stack

This drill helps gymnasts kick the legs with more force and it allows even the weakest gymnast to successfully stand up from the round-off.

- Stand on the mat stack in gymnastics point.
- Place hands in round-off position on the stacked mat.
- Lift back leg and push with lunge leg to perform a round-off.
- Turn the shoulders and then the hips and bring the legs together as quickly as possible.
- Land on both feet on the floor facing the direction of takeoff.
- Sequence is lunge, lever, half turn handstand, snapdown, finish.

Handstand Snapdown

The handstand snapdown helps the round-off stand up and is essential to the success of round-off straddle jumps, round-off back handsprings, and other combinations. Perhaps this should really be called a snapup because the focus is on lifting the chest up, not snapping the feet down.

The snapdown assists in getting gymnasts to finish the round-off with the body in an upright position with arms overhead when the feet hit the floor. This drill is a lead-up but can also be used as an enhancement after the basic round-off is learned. To do the drill, the gymnast will perform a handstand, then block by pushing with the hands and shoulders as he or she quickly brings the chest and arms up and snaps the feet down to the floor. Sequence is gymnastics point, lunge, kick, handstand, block, snapdown.

Round-Off

After the lead-ups, gymnasts are ready to perform the round-off. The round-off is basically a quarter turn into a cartwheel into a handstand, then a quarter turn and snapdown. Beginning gymnasts do not have the shoulder strength and skill to perform a round-off from a standing position on a regular mat. Therefore, when gymnasts are first learning the round-off they should perform it off a stacked mat.

Learning Cues for Round-Off

Verbal/Linguistic

- Start in gymnastics point.
- Step into a lunge and pass through lever.
- Reach forward, placing first hand on mat.
- Then place the second hand slightly turned in with fingers facing the other hand as you kick into a handstand.
- Do a quarter turn with legs together.
- Push explosively off the floor with the arms and shoulders and do a quarter turn.
- Snap down with feet landing on the floor and body in hollow straight position.
- Salute.

Logical/Mathematical

- Sequence is lunge, kick, lever, quarter turn handstand, quarter turn block, snapdown.
- Stay on one line from lunge through to snapdown.
- Place hands parallel on floor but with second hand slightly turned in.

Visual/Spatial

- Kick off front leg when chest is directly over thigh (kicking late will pike the round-off).
- Stretch arms out to place both hands on same line as lunge. (Place chalk on hands to see if your handprints are crooked or in a straight line. A common mistake is turning the round-off too early.)
- Turn second hand slightly to help turn body.
- Reach out with the arms and push the mat away.
- Turn the shoulders and then the hips.
- Keep stretching legs away from the mat, and quickly bring them together.
- Snap down with a slight hollow in upper back.
- Land on both feet facing the direction of takeoff.
- Kinder cue: Do a cartwheel that lands on two feet.

Bodily/Kinesthetic

- Feel straight arms and shoulders lifted by ears.
- Push off lunge leg to kick over as hard as you can.
- Push floor away and turn shoulders with arms.

Musical/Rhythmical

- Rhythm is:

  Kick, push, snap.

  1 and 2.

Assist

- Always stand on the lunge side and spot the torso after the turn to guide the landing.

Common Errors

- Arms drop below head.
- Hands are placed incorrectly.
- Arms are bent.
- Landing is piked.
- Snapdown happens before body is vertical and before legs come together.
- Arms give in instead of pushing away from floor.
- Push is ineffective and incorrectly timed.

Round-Off, Rebound

Many instructors prefer to teach a rebound with the round-off because the round-off usually leads into another skill from which a rebound is necessary. A rebound is a quick upward jump or punch using very little flexion of the hips, knees, or ankles. The rebound is performed immediately on landing on the snapdown of the round-off. As you land on the balls of the feet, immediately punch or push off with the feet into a stretch jump using the landing as the takeoff.

Variations:

- Perform a run, hurdle, round-off, rebound.
- For a challenge, add a jump half turn, straddle jump, tuck jump, or any other jump. (Progress slowly; beginners may not be able to control a movement from the rebound momentum.)

HORIZONTAL CIRCULAR ROTATIONS: BACK WALKOVERS

Review

Bridge

Back Walkover Progression

Rocking bridge

Jumping bridge

One-leg hopping bridge

Bridge kickover

Wall touch from a kneel

Backbend

Backbend to kickover

Back walkover

There are two main terms used in lead-up and skill development for walkovers. The *bridge* starts on the floor and is an arched position with the hands and feet flat on the floor and the abdomen up. The *backbend* starts from a standing position and the gymnast arches the back into a bridge. Review the bridge skill in chapter 3, page 83, and remember that back arching is not recommended for some people.

Rocking Bridge

This exercise is primarily designed to get more weight forward on the hands and less weight on the feet. It also develops shoulder and upper-back flexibility. Too much rocking to the feet can stress the lumbar spine. Because the correct position for a bridge is with the shoulders directly above the hands, the forward shift of weight is the one to be emphasized.

- Assume a bridge with equal weight placement on hands and feet.
- Rock weight to feet (where it should not be) and back to hands (where it will be eventually).
- With the weight over the hands, find the maximum range of motion as the arms and legs are straightened.
- Do not push into the lumbar spine.
- Use a slow, gentle push; never try to jerk the spine into a position.

Jumping Bridge

This skill teaches gymnasts to push with the legs.

- From a bridge position, jump off both feet and return to bridge.
- Keep the weight over the hands.

One-Leg Hopping Bridge

The one-leg hopping bridge teaches gymnasts to push and kick with one leg.

- Begin in a bridge position with one leg lifted.
- Push and kick off one foot.
- Return to starting position.

Bridge Kickover

Perform the bridge kickover with feet on elevated mat or at the top of an incline mat before performing on a flat surface.

Learning Cues for Bridge Kickover

Verbal/Linguistic

- Begin in a bridge.
- Shift weight, aligning shoulders directly above the hands.
- Push off support leg.
- Kick your stronger leg up and over bridge in a stride split as you shift weight back over hands.
- Step down into lunge.

Logical/Mathematical

- Sequence is bridge, kick, handstand stride split, lever, lunge.
- Inner thighs share a center line.
- Kick, trying for 180-degree inverted split.
- Shift weight to hands before pushing off the incline or mat with the legs.

Visual/Spatial

- See parallel hands on wedge.
- Keep arms straight throughout.
- Kick your good leg first.
- Pull legs apart in split.
- Turn lead leg out slightly for maximum split.
- Push support leg until it straightens.
- When you see front foot land, push hands on mat and lift chest and arms up to stand up quickly in lunge.

Bodily/Kinesthetic

- Swing lead leg up as you push hard off support leg.
- Feel hips directly above shoulders in walkover.
- Feel legs slightly turned out in lunge.

Musical/Rhythmical

- Straighten both legs at the same time.
- Rhythm is:

  Shift, kick, lunge.

  And 1, 2.

Assist

- Support gymnast on back of hips, pushing backward and upward to assist the kickover.

Common Errors

- Legs are bent.
- Shift of hands and weight is not adequate to get over.
- Shoulders and hips are not over the top of the hands.

Backbend Progression

Safety issue: A bridge kickover down an incline or off a mat stack is actually much less taxing to the spine than a backbend. Gymnasts should only do backbends when they have very good shoulder flexibility as well as the back and abdominal strength to hold a handstand. Once in a backbend, gymnasts should not try to stand, but lower the back by rounding down to floor.

Wall Touch From a Kneel

Begin in a kneel with back to the wall. Reach upward and backward with straight arms. Hold abdomen tight and watch hands until they touch the wall. Arch the spine from the shoulders down, one vertebra at a time, to touch the wall. Push away from the wall back to starting position. Sequence is kneel, reach, touch, push, kneel.

Backbend

In the backbend progression it is easier and safer to start with mats at a higher elevation and lower them a little at a time until you reach a floor level. An octagon can be used for teaching this skill. The progression is as follows:

- Do a backbend up incline.
- Do a backbend to stacked mat.
- Do a backbend to 8-inch mat.
- Do a backbend to flat mat.
- Do a backbend to stand.

Learning Cues for Backbend

Verbal/Linguistic

- Stand in a vertical straight-body position.
- Lift straight arms upward and backward to arch first in the shoulders, then the upper back, middle back, and lower back.
- Press the hips and thighs forward.
- Continue reaching backward and place the hands on the floor side by side, shoulder-width apart.
- Immediately press the hips and thighs forward, pushing from the hands to stand up.
- Finish in a straight stand.

Logical/Mathematical

- Sequence is stretch body, reach and arch, bridge.
- Create a sequential curve in the spine, one vertebra at a time, starting in neck and upper back.
- Curve the spine evenly.

Visual/Spatial

- First take your arms back as far as you can, then watch them as you go backward until they touch the mat. Maintain focus on hands.
- Lift abdomen and rib cage up, then extend arms up and back until hands touch the mat.
- Keep shoulders directly over the hands.
- Keep head inside arms; do not let it drop back to rest on upper back.
- Keep feet flat on floor.
- Push hips forward while going back.

Bodily/Kinesthetic

- Reach arms up and back until you feel your shoulders stretch.
- Feel an arch in your upper back, then middle back.

Musical/Rhythmical

- Arch back in a smooth, slow motion.

Assist

- As the gymnast goes back, support the shoulders and upper back so that gymnast avoids stressing the lumbar spine.

Common Errors

- Arch starts in the lumbar spine and goes back from that part of the spine.
- Lower back is overarched.
- Heels lift off the floor.
- Head does not stay in line with arms and focus is not on hands.
- Hips don't push forward.

Backbend to Kickover

- Combine the backbend with the kickover.

Back Walkover

The difference between the backbend kickover and the back walkover is that the back walkover starts on one leg from a gymnastics point and progresses through a standing backbend.

Learning Cues for Back Walkover

Verbal/Linguistic

- Begin in gymnastics point.
- Keep the standing leg straight and extended.
- Reach upward and backward, arching and progressing downward through the spine as the leg begins to lift.
- Coordinate the push and shift. When hands touch the floor, immediately push off the standing leg, shifting the weight of shoulders back over hands.
- Pass from inverted split in handstand to a lever.
- End in a lunge.

Logical/Mathematical

- Sequence is gymnastics point, bridge with leg extension, push and kick to inverted split in handstand, lever, arabesque, lunge.
- Take arms up and back on a diagonal line to maximum shoulder flexibility before arching.
- Point front foot on same line as back foot.
- Bring front leg up through center line of the body.
- Create a sequential and uniform curve of the spine.
- Keep a vertical line up through legs. If hips push forward, lower back is taking too much stress!
- Handstand goes through vertical.
- Land front foot on same line as the takeoff occurred.

Visual/Spatial

- Reach arms behind ears, then begin to reach up and back.
- Turn out free leg slightly, lifting it to keep it in line with belly button, nose and spine.
- Pretend you're doing this on the balance beam and stay on line of the beam.

Bodily/Kinesthetic

- Keep standing leg tight (bending the knee puts pressure on the lower back).
- Feel arms straight and behind ears as if hanging from a bar, then reach back.

Musical/Rhythmical

- Walkover should be done smoothly.
- When hands make contact with floor, push off standing foot.

Assist

- Support the gymnast's upper and middle back to keep stress off of the lower back.

Common Errors

- Feet push too early, which causes a jump to hands.
- Feet push too late, which shifts weight to the lower back.
- Support leg bends, which shifts hips and weight forward instead of over hands.
- Chest drops at end of skill.
- Lower back arches first.
- Arms bend or standing leg bends.
- Free leg doesn't lift enough.
- Legs don't pull apart to create a stride split.
- Push from support leg is not strong enough.
- Gymnast doesn't push into shoulders.

HORIZONTAL CIRCULAR ROTATIONS: FRONT WALKOVERS

Review	New Skill
Handstand	***Front Walkover Progression***
Bridge	Backbend to stand
Rocking Bridge	Handstand to bridge
	Front limber
	Handstand split to one-leg bridge
	Front walkover

Backbend Rock to Stand

- Perform a backbend, then rock to stand—first over octagon, then on incline.
- From a backbend, rock and shift weight over the feet and rise to a standing position.

Handstand to Bridge

Do not have the students attempt to stand up from this position.

- Begin in a stand at bottom of incline.
- Lunge, lever, and then perform a handstand.
- Hold handstand momentarily.
- Push forward into shoulders, arch the back, and bend knees slightly until feet touch the mat, creating a bridge position.
- Land in three-quarter bridge at top of incline.
- Variations include handstand to bridge onto mat stack, down the incline, and on the floor.
- Sequence is straight-body stand, lunge, lever, handstand, bridge.
- Assist: Spot the descent to bridge by placing near hand on upper back and one arm along the lower back or upper thighs. (The hand on the upper back can push to remind the gymnast to arch upper back and shoulders first.)

Front Limber

The front limber is a skill by itself or it can be used as a lead-up for front walkovers. Many teachers do not teach or spend much time on the front limber. It is really more stressful on the back than the front walkover. Some instructors go immediately to the front walkover.

- Move through lunge.
- Lever to handstand, bridge, then push through shoulders and upper back.
- Rise to a straight-body stand with arms by ears and head neutral.
- Sequence is gymnastics point, lunge, lever, handstand, bridge, push through shoulders, straight-body stand.
- Assist: Spot the descent to bridge by placing one hand on upper back and one hand on the back of thighs or lower back. Spot the rise to stand by placing near hand on top of shoulder to lift and far arm along the upper back for support. Slide hand from shoulder to stretch arm above head to emphasize correct alignment at end.

Handstand Split to One-Leg Bridge

- Purpose is to give a transition from a two-leg landing to the split used in the walkover.
- Start in a lunge.
- Lever and perform a handstand to inverted stride split.
- Land in a bridge with the leading leg supporting.

Front Walkover

The front walkover is a lunge to handstand split that arches over until one foot makes contact with the floor, then the other foot, then to stand. This skill can progress down an incline, then on floor.

Learning Cues for Front Walkover

Verbal/Linguistic

- Move through lunge and lever to handstand split.
- Push down on floor to extend through shoulders and upper back.
- Keep the legs in a maximum stride split and allow the back to begin the arch.
- Continue moving through the arch.
- Place the lead leg on floor and watch the hands.
- Push through the shoulders to rise up to a straight-body position as the other leg reaches the floor.

Logical/Mathematical

- Sequence is stand, lunge, lever, extend shoulders, handstand split, arch and push with arms, front lever, front scale, straight-body stand.
- Handstand is vertical and legs are in wide stride split.
- Create a vertical line from wrists through front of hips in handstand.

Visual/Spatial

- Keep arms by ears and head neutral.
- Focus on hands throughout, even while standing up (to keep head in position).
- Keep weight over palms in handstand.
- Push into shoulders to arch over; push into upper back to stand up.
- Keep arms an extension of torso throughout.

Bodily/Kinesthetic

- Keep legs in stride split from lever to front scale.
- Feel the push through upper back, not the lower back to stand.
- Lower with control; try not to fall into it.

Musical/Rhythmical

- The only stop is in a momentary handstand split.

Assist

Spot the ascent by placing one hand on upper back and one hand on the shoulder. Lift the shoulder as needed. Slide hand to stretched arm overhead at finish to emphasize correct alignment.

Common Errors

- Chin is tucked, which rounds the spine.
- Gymnast doesn't look at hands on the ascent, which rounds the spine.
- Arms are bent.
- Shoulders are not extended.
- Split is not maintained.
- Legs go to side rather than moving through a vertical plane.
- Hands don't push off and upper body is not lifted as foot makes contact.
- Hips are not shifted over knees before upper body is lifted.
- Head is not kept back, which causes gymnast to lose sight of movement path.

HORIZONTAL CIRCULAR ROTATIONS: HANDSPRING

Review	**New Skill**
Handstand	***Front Handspring Progressions***
Hurdle cartwheel	Blocking
Round-off	Handstand to flatback
	Block to flatback
	Front handspring

Handsprings are considered advanced skills that utilize the handstand as the core skill. Therefore, a gymnast must have a sound handstand to be successful in handsprings. Review the hurdle used in the hurdle cartwheel (page 147).

There are three main parts of the handspring that need to be practiced before putting the skill together.

1. Block with shoulders. This gives the body flight.
2. Snap feet together early so that the body does not arch.
3. Keep a straight body throughout. Maintain straight body after feet come together. (Upper back arches on the finish position.)

Blocking

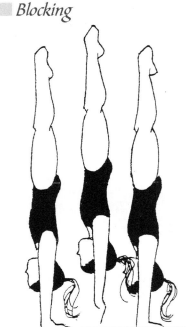

A block occurs in extension of the shoulders, not bending of the arms, while moving into the handstand position. The block takes place from the push of the arms on the floor and the opening of a slight shoulder angle. The opening of the shoulder angle occurs as the arms move from beside the cheeks to behind the ears. The block is what gives a gymnast flight to land the front handspring standing up. It is a drill that needs extensive repetition.

- Perform a handstand.
- When vertical, block (jump) hands off the floor by extending shoulder girdle (a block is impossible if handstand is compressed or collapsed).
- Thrust shoulders back behind ears, which will repel hands away from floor.
- Both hands must leave the floor simultaneously to hop up and forward.
- The block will lift the entire body vertically from floor.
- Return to lunge.
- Assist: Stand beside gymnast and guide the handstand hop by holding gymnast's thighs or lower legs.
- Other challenges: Consecutive hops on floor, two fast hops in a row, three fast hops in a row.

Handstand to Flatback

This skill gets gymnasts to snap the feet together early and to learn to keep the body tight and straight (every body part has to hit the safety cushion simultaneously). When first teaching this skill, have the gymnast begin in a gymnastics point and then perform a handstand in front of safety cushion (8-inch mat) or on springboard with a spot. The gymnast can proceed to use a hurdle, rebound into a handstand.

- Perform a handstand onto safety cushion.
- Bring legs together quickly and keep head inside arms.
- Keep hips forward directly above shoulders.
- Hold tight handstand position.
- Bring entire body to a fall flat onto safety cushion.
- Assist: Stand beside gymnast and, if necessary, stop the legs to make sure the body is vertical. Assist in the fall to flatback on the cushion.

Block to Flatback

These drills should be performed on 8-inch safety cushions. The progression for combining the block with flatback is as follows:

- Block with the handstand to flatback.
- Hurdle, lunge, handstand, block to flatback.
- Short run, hurdle, lunge, handstand, block to flatback.

Learning Cues for Block to Flatback

Verbal/Linguistic

- Stand in front of safety cushion in gymnastics point.
- Kick to handstand.
- Upon touching floor (mat) with hands, immediately elevate shoulder girdle (block) to raise entire torso upward off floor.
- Continue to hold handstand position.
- Fall onto flatback on safety cushion.

Logical/Mathematical

- Sequence is lunge, lever, handstand, block, flatback.
- Kick to a three-quarter handstand, bringing legs together as quickly as possible.
- Thrust shoulders back behind ears, which will repel hands away from floor.
- Block will lift entire body vertically up off floor.
- Keeping body in straight line, fall onto safety cushion.

(continued)

(continued)

Visual/Spatial

- Keep your arms up and by ears. If you can see your arms, they have dropped.
- Bring legs together quickly and keep them together.
- See hands but do not lift head; look with eyes only.
- Watch hands throughout.
- Watch hands throughout skill and "hop" on floor.
- Keep hips directly above shoulders.
- Kinder cue: Handstand, kaboom!

Bodily/Kinesthetic

- When almost in handstand, block shoulders (feel the block in shoulders).
- Pop shoulders up and back.

Musical/Rhythmical

- Kick to hold a momentary handstand before fall starts.
- Rhythm is:

  Touch, block.

  And, 1.

Assist

- Spot the descent by placing one hand on upper back and one hand on lower back.

Common Errors

- Arms drop or bend.
- Block doesn't happen at the right time.
- Legs don't get together quickly.
- Back arches.

Front Handspring Stepout

A variation or lead-up to the handspring is the finish of stepping out. The progression for front handspring stepout is as follows:

- Short run, hurdle, lunge, handspring over octagon.
- Short run, hurdle, lunge, handspring with hands on mat stack.
- Short run, hurdle, lunge, handspring on mat stack to incline.
- Short run, hurdle, lunge, front handspring stepout.

Front Handspring

The skill of the handspring should be learned first from an elevated mat.

Learning Cues for Front Handspring

Verbal/Linguistic

- Run, hurdle, and lunge keeping the lever line, and place hands on mat as the legs kick up to handstand.
- Upon hitting handstand, block and immediately elevate shoulder girdle to raise entire torso upward off the floor.
- Hold the handstand position as the body rotates around, slightly arching the upper back.
- Land in a straight-body stand or stepout.

Logical/Mathematical

- Sequence is run, hurdle, lunge, lever, handstand, block, stand or step out, lunge at 60 degrees.
- Reach out but don't drop arms in lunge to get the most powerful block that you can get.
- At three-quarter handstand, block through shoulders.
- Keep arms in one line (do not create a shoulder angle) to stand up.
- Open angle of legs slightly to stand up in stepout.

Visual/Spatial

- Keep your arms up. If you can see your arms, they have dropped.
- Reach your arms as far out in your lunge as possible.
- Bring legs together quickly and keep them together.
- Watch hands throughout, especially on the return to standing.
- Keep chin and head up while watching hands (tucking chin will round upper back, causing a fall backward).
- Keep arms and legs straight throughout.

Bodily/Kinesthetic

- Feel the powerful push of the legs in the hurdle lunge.
- Feel the block.
- Squeeze legs and buttock muscles, pushing hips forward to keep from piking.
- Feel a slightly arched upper back on stand up.

Musical/Rhythmical

- Block immediately upon reaching mat.
- Block as quickly as possible by quickly extending shoulders ("pop the shoulders").
- Bring your legs together quickly for the block, then step out to stand up.
- Stand up will happen more quickly on incline.

Assist

- Reach under the handspring to support the gymnast on the upper back and assist the rise back to standing.

Common Errors

- Arms drop in the reach through the lunge.
- Block doesn't happen or it happens at the wrong time.
- Arms and legs bend.
- Legs don't come together.
- Chin is tucked so that the back straightens or rounds, pulling gymnast back to floor.
- Back arches in the entry and handstand.
- Hips drop, which causes a squat on the landing.

Back Handspring Progression

There are four parts of the handspring that need to be practiced before putting the skill together:

1. Shift the weight (sit back) to get the correct initial body angle.
2. Push upward and backward forcefully off the legs.
3. Hit the handstand position.
4. Repel (block) off the hands.

Shift Back

The purpose of this skill is to get correct flight angle and feeling of the weight shifting back. The first part of the back handspring is a shift of the weight backward. The sensation of shifting back is similar to that of sitting back into a chair. It is important to experience the feeling of shifting the weight back and momentarily going off balance. This will aid in proper flight angle and take some of the weight off the hands.

- Use a mat set at knee height and stand facing away from the mat about a foot away.
- Stand in hollow body position, arms by ears overhead, and with the weight equally distributed over the feet.
- Maintain hollow as body weight shifts back quickly with a feeling of weight over the heels.
- Bend the hips and knees and keep the torso vertical and almost on the stacked mat. You should be able to see your toes.
- Repeat several times.

Shift Back, Jump to Flatback

Gymnasts must learn to push strongly with the legs and hold a straight body, which is crucial when the hands touch the floor in the handstand.

- Use a safety cushion (at least 32 inches high) or two folded stacked mats and stand facing away from the cushion about a foot away.
- Begin in hollow body position, arms by the ears overhead, and with weight equally distributed over the feet.
- Maintain hollow as the body weight shifts back. Quickly bend the hips and knees, keeping the torso vertical.
- Quickly straighten the hips and knees, pushing forcefully off the floor, keeping the torso vertical.
- Jump backward to land on a flat back on a soft waist-high mat. Arms are extended above head and body is very tight. The whole body must hit the mat at the same time. If one part hits the mat before another, you will not reach a handstand position in the back handspring.

Note: This drill can be practiced with or without an arm swing. The back handspring is usually in a sequence after a skill in which the arms are by the ears (for example, a round-off back handspring). Some gymnasts need or feel more comfortable with an arm swing when first learning the back handspring; the arm swing can also add more power to the weaker gymnast. However, many gymnasts typically pike and drop the torso forward with the arm swing. It is very important to keep the torso vertical to avoid shifting the weight forward, which puts too much weight on the hands at contact.

Back Handspring

- First perform back handspring over an octagon or down an incline mat.

Learning Cues for Back Handspring

Verbal/Linguistic

- Begin in a stretched hollow body position with arms by ears.
- Shift weight backward and lower arms behind body.
- As arms pass knees, quickly bend and straighten legs as the arms swing upward.
- Jump backward at 70 degrees to handstand.
- Block to bring torso and arms through to a stretched hollow body position.

(continued)

(continued)

Logical/Mathematical

- Sequence is hollow body with arms by ears, shift weight, jump, handstand, block to stand.
- Shift weight to sit back with knees and hips at 90 degrees, thighs parallel to floor.
- Jump backward at 70 degrees.
- Pass through vertical in handstand.

Visual/Spatial

- In hollow, shift weight back until you can see your toes.
- Watch hands reach backward to mat.
- Keep arms straight; reach back with extended shoulders.
- Keep hips under; do not pike backward.
- Stretch your jump out backward.
- Quickly lift chest and arms back to vertical.
- See feet land, then look to wall to continue chest rotation.

Bodily/Kinesthetic

- Feel abdomen and buttocks tight in handstand.
- Start with weight on front of feet, then rock back to heels to pick up the energy of the fall.
- Feel the weight shifted back (almost like you are going to fall).
- Feel shoulders press on hands hitting floor and then block away from floor.

Musical/Rhythmical

- Rhythm is:

  Sit, jump, hands, feet.

  And a 1, 2.

Assist

- Place dominant hand across the lower back to let gymnast know that you are ready.
- Grasp both hips firmly to fully support gymnast and facilitate skill.

Common Errors

- Head is thrown back first.
- Arms reach back before the feet push off, causing back to arch.
- Knees are pushed forward; weight doesn't shift back.

COMBINATIONS AND ROUTINES

Many different skill combinations can be performed in floor exercise. As suggested earlier, allow students the chance to problem solve and put combinations and routines together. You can choose a skill and let students choose an introduction into the skill and an exit out of the skills. Link several skills together to perform a routine. The movement chart will also assist you in the creation of a routine.

5

Balance Beam

FOUNDATIONAL POSITIONS ON BEAM

Hand placements	Approaches	Basic body positions (review)		
Parallel English Cartwheel Round-off	Front Rear (back) Side/cross Front diagonal	Sitting tuck Sitting pike Standing straight body Standing straddle Stride Lunge Arch stand Hollow stand Stride Gymnastics point Supported tuck Supported pike	Squat stand Prone—straight body Supine—straight body Supine tuck Standing pike Supine pike Sitting straddle Piked straddle stand Piked supine straddle Supine straight body	Inverted tuck Inverted pike Piked inverted straddle

NONLOCOMOTOR SKILLS ON BALANCE BEAM

Balance			Support
Standing balances (straight line from supporting foot to head) Relevé hold Coupé Passé Front attitude Battement **Standing balances (straight line from nonsupported foot to head)** Arabesque Front scale Lever	**Standing Balance** Side scale Y scale **Nonstanding balances** Stride split Straddle split Candle **Knee balances** Knee stand Knee lunge Half split Knee scale Balance in knee scale	**Standing balances** Front support with feet on beam Rear support with feet on beam V-sit with hands on beam **Supports with arms** Front support Stride support Front support, single-leg cut to stride support Rear support Stride support, single-leg cut to rear support **Supports with arms: holds** Tuck support L or pike support Straddle L support Stride support V-sit support	**Handstand progression** Tuck support, kick up one leg Lunge, lever, single leg up, lever, lunge (single leg swing up to handstand) Lunge, lever, feet together, lever, lunge English handstand

(continued)

LOCOMOTOR SKILLS ON BALANCE BEAM

Mounts	Using feet	Dismounts	Rotational movements
Lead-ups using stacked mats	**Alternating feet**	Step off dismount	**Turns in place**
Squat on	Forward walks	Stretch jump dismount	Pivot (180-degree relevé turn)
Straddle on	Backward walks	Tuck jump dismount	Squat turn
Wolf mount	Lateral walks	Straddle jump dismount	Pirouettes
Beam mounts	Dip walks	Pike jump dismount	**Cartwheel**
Jump to front support	Relevé walks	Jump half turn dismount	Lunge, cartwheel, lunge
Front support to supported straddle	Grapevine	Front support (push-up	**Back walkover progression**
Front support to straddle sit, knee	Waltz step	position) to front dismount	Rocking bridge
scale, knee lunge, and stand	Chassé	Cartwheel to side handstand	Bridge kickover
Whip-up	Side chassé	dismount	Walk touch from a kneel
Front support, stag sit	Back chassé	Round-off dismount off end	Backbend
Mount straddle, V-sit, tuck to stand			Backbend to kickover
Step to squat	**Jumps landing on two feet**		Back walkover
Step on to balance stand	Safe landing position		
Jump to squat-on	Small bunny jumps (stretch		
Jump to straddle-on	jumps)		
Wolf mount	Stretch		
Scissor mount	Tuck		
	Stride		
	Assemblé		
	Landing on one foot		
	Stride split leap		

Equipment: The regulation balance beam is 4 inches wide and 16 feet long. Beams vary from 6 inches to 50 inches off the floor.

Spotting and safety: The entire beam area and the ends should have safety mats underneath. Additional matting can be placed under the beams and built up to a height at which the gymnasts will feel safe as the beam height is increased. If skills are initially learned on a high beam with mats built up, gymnasts' spatial orientation can stay the same and mats can gradually be taken away. Different beam widths can also be used to help gymnasts build confidence. Some teachers feel that the use of 12-, then 8-, then 6-inch-wide regulation-height beams are good for progressions.

If a springboard is used for mounting the beam, spot the mount and then remove the springboard after the mount; this ensures the safety of the gymnasts. Assist athletes by standing or walking next to them and holding the hips. To assist, you can also hold the same-side hand up and the gymnast can press against the hand as a balance point. Review falling and rolling techniques and teach gymnasts how to twist out of a handstand and cartwheel (chapter 1, page 11) to avoid hitting the beam in a fall.

School and outdoor recreation facilities: Low balance beams that are permanently placed in the ground can be found at most outdoor school areas. Wooden rail-like beams, posts, or other types of balance areas are also part of most parks. Chalk, paint, tape, or ropes can be used to simulate the lines of a balance beam. Sturdy benches can also be used as the platform to perform many of the balance, locomotor movements, or dismounts on the balance beam.

In this chapter: Many of the exploratory movements, basic body positions, balance, support, and locomotor movements that are performed on the floor can be performed on the beam. Refer to those sections for descriptions and learning cues. Skills to be performed on the beam should first be mastered on the floor, then on a line on the floor, and slowly progress to a low beam, then to a higher beam.

HAND PLACEMENTS FOR BALANCE BEAM

New Skills	
Hand placements	Cartwheel
Parallel	Round-off
English	

Parallel Hand Placement

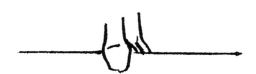

- Face the beam crosswise and place hands palms down, shoulder-width apart. This position is also known as overgrip and is used for the cartwheel.

English Hand Placement

- Face the beam lengthwise and place hands on top with fingers around the edge of the beam and thumbs touching each other.

Cartwheel Hand Placement

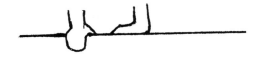

- Place hands on top of beam with dominant hand placed sideward. Nondominant hand is turned slightly inward.

Round-Off Hand Placement

- Place hands on top of beam with dominant hand placed sideward. Nondominant hand is turned slightly inward.

APPROACHES TO BALANCE BEAM

New Skill	
Front	Side/cross
Rear	Front diagonal

Front Approach

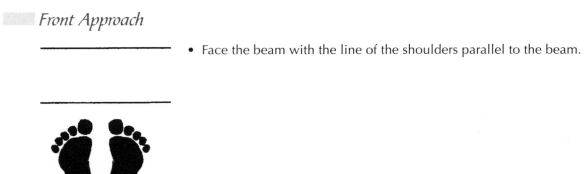

- Face the beam with the line of the shoulders parallel to the beam.

Rear Approach

- Face away from the beam with the line of the shoulders parallel to the beam.

Side/Cross Approach

- Face the beam with the nose parallel with the beam and the line of the shoulders perpendicular to the beam.
- First learn a side sit and then progress to the scissor mount. A springboard can be used.

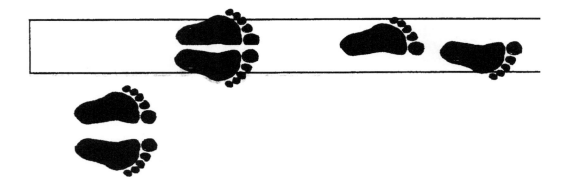

Front Diagonal Approach

- Face the beam at a diagonal between a front and side approach with shoulders at a 45-degree angle to beam.

BASIC BODY POSITIONS AND BALANCES

Practicing the basic body and balance positions on the beam is much different than practicing them on the floor. Therefore, gymnasts should move slowly and with control when moving into or out of positions. Begin practicing on a low beam, and as gymnasts become more confident, progressively move them to higher beams.

In the standing positions on beam, gymnasts may either face the side of the beam or face the end of the beam and place the feet in "train" position with one foot directly behind the other and slightly turned out. In sitting and supine positions, hands should be placed in English hand placement or overgrip.

In general, the spotter should stand beside the beam so that a gymnast can place his or her hand on the spotter's hand for balance. The spotter may also hold at the hips or place a hand on the back, abdomen, or under legs of the gymnast, depending on the position or balance.

Review Body Positions on Balance Beam

Beginning Skills
Sitting tuck
Sitting pike
Standing straight body
Standing straddle
Stride
Lunge
Arch stand
Hollow stand
Stride
Gymnastics point
Supported tuck
Supported pike

Intermediate Skills
Squat stand
Prone straight body
Supine straight body
Supine tuck
Standing pike
Supine pike
Sitting straddle
Piked straddle stand
Piked supine straddle
Supine straight body

Advanced Skills
Inverted tuck
Inverted pike
Piked inverted straddle
To review and perform these skills, have just a slight lift of the hips off the beam.

Review Balance Positions on Balance Beam

Beginning Skills
Relevé hold
Coupé
Passé
Front attitude
Battement
Knee stand
Knee lunge
Half split
Knee scale

Intermediate Skills
Arabesque
Front scale
Stride split
Straddle split
Balance in knee scale

Advanced Skills
Inverted shoulder stand (candle)
Side scale
Y scale
Lever

SUPPORT POSITIONS

Supporting one's body weight and developing upper body strength will enhance mounts, dismounts, and skills on the beam.

Supports on Three or Four Body Parts

Supports on three or four body parts will prepare gymnasts for the balance and strength necessary for mounts, rolls, and handstands.

Review Support on Three or Four Body Parts	
Standing Balances	Rear support with feet on beam
Front support with feet on beam	V-sit with hands on beam

Supports With Arms

The front, stride, and rear support on the beam will prepare gymnasts for similar movements on the horizontal bar.

New Skill	
Supports With Arms	
Front support	Front support, single-leg cut to stride support
Stride support	Rear support
	Stride support, single-leg cut to rear support

Front Support on Beam

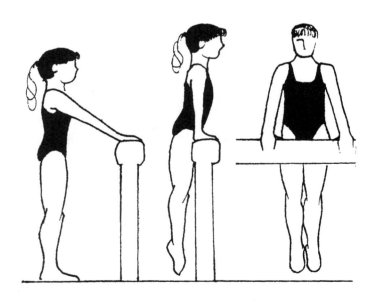

- The front support is one of the basic mounts for beam and bars.

Learning Cues for Front Support

Verbal/Linguistic

- Stand facing balance beam in straight-body position.
- Place hands in parallel, shoulder-width apart on beam.
- Jump off floor.
- Push down on beam until arms are straight and shoulders are down.
- Keep body straight and tight with the legs together.
- Keep hips just above the beam, head up, and shoulders over the beam in straight-body position.

Logical/Mathematical

- Make a straight, slightly diagonal line from head to toes.
- Keep weight distributed over the knuckles of hands with thumbs pressed against index fingers.

Visual/Spatial

- Get shoulders in front of wrists.
- Focus straight ahead.

Bodily/Kinesthetic

- Push on beam until arms are straight and shoulders are down.
- Distribute weight evenly on both hands.
- Feel abdominal muscles pulled tight, not resting on the beam.
- Keep legs straight by squeezing muscles above knees.
- Keep body tight.
- Feel feet pointed.

Assist

- Stand behind gymnast and hold at hips and assist in the lift.

Common Errors

- Arms are bent.
- Lower back is arched.
- Head is not in neutral.
- Body is resting on beam.
- Keep shoulders in front of wrists.

Stride Support

- Sit in stride position across the beam with hands outside of legs.
- Extend arms and support stride split with front thigh on beam.
- Keep both legs straight.
- Assist: Stand behind gymnast and hold at waist to help balance and support.

Front Support, Single-Leg Cut to Stride Support

Single-leg cuts to the front and rear help develop strength and spatial awareness on beam. A successful leg cut on beam helps ensure a successful leg cut on bars.

- Begin in front support in overgrip.
- Lift one hand off beam.
- Swing leg quickly on same side as lifted hand over beam to the front.
- Immediately replace hand on outside of leg.
- Arrive in stride support.
- Keep both legs straight.
- Assist: Stand in front of gymnast on opposite side of swinging leg. Hold under arm of gymnast to support arm and torso as leg swings to the side. As leg swings to the front, place other hand under leg to keep gymnast from falling forward.
- Challenge: Perform skill with other leg.

Rear Support on Beam

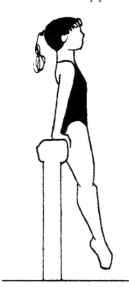

First review the front support (page 182), which is usually used in mounts on the beam and bars. The rear support is used for dismounts or changing positions on the beam or bars.

Learning Cues for Rear Support on Beam

Verbal/Linguistic

- Sit on side of balance beam.
- Place hands in overgrip and keep arms straight.
- Keep body straight and tight with the legs together.
- Keep head and chest up with shoulders over the beam in a balanced position.

Logical/Mathematical

- Make a straight, slightly diagonal line from head to toes.
- Keep spine vertical; don't round.
- Keep both arms equal.
- Lift legs to horizontal.
- Keep weight evenly distributed on both hands.

Visual/Spatial

- Keep hands shoulder-width apart with fingers slightly open.
- Keep shoulders directly above hands.
- Keep head up and chin lifted.
- Focus straight ahead.
- Point feet.

Bodily/Kinesthetic

- Keep body tight.
- Stay centered so that body does not pike.
- Push down on beam.
- Lift hips up and tighten buttocks muscles so that you are supported, not sitting, on beam.
- Feel arms and legs straight.

Assist

- Stand behind gymnast and hold at waist to help balance and support.

(continued)

(continued)

Common Errors

- Body is too loose.
- Body is piked.
- Body is rounded.
- Body falls backward.
- Gymnast loses balance.

Other Challenges

- Lift legs to a pike support.

Stride Support, Single-Leg Cut to Rear Support

- Begin in stride support with hands in overgrip and torso vertical.
- Quickly swing back leg forward, lifting and replacing hand as leg passes under hand.
- Leg arrives beside existing front leg in rear support.
- Create a straight diagonal line in rear support, but don't pike.
- Assist: Stand behind gymnast slightly to the side to avoid swinging leg. Hold gymnast at waist.

Supports With Arms: Holds

Review	New Skill
Supports With Arms on Folded Mats	***Supports With Arms on Beam***
Tuck support	Tuck support
L or pike support	L and straddle L support
Straddle L support	Stride support
	V-sit support

Holds require a lot of upper-body strength; they help prepare gymnasts for more advanced skills on the beam and especially the bars. In a hold, the gymnast presses or lifts the weight away from the beam. The entire weight is on the hands and only the strongest gymnast can support one's entire body weight for any length of time. This is still a good skill to practice because even a temporary support of the body weight helps to develop upper-body strength. It is common for the gymnast to lose balance when lifting one's weight; therefore, a spotter must support at the waist to help gymnast maintain his or her balance.

Holds on Beam

- Perform a stride support (page 184) and lift the body, keeping the thigh off the beam.
- Perform a V-sit and lift the body off the beam.
- Perform a tuck support and lift the body off the beam.
- Perform a straddle support and lift the body off the beam.
- Perform an L support and lift the body off the beam.

INVERTED SUPPORTS: HANDSTANDS

Review Inverted Supports

Handstand Progression

Tuck support, kick up one leg	Lunge, lever, feet together, lever, lunge
Lunge, lever, single leg up, lunge (single leg swing up to handstand)	English handstand

Handstands are listed in this section because they are support skills. However, they should be practiced after mounts.

Review and perform the lead-ups from chapter 4, page 110, for the handstand on the floor. Then begin the handstand progression on the beam. The handstand on the beam is performed in both the cross stand and English hand placement. The spot is the same as on the floor; however, the spotter may need to use a spotting block to elevate his or her body to be in a good position to handle the gymnast's body weight.

MOUNTS

Mounts are the skills used to get onto the beam. Begin with exploration using low beams, cartons, benches, or folded mats. The squat-on, straddle-on, and wolf mounts on folded mats give gymnasts experience where there is plenty of room to place the entire surface of the feet and hands. In beginning and intermediate skills, the hands support the body, or the center of gravity is close to the beam on the mount. The jump to a balanced stand is an advanced skill because it does not use a hand support and it requires more balance and precision than the beginning and intermediate skills require.

Lead-Ups for Mounts

Review	**New Skill**
Exploring Mounts	*Lead-Ups Using Stacked Mats*
Front support	Squat-on
Front support on floor series	Straddle-on
	Wolf mount

Squat-On Mount

- Begin in a stand or tuck stand position on floor in front of mat stack.
- Place hands on mat stack.
- Keeping legs together, push off with feet to straighten legs.
- Raise hips while supporting with arms.
- Push down and back on mats with arms as hips rise up.
- Tuck knees and land in squat position on top of folded mat.
- Place feet between hands.
- Keep chest up and torso vertical.
- Assist: Assist by lifting hip or holding waist.

Straddle-On Mount

- Begin in a stand or tuck stand position on floor in front of mat stack.
- Place hands shoulder-width apart on mat.
- Jump from floor.
- Push down on mats with arms as hips come up and forward over the hands.
- Immediately open legs sideward to straddle.
- Place feet to the outside of hands in a piked straddle on top of mat stack or beam.
- Assist: Reach over mats and hold the gymnast's hips or reach over mat with one hand and place it on gymnast's waist while placing the other hand on the upper arm.

Wolf Mount

- Begin in a stand or tuck stand position on floor in front of mat stack.
- Place hands on mat shoulder-width apart.
- Jump from floor.
- Push down on mats with arms.
- Lift hips and place feet on stacked mat with one leg between hands in tuck, the other leg outside the hands in straddle.
- Assist: Reach over mat and hold the gymnast's hips or reach over mat with one hand and place it on gymnast's waist and place the other hand on the upper arm.

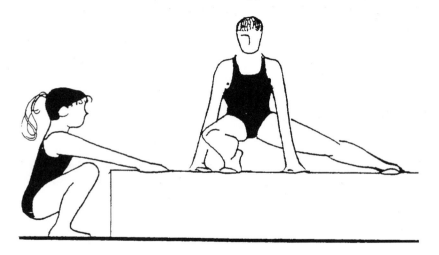

Beam Mounts

Review Mounts

Beam Mounts

Jump to front support	Step to squat
Front support to supported straddle	Step on to balance stand
Front support to straddle sit	Jump to squat-on
Whip-up	Jump to straddle-on
Mount, straddle, V-sit, tuck to stand	Wolf mount
Front support, stag sit, knee scale, knee lunge, and stand	Scissor mount

Review jump to front support (page 182).

Front Support to Supported Straddle

- Begin in a front support.
- Lift legs in straddle and place feet on top of the beam in a supported straddle.
- Assist: Stand in front of the gymnast on other side of beam to keep the gymnast from going head first over the beam. Reach over the beam and hold hips to help gymnast lift hips, straddle legs, and bring them on to beam.

Front Support to Straddle Sit

- Jump to front support on beam.
- Swing one leg sideward and up over the beam.
- Turn the body to a straddle sit position on top of the beam, facing the end of the beam, and change inside hand to create the English hand placement.
- Sequence is jump, front support, leg cut, straddle sit.
- Assist: Stand behind gymnast. Lift hips, stepping slightly behind as legs straddle.

Whip-Up

This drill is also known as a swing-up or a tuck-up.

- Start in push-up position on floor.
- Push both feet up in the air so that you are stretched in the air for a second with just your hands on the mat.
- Pull your knees in and squat with your feet on the floor between the spots where your hands were as you lift your arms and chest to finish in a squat stand.

Note: Feet should be in train position (one foot in front of the other) for the beam drill. Use the same drill but land with feet parallel for squat vault drill.

Mount, Straddle, V-Sit, Tuck to Stand

- Begin in a front support.
- Swing one leg over beam and turn to straddle sit while placing hands in front in English placement.
- Change hands to rear English placement.
- Shift weight back to the buttocks.
- Straighten legs into V-sit with the torso extended.
- Place hands down on beam in front English position as legs swing down through straddle and behind torso.
- In the swinging of the legs, push with arms to transfer the momentum to hips, then torso.
- In the straddle swing-through, push up, stay tight, then tuck on to the beam.
- Land on balls of feet in tuck. When balanced, move arms out to side middle.
- Stretch up into standing position.
- Sequence is mount, straddle, V-sit, straddle swing-through, push up, squat, tuck stand, stand.
- Assist: Stand on side of beam and reach in to hold hips on the swing-through and stand.

Front Support, Stag Sit, Knee Scale, Knee Lunge, and Stand

- Jump to front support.
- Press down against beam and lift a straight leg sideward to place on top of the beam.
- Bend the other leg upward and place in a side stag position, arriving at a stag sit position with hips parallel to beam and torso straight.
- Rotate the torso while adjusting the hand to support weight as the hips are lifted off the beam to a modified knee scale with back toes touching the beam.
- As the torso straightens, swing the straight back leg downward, forward, and upward.
- Bend the knee of the swinging leg to place the foot on the beam in front in a knee lunge.
- Keep weight on the front leg and rise to a standing position.

Step to Squat

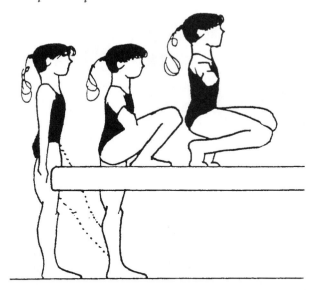

- Stand facing the end of the beam with the beam to the side of the body (cross or side approach). Place inside hand on top of the beam.
- Step onto beam with inside foot (in front of hand), then outside foot in front into tuck position.
- Lift arms to the sides for balance as the outside foot lands on beam.
- Balance body in a squat position with head up, torso straight.
- Assist: Stand on the side of gymnast and hold waist with both hands. Move forward with the gymnast. Another spot is to hold the hand opposite the push leg to assist with lift onto the beam as gymnast pushes down on the palm of spotter's hand.

Step on to Balance Stand

This step-on skill becomes more advanced on a higher beam. If the beam is low, it is relatively easy to just step on, but as the beam becomes higher, momentum of the approach or jump, positioning of the feet, and balance once arriving on the beam become factors in the success of this mount.

Learning Cues for Step on to Balance Stand

Verbal/Linguistic

- Stand facing the end of the beam.
- Step forward on floor or springboard.
- Push off nondominant foot. Arms reach in opposition during push.
- Push off the floor before trying to step onto beam; don't rush it or you will lose flight.
- Pass the dominant foot through to step onto beam as push leg passes through a low arabesque to balance on the beam. Support leg turns out slightly so that the little toe will be on one side of the beam and the heel will be on the other.
- Bring arms forward with an underswing and then to oblique in arabesque or directly overhead.
- Maintain a vertical line from head to toe.
- Look to the end of the beam.
- Sequence is step, push, step on beam, low arabesque, stand.
- Assist: Hold the hand opposite the push leg to assist with lift onto the beam as gymnast pushes down on your palm.
- Challenges: Add springboard and add height to beam. Remain in arabesque upon landing.

Jump to Squat-On Mount

A good lead-up is a jump to one-foot squat support. In this lead-up, the gymnast jumps from the floor, pushing down with arms as hips are directed up in pike. One knee comes to the chest in tuck and that foot is placed on the beam.

Learning Cues for Squat-On Mount

Verbal/Linguistic

- Begin in a front approach.
- Face the side of balance beam and place hands on beam in parallel hand placement.
- Jump from floor or springboard, pushing down with arms as hips are directed up in pike and forward over the hands.
- Bring knees to the chest in tuck and feet on the beam inside the hands.
- Keep head up and hands on the beam.
- For a challenge, lift arms out to sides immediately to balance in tuck stand.

(continued)

(continued)

Logical/Mathematical

- Sequence is jump, push, squat on.
- Keep jump vertical.
- Make a vertical line from shoulders through hands.
- Close angle of pike.
- Bring torso to vertical as quickly as possible.
- Place feet on beam simultaneously.

Visual/Spatial

- Straighten arms before squatting as support leg punches.
- Lift hips high and up to pike before landing on beam.
- Lower hips as feet contact beam.
- Keep shoulders over beam.
- Bring torso to vertical; don't let chest rest on thighs.
- Keep space between buttocks and heels (don't "bottom out").

Bodily/Kinesthetic

- Feel body weight on front of hands.
- Feel knees, toes, and heels together.
- Feel knees pull in toward chest.
- Feel feet point in pike, then flex to squat on beam.

Musical/Rhythmical

- Jump, hips up, tuck, feet on, torso up.
- Give yourself time to lift up in pike so that legs clear beam.
- Punch equally with both legs.

Assist

- Assist by supporting upper arm and lifting abdomen, or stand behind gymnast and hold the waist or hips to lift the gymnast.

Common Errors

- Hips don't rise above shoulders.
- Body doesn't tuck and feet don't land on beam.
- Heels are down and weight is on heels on landing.
- Weight doesn't shift forward on takeoff, which causes a fall backward.
- Weight sits on heels.

Jump to Straddle-On Mount

- Begin in a front stand facing the side of the beam. Place hands in parallel shoulder-width apart on the beam.
- Push the legs off the floor and push the arms down on the beam.
- Keep head up while the hips rise.
- Straddle legs, move shoulders forward, and move hips up and forward over hands.
- Place feet on top of beam in a supported straddle, then lift chest and bring arms to the side and bring head up.
- Assist: Stand in front of the gymnast and hold upper arms.

Wolf Mount

- Begin in a front stand facing the side of the beam. Place hands in parallel shoulder-width apart on the beam.
- Push the legs off the floor and push the arms down on the beam.
- Keep head up while the hips rise.
- Land on beam with one leg between hands in tuck and the other leg outside the hands in straddle.
- Assist: Reach over beam and hold the gymnast's hips or reach over beam with one hand and place it on gymnast's waist while placing the other hand on the upper arm.

Scissor Mount

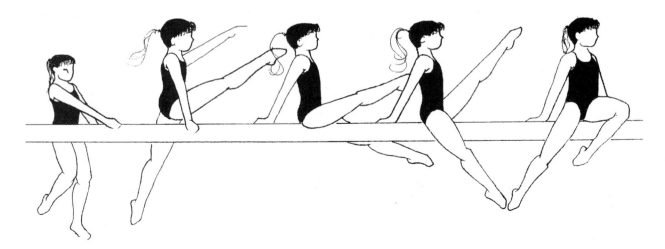

Learning Cues for Scissor Mount

Verbal/Linguistic

- Begin in a front diagonal approach with springboard angled.
- Walk or run to board.
- Place inside hand on the beam.
- Push off board with outside leg.
- Lift straight inside leg up and over beam in front of hand.
- Follow with second leg.
- Place outside hand in front of body to finish in a side sit.

Logical/Mathematical

- Sequence is hand on beam, push, lift leg over beam, follow with other leg, other hand on beam in front, side sit.
- Square shoulders throughout.
- Keep torso straight but lean back at a diagonal while legs go over beam.
- Lift legs above 90 degrees to scissor over beam.
- Make an elliptical pattern over the beam with the legs.
- End with torso vertical.

Visual/Spatial

- Place inside hand on top of beam.
- Spot end of beam throughout.
- See straight legs with pointed toes scissor over beam.
- Lift legs to chest height.

Bodily/Kinesthetic

- Feel abdomen and rib cage lifted throughout.
- Push down on board and beam.

Musical/Rhythmical

- Step kick, kick, switch hands.
- Push down on beam and board at the same time.

- Rhythm is

  Leg, leg.

  1, 2.

Assist

Hold outside hand of gymnast until it is placed on the beam. Move with gymnast and assist as necessary. Place hands on the hips as the gymnast sits on the beam.

Common Errors

- Legs don't get up in scissors.
- Weight is not centered on finish.

LOCOMOTOR SKILLS: ALTERNATING FOOT PATTERNS

First review alternating foot patterns from chapter 3, then perform skills on a line on the floor, beam on floor, then low beam.

Review Alternating Foot Patterns on Balance Beam

Beginning Skills
Forward walks
Backward walks
Lateral walks
Relevé walks (fully point toes between steps: point, step, point, step)
Grapevine (keep hips square)

Intermediate Skills
Runs
Prances

Waltz step
Chassé
Side chassé (slide steps)

Advanced Skills
Back chassé

New Skill

Alternating Foot Patterns
Dip walks

Dip Walks

It is difficult to practice this skill on the floor, as it involves dipping the foot below the surface of the beam. The gymnast will dip the free foot below the level of the beam while walking.

Learning Cues for Dip Walks

Verbal/Linguistic

- Execute a forward walk across beam.
- Bend the standing leg and swing the free leg downward along the side of the beam with each step.

Logical/Mathematical

- Draw undercurves on the sides of the beam.
- Keep hips and shoulders parallel with end of beam.
- Keep torso vertical.
- Keep arms parallel with the floor.

Visual/Spatial

- Keep legs slightly turned out.
- Keep arms out to side middle.
- Place standing leg in plié as free leg swings alongside the beam.
- Lift foot slightly above beam before and after each dip.
- Kinder cues: Dip your foot in the water to see how warm it is. Test it with just your toes. These beams don't look too happy. Let's make them happy beams. We need to paint smiles on them to make them happy sunbeams! Make your foot a paintbrush and draw a big smile on the beam. Try it with the other leg on the other side.

Bodily/Kinesthetic

- Feel chin and rib cage lifted.
- Feel free leg straighten and foot point in each step.

Musical/Rhythmical

- Rhythm is even and smooth: dip, step, dip, step.

Assist

- Stand on floor or mat next to beam and allow gymnast to push against your hand, or hold gymnast's hips while walking to end of beam.

Common Errors

- Free foot is not pointed.
- Free foot "sickles" (turns inward).

Challenge

- Lift leg to 45 degrees each time before stepping.

LOCOMOTOR SKILLS: LANDING ON TWO FEET

Review Jumps on Balance Beam

Beginning Skills	*Intermediate Skills*
Safe landing position	Stretch
Small bunny jumps (stretch jumps)	Tuck
	Stride split
	Advanced Skills
	Assemblé

Students will need assistance when first performing jumps on the beam. Gymnasts begin by jumping straight up a short distance on a low beam. As skill, confidence, and body and spatial awareness become evident, gymnasts will gradually try to jump higher and on higher beams. In a cross stand (with shoulders perpendicular to beam), one foot needs to be placed in front of the other in the train position. All jumps should be lengthwise. Do not try to put feet directly parallel to each other on the 4-inch width of the beam. Side jumps are not recommended.

The landing of the feet and the alignment of the body are very important to the success of jumps on beam:

- Lift head slightly and focus on end of beam.
- Bend (demi-plié) legs and push off beam.
- Extend legs through hips, knees, ankles, and toes.
- Press the heel of the front foot against the front of the back foot during the stretch jump or perform tuck, straddle, or pike. Torso makes a straight line.
- Land on balls of feet with one foot in front of the other (train position). Don't land on the heels.
- On landing, bend the knees and press the balls of the feet to lower the heels on the beam.
- Knees pushing over the toes.
- Keep arms in line with torso on landing.

First review and perform jumps from chapter 3 on a line on the floor.

LOCOMOTOR SKILLS: LANDING ON ONE FOOT

> **Review**
>
> ***Landing on One Foot***
> Stride split leap

As with all other jumps that land on two feet, assistance is needed when gymnasts first perform the one-foot landings on the beam. Gymnasts begin by jumping only a short distance and on a low beam. Gradually have gymnasts try the skills on higher beams. Begin standing in a cross stand (with shoulders perpendicular to beam). All one-foot landings should be lengthwise.

DISMOUNTS

> **Review**
> Jumps
> Handstand
> Cartwheel
> Round-off
>
> ***Dismounts***
> Step off dismount
> Stretch jump dismount
> Tuck jump dismount
> Straddle jump dismount
> Pike jump dismount
> Jump half turn dismount
>
> **New Skills**
> Front support to front dismount
> Cartwheel to side handstand dismount
> Round-off dismount off end

A dismount is a controlled, upright landing from the beam or apparatus. Jumps are one type of dismount from the beam. Begin jumping dismounts on a low beam first. Make sure gymnasts jump upward and forward to clear the beam. Review and perform the jumps from chapter 1. Also review the safe landing position because gymnasts will jump down from the beam, which will apply more force to the body on the landing. Avoid side landings that have a lot of momentum because they put much more torque on the knees than forward landings do.

Front Support to Front Dismount

- Begin in a front support (push-up position).
- Bend knees and push with feet.
- Extend upward then sideward off the beam.
- Remove the outside arm to the side for balance.
- Lower legs and land on two feet with bent knees.
- Salute.

Cartwheel to Side Handstand Dismount

There are two different cartwheel dismounts. One is a cartwheel to handstand that pushes off both hands and comes straight down on the side of beam opposite the one the fingertips were touching while in the handstand, similar to the ending of the round-off. The second is a cartwheel to handstand that shifts forward. The second hand lifts while gymnast pivots over the first hand to land, with the side of the body to the beam, on the side of the beam that the fingertips touch while in the handstand. The first cartwheel dismount is the easiest to learn and will be described here.

- Stand in gymnastics point with arms up.
- Lunge, then lever into a cartwheel, placing both hands shoulder-width apart on the beam.
- Bring both legs together in handstand position.
- As body reaches vertical, push away from beam.
- Keep both hands overhead by ears.
- Land facing beam on landing mat.
- Assist: Stand to lunge leg side of beam. Hold at the waist and make sure hands are secure on beam. Spot torso area with hands to guide landing.

Round-Off Dismount Off End

- Start in gymnastics point.
- Step into a lunge.
- Kick hard when chest is over thigh.
- Place hands on beam with the second hand slightly turned in.
- Bring both feet together before handstand.
- Make a quarter turn with entire body.
- Push away from beam with both hands.
- Land facing beam on landing mat.

LONGITUDINAL ROTATIONS: TURNS

Review

Turns in Place
Pivot (180-degree relevé turn)
Squat turn
Pirouettes

Review and perform pivot (180-degree relevé turn, page 102), pirouettes (half and full turns, page 123), and squat turns (page 101) on the floor first. Then perform beam progressions.

SIDEWARD ROTATIONS: CARTWHEEL

Review

Cartwheel
Lunge, cartwheel, lunge

Review and perform cartwheel to lunge on floor (page 145). Perform the cartwheel to lunge on a line on the floor, then low beam, then medium beam. Cartwheels on the beam are considered advanced skills and gymnasts must have secure cartwheels on floor before progressing to cartwheels on beam. A good spot is necessary on beam and is the same as the spot on the floor.

HORIZONTAL CIRCULAR MOVEMENTS

Review and perform formal lead-ups and back walkovers from chapter 4, page 161.

Back Walkovers

Review

Back Walkover Progression

Rocking bridge	Backbend
Bridge kickover	Backbend to kickover
Wall touch from a kneel	Back walkover

6

Springboard and Vault

FOUNDATIONAL POSITIONS ON VAULT

Approach and springboard skills	Vault lead-ups	Vault
Explore Run Run, land on target Run, land on target, jump (knee slapper) Run, land on target, stretch jump 　(then a variety of jumps) **Approach skills in isolation** Run Step-hurdle (assemblé) Arm circle Step-hurdle with arm circle **Approach and springboard skills** *Perform on floor with target then use* 　*springboard* Step-hurdle with arm circle, jump Run, step-hurdle with arm circle, jump 　(then a variety of jumps)	**Squat-on/squat through** **vault lead-ups** *On floor* Front support to supported tuck Front support to squat-through *On mats* Traveling jumps on, off, and over Squat-on Squat-between Squat-through **Straddle-on/straddle-through** **vault lead-ups** *On Floor* Front support to supported straddle *On Mats* Straddle-on Straddle-over Straddle-through **Flank vault lead-ups** *On Mats* Tucked front vault Flank vault **Handspring vault lead-ups** Handstand block from springboard Step-hurdle, lunge, handstand to flatback Run step-hurdle, lunge, handstand to 　flatback	**Vault techniques** Jumps with hand on horse (pike, squat 　straddle) Approach, hurdle/rebound, jump with 　hands on horse (pike, squat, straddle) **Flank vault** Three jumps, flank Flank vault **Squat-on/squat-through vault** Three jumps, squat-on Squat-on **Straddle-on/straddle-through vault** Three jumps, straddle-on Straddle-on **Handspring vault progression** Short run, step-hurdle, lunge, handspring 　over mat stack Short run, step-hurdle, lunge, handspring 　on mat stack to incline Short run, step-hurdle, lunge, 　front handspring stepout

Equipment: For competition, both men and women's vaulting horse is 14 inches wide. Women's vault is 4 feet high and 5 feet long and men's vault is 4 feet 6 inches high and 5 feet 3 inches long. Women vault widthwise and the men vault lengthwise. The vault is also called the "horse." Both men and women use an 80-foot runway with a springboard to propel the body up and onto the horse. The preflight is the span of time in which the gymnast leaves the springboard with two feet and briefly touches the horse with both hands.

Spotting and safety: Vaulting requires gymnasts to become airborne, so it is important to review and perform the fundamental skills and follow a safe progression. Review safe landings (chapter 1, page 9) and make sure that gymnasts communicate with you so that you can be prepared for the skill and spot correctly. A panel mat is not sufficient for landings from the springboard or vault. The landing mat should be a minimum of 4 inches thick; for landings with more force, two pads or a mat of at least 8 inches should be used. Mats tend to shift with each gymnast's landing and should be checked frequently; the springboard's position should be checked as well.

School and outdoor recreation facilities: Folded mats, benches, milk crates, and wooden vaulting boxes can substitute for a standard vaulting horse. Ensure that there are adequate landing mats and that the mats and equipment are stable and not in danger of sliding. A covered bed mattress can be a substitute for the thick mat that is needed for landings. All the educational and exploratory skills as well as the lead-up skills with one folded mat should be taught in the school setting.

In this chapter: For the skills in this chapter, the vault will remain widthwise. Folded mats or trapezoid mats may be used for lead-ups to the vault. The skills will begin on the floor and progress, skill by skill, to the vault. Gymnasts should review the skills in "Exploring the Vault Approach" in chapter 2, page 45.

VAULT APPROACH AND SPRINGBOARD SKILLS

Explore	Approach and Springboard Skills
Run	Run
Run, land on target	Step-hurdle (assemblé)
Run, land on target, jump (knee slapper)	Arm circle
Run, land on target, stretch jump (then a variety of jumps)	Step-hurdle with arm circle
	Step-hurdle with arm circle, jump
	Run, step-hurdle with arm circle, jump (then a variety of jumps)

The essentials of the vault approach include the run, step-hurdle (assemblé—one foot takeoff to two-foot landing) with a quick arm circle, and the jump from the target or springboard. Teaching the individual elements, or motor notes, and slowly combining the pieces will help the gymnasts be successful with the vault approach. The sequence should begin with exploration on the floor, then a progression of skill development on the floor to a target, before the springboard is incorporated into the sequence.

Exploration

Give the gymnasts plenty of opportunities to practice running and jumping on and off a target on the floor. The exploration activities for springboard and vault in chapter 2 will help prepare gymnasts for the approach and landing on the springboard. Jumping on a target from a run teaches the hurdle automatically.

Approach Skills in Isolation

After exploration, teach each element of the skill in isolation before combining the elements to form the whole skill. Learning and practicing the hurdle and arm circle in isolation will improve the technique. Then the gymnasts will combine the hurdle with the arm circle as soon as possible. (The term *step-hurdle* includes the arm circle unless stated otherwise.)

Note: The trick of slapping the thighs (knee slapper) as you hurdle is a good drill to get the arms down into the circle, but if it is practiced too much there will be problems breaking the touch to the thighs in the circle. Gymnasts should get into the habit of bringing their arms up quickly overhead after slapping the thighs.

Run

Running is an essential skill for vault. It is often said that good runners are good vaulters. The power of the run determines the power of the vault. Students of gymnastics need to train in different ways to make their runs more powerful. They must also be aware of the role the arms play in powerful running.

However, gymnasts need to be able to handle their runs. It's very common for a gymnast to start with a very quick and powerful run, then slow down to almost half his speed a few feet before the board, usually by stuttering his steps. The common reaction is to address the number of strides as the gymnast thinks that his steps were off. Actually, what is happening is that the gymnast realizes that he cannot handle the amount of power his great run generates and instinct slows him down. It is better for a gymnast to have a consistent run, even if he must run a little slower rather than vary the speed by starting fast and then slowing down in fear. A fast run requires a low, fast hurdle with a very quick arm circle. This will cause a very powerful vault, but the gymnast must be able to control the body during the large flight path generated and land safely. The instructor should work on correct running technique, but remain aware that the gymnast must also be able to handle the power of the run throughout the vault.

Learning Cues for Vault Running Approach

Verbal/Linguistic

- Run with slight forward lean.
- Move arms in opposition to legs, pulling elbows back.

Logical/Mathematical

- Flex arms at 90 degrees.
- Lift front knee to horizontal with 90-degree bend.
- Lift knees high enough so that push will help forward velocity.

(continued)

(continued)

Visual/Spatial

- Run on balls of feet—do not let heels come in contact with the floor.
- Hold head neutral with top of head parallel to ceiling.
- Focus on springboard or target.
- Keep back straight.
- Bring heel close to the buttocks before striding forward.

Bodily/Kinesthetic

- Feel a forceful back leg push downward and backward with balls of feet.
- Push the floor away with feet.
- Feel relaxed shoulders.

Musical/Rhythmical

- Make a steady pattern.

Common Errors

- Body leans too far forward or backward.
- Arms cross in front of torso or are not in opposition.
- Run is on heels or flat feet.
- Feet do not push.
- Stance is too wide.
- Knees are not lifted high enough.
- Heels come up too high.
- Run is too slow.

Other Challenges

- Run with seat kicks.
- Run in place with knees up.
- Run in place with fast feet.
- Run, stepping up and down off mat stack.

Step-Hurdle in Isolation

The hurdle is an essential element to successful springboard and vault skills. A good lead-up is the assemblé (chapter 4, page 119). If children are adept at this skill, they will find the vault hurdle quite easy. The vault hurdle is different than the hurdle for the cartwheel. In the hurdle for the cartwheel there is a step-hop into a lunge with one foot in front of the other. In the vault hurdle, there is a one-foot takeoff to a two-foot landing and the two feet come together, or assemble, in the air before landing.

- Stand on one foot with other foot pointed in front at base of target or springboard.
- Step on pointed foot, pushing off the ground for one-foot takeoff.
- Brush other leg to front to land, or assemblé, on both feet on target or curve of springboard.
- Land with bent knees with the feet under and slightly in front of a vertical torso.
- Keep landing light with slight hip and knee flexion.
- Sequence is step off one foot, assemblé, land on two feet.

Arm Circle in Isolation

The most common mistake in the arm circle is to make the circle too big. This takes too much time, slows the gymnast down, and affects the timing of the skill.

- Stand on both feet with chest up and arms down by sides.
- Circle arms forward, upward, then backward in a small fast circle, with arms finishing by the legs.
- Create the fastest circle possible from the shoulders.
- Complete one circle in a fluid motion.
- Feel a fast circle: up, back, down.

Learning Cues for Step-Hurdle With Arm Circle

Verbal/Linguistic

- Begin in gymnastics point.
- Step on pointed foot, pushing off the floor for a one-foot takeoff.
- Begin to swing arms upward and around.
- Bring straight back leg through to front in a 45-degree angle to the body.
- Brush other leg to front to land on both feet with arms slightly in front of legs and entire body in a hollow C curve landing on target or springboard.

Logical/Mathematical

- Sequence is straight body, step-hurdle with arm circle, land in hollow.
- Body moves up vertically and forward in hurdle.
- Arms complete a small, quick, 360-degree circle.

Visual/Spatial

- Focus straight ahead.
- Push off on one foot, land on two feet.
- Move up and forward in hurdle.
- Complete one circle of the arms in a two-foot landing.
- Keep head neutral.
- Bend knees on landing.
- Bring both feet in front of torso in hurdle.
- See arms quickly brush up in front of torso.

Bodily/Kinesthetic

- Push off as hard as you can.
- Feel abdomen tight.
- Feel straight arms on circle.

Musical/Rhythmical

- As arms circle upward and backward, push off one foot.
- Arm circle and step-hurdle is a fluid motion.
- Arms move faster than legs.
- Arms complete one circle in a two-foot landing.

Common Errors

- Arms don't get up in front as feet land.
- Arms are too slow or aren't used for momentum.

Approach and Springboard Skills

Once the gymnasts practices the approach skills in isolation, they are ready to put all the skills together and perform on the floor using a target, then practice the same skill using the springboard progression. Make sure that gymnasts develop a sound step-hurdle with arm circle as described in the isolated approach skills. Another important factor in preparing the gymnasts for the power for the lift off the springboard is the heel drive. Remind gymnasts as they rebound off the springboard to push from their heels.

Emphasize the importance of tight muscles in vaulting skills! When gymnasts jump off the board they must squeeze the buttocks muscles tight. This will help them avoid the most common mistake, which is a pike off the board. The following activities will help gymnasts understand this concept.

Have gymnasts stand up and tighten their buttocks muscles. Ask them to keep the muscles tight and try to pike. They can't! Tell them that they must tighten the muscles as their heels drive off the springboard.

Have gymnasts lie on the floor with legs together. Tell them that they should tighten their buttocks muscles. Ask for a volunteer. Tell them that you will try to separate their legs. Usually when you try the legs come apart easily, which means that their muscles are not tight. Ask them to touch their own hips and buttocks and see if they are tight as possible.

Review and practice jumps (chapter 2, page 40) on the floor before trying them from an approach and jump on the springboard.

Step-Hurdle With Arm Circle, Jump

- Perform a step-hurdle with arm circle, landing with both feet on target or springboard.
- Land with knees bent, feet under body, arms back, chest up, and head neutral.
- The takeoff (rebound) for the jump happens immediately by bending the knees on landing and immediately pushing off with heel drive.
- The punch (rebound) is timed with an arm swing forward and overhead for momentum.
- At the same time, the legs straighten, pushing through the feet equally to extend the entire body into the air vertically in a straight body position with arms above head.
- The jump is up and forward.
- Upon landing, lower the arms sideward, downward, then to a forward low diagonal.
- Stick the landing and extend arms to balance with salute.
- Sequence is run, step-hurdle, jump (stretch, tuck, straddle, pike), bend knees, balance, salute.

Run, Step-Hurdle With Arm Circle, Jump

- Take running steps, reaching and maintaining maximum speed midway to target.
- Focus on target.
- On last running step before target, hurdle from one foot to target with two-foot landing.
- If the correct run technique is used, the arms will be bent and pump in opposition to the legs.
- As the right leg hurdles forward to join the left leg, the right arm (if in front) does a small, quick semicircle to catch up with the left arm. Then both lift up forcefully into the jump.

Learning Cues for Run, Step-Hurdle With Arm Circle, Jump

Verbal/Linguistic

- Begin with a short approach (approximately 25 feet) to aid in body control to land on the target. As you become more proficient, increase the distance to a long approach (60 to 80 feet).
- Run, step-hurdle, and land with both feet on floor or springboard.
- Land with the knees slightly bent, feet under body, arms back, chest up, and head neutral.
- Immediately push off for the takeoff of the jump.
- Time the punch off the board with the arm swing forward and overhead for momentum as legs straighten and push through the feet equally.
- Extend the entire body into the air vertically with arms above head.
- Stretch body up and forward in jump (momentum carries you forward), maintaining a straight hollow body position.
- Land on both feet with hip and knee flexion, keeping the chest up.
- Upon landing, lower the arms sideward, downward, then to a forward low diagonal.
- Stick the landing and extend arms to balance with salute.

Logical/Mathematical

- Take off on one foot, land and jump immediately from two feet.
- Send a vertical line up.

- Stretch body up and forward in jump.
- Kinder cue: Blast off like a rocket!

Visual/Spatial

- Hold head neutral and parallel with ceiling.
- Keep chest up and focus straight ahead.
- Jump as you see your arms come up in front of you.
- Bounce off the board as quickly as a ball bounces off the wall when you throw it hard.
- Kinder cue: Keep your body straight like a pencil (your pointed feet are the sharp pencil tips).

Bodily/Kinesthetic

- Push off the floor as you feel your arms brush past your legs.
- Feel your feet push away from the floor or springboard.
- Feel your knees quickly bend and straighten.
- Let your arm swing pull you up into the air.
- Feel abdomen and muscles above your knees tighten in the air.
- Feel legs bend on landing.

Musical/Rhythmical

- Step-hurdle, punch, stretch tall, bend knees, balance, salute.
- Make the tempo of the arm swing fast—as fast as you can lift your arms.
- Make the landing on the target or springboard the takeoff for the jump.

Assist

- Stand to side of gymnast, holding gymnast at waist to support abdomen and back on landing and to prevent falls in either direction.

Common Errors

- Arms move too slowly.
- Arms are not used for momentum.
- Push through legs and feet is insufficient.
- Body is loose.
- Timing is off.
- Body leans forward (pikes).
- Entire body is not stretched in jump.
- Jump is directed forward instead of up.
- Knee bend is not adequate to absorb landing and help gain balance.
- Time spent on the board is too long (a push off the board instead of a rebound off).

VAULT LEAD-UP SKILLS ON FLOOR AND FOLDED MATS

Gymnasts need a lot of experience with drills such as supporting their own body weight, blocking and rebounding off a mat, transferring their weight, and becoming familiar with the hand positioning. These drills prepare them for vaulting activities. A squat-on or squat-through is usually the first vaulting skill that gymnasts learn, so they need experience using a flat mat or low folded mats so that they can improve technique and gain confidence. Many school physical education programs do not have springboards or vaulting horses. The following drills are very useful in developing skills in those programs.

Squat-On and Squat-Through Lead-Ups

Squat-On/Squat-Through Vault Progression (On Floor)	
Front support	Front support to squat-through

On Floor

Review the front support to supported tuck (chapter 3, page 82).

Front Support to Squat-Through on Floor

- Begin in a front support.
- Push off feet and shift weight forward so that arms support weight.
- Lift hips, keeping legs together, and bend knees to achieve a tuck position. Shoot through arms to sitting L position.
- Push down with hands and lift torso with arms to tuck legs back through.
- Push with feet and extend legs and body to resume the front support position.
- This can also be performed with hands slightly elevated on folded mats to give more space to bring legs through.
- Sequence is front support, push, lift hips, squat through, push down, lift, front support.

On Stacked Mats

Squat-On/Squat-Through Vault Progression
(On Mats)

Traveling jumps on, off, and over	Squat-between
Squat-on	Squat-through

Review squat-on for beam (chapter 5, page 188).

Traveling Jumps On, Off, and Over Folded Mats

- Stand in a cross approach to panel mats placed end to end.
- Push sufficiently from mat or floor to extend arms and lift hips simultaneously.
- Push hips up high as you tuck knees.
- Squat and place hands on either side of center line on mat in a supported squat position.
- Keep arms extended and pushed out at shoulders.
- Stay slightly rounded in shoulders and upper back.
- Lower hips as feet contact mat or floor.
- Place feet on mat or floor simultaneously.

Jump On and Off Mat:

- Land in a squat position on top of folded mat.
- Jump to other side of the mat to floor.
- Sequence is jump, squat on, jump, squat off, hands forward.

Jump Over Mat:

- Land in a squat position on other side of the mat without touching feet on top of mat.
- Immediately upon landing in squat on floor, move hands forward.
- Continue jumping, moving the hands 6 to 12 inches forward each time.
- Sequence is jump over, squat, hands forward.

Other Challenges:

- Try doing same skill with extended legs and body.
- Try to raise hips and legs higher on the jumps.

Squat-Between on Folded Mats

- Begin in a squat position on floor in front of mat stack.
- Place hands on mat stack.
- Keeping legs together, push off with feet and raise hips while supporting with arms.
- Push down and back with arms as hips come up and forward.
- Tuck knees as legs move between the stacked mats in squat support.
- Hands rebound off mat.
- Lift arms and stretch body up as legs extend before landing. This drill will help eliminate the fear of feet not clearing the mat. A ribbon or something that will "give" if feet make contact can be used as a challenge to tuck over.
- Assist: Support upper arm and lift on belly or hold on to waist.

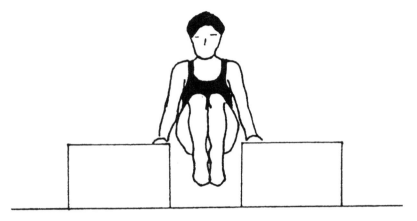

Squat-Through on Folded Mats

- Begin in a squat position on floor in front of mat stack.
- Place hands on mat stack.
- Keeping legs together, push off with feet and raise hips while supporting with arms.
- Push down and back with arms as hips come up and forward.
- Push with arms on mat.
- Tuck knees to chest and pull knees through arms and over mat.
- Do not touch the feet to the mat stack; feet should clear it.
- Lift arms and stretch body up before landing.
- Land vertically as feet are placed on mat or floor simultaneously.
- Assist: Support upper arm and lift on belly or hold onto waist.

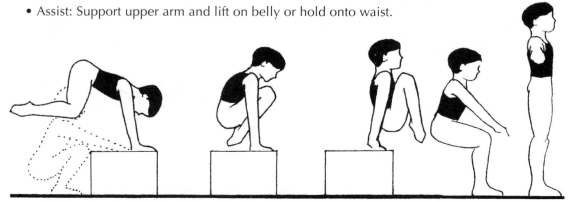

Straddle-On and Straddle-Through Lead-Ups

On Floor

Straddle-On/Straddle-Through Vault Progression (On Floor)
Front support to supported straddle

Review the front support to supported straddle for beam (chapter 5, page 189).

Note: These lead-ups and drills for the straddle vault are included for those who want this vault to be included in their gymnastics programs. However, this skill has a higher risk for injury than the squat vault, because the feet can hit the horse and cause a fall, and the direction of the fall sends the gymnast forward head first. A spotter must position oneself to avoid this type of fall and be confident enough to control the gymnast's weight and forward momentum. Some of the beginning lead-ups include straddle vaults in which the feet would not catch on the mats.

On Stacked Mats

Straddle-On/Straddle-Through Vault Progression (On Mats)
Straddle-on   Straddle-over
                                                 Straddle-through

Straddle-Through on Folded Mats

In the beginning, turn the mats so that gymnasts go over the narrow section of folded mats and they straddle over as if jumping a post. If the feet do not clear the mat they will not go forward. Each time gymnasts jump, encourage them to open the straddle.

- Begin in a squat position on floor in front of mat stack.
- Place hands on mat stack shoulder-width apart.
- Push off with feet and raise hips while supporting with arms.
- Open legs to a straddle, clearing the mat.
- Lift arms, stretch body up, and bring straight legs together in postflight.
- Land in straight body position, arms overhead, chest up.
- Assist: Reach over mats and hold gymnast's upper arms for support or reach over mat with one hand and place it on the gymnast's belly to lift while placing the other hand on the upper arm for support.

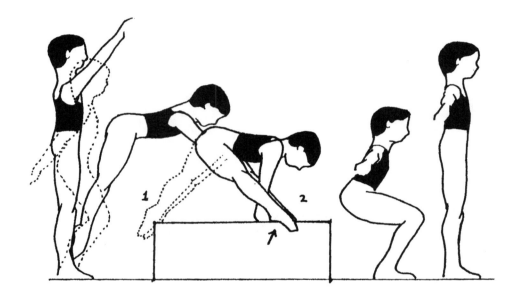

Flank Vault Lead-Ups

On Stacked Mats

Flank Vault Progression (Using Mats)	
Tucked front vault	Flank vault

Tucked Front Vault Over Folded Mats

- Begin in a squat position on floor in front of mat stack.
- Place hands shoulder-width apart on mat stack.
- Push off from both feet to lift hips and knees up into tuck position.
- Torso and legs complete 90-degree turn to land on the other side of mat stack and end sideways to the mat stack.
- Land on both feet, bending knees, and then stretch up into salute position.
- Assist: Stand on the back side of mat stack and support under hips, if necessary, as gymnast passes over the top. Help to support upper arm and torso on landing.

Flank Vault Over Folded Mats

- Begin in squat position on floor in front of mat stack.
- Place hands shoulder-width apart on top of mat stack.
- Push off both feet to lift legs into a straight body position.
- Swing both legs to one side, shifting weight to outside arm and lifting inside arm to vertical.
- As legs continue to swing toward floor, lift outside arm up to vertical.
- Land on both feet, bending knees.
- Finish in salute.
- Assist: Stand on the back side of mat stack and support under hips, if necessary, as gymnast passes over the top. Help to support upper arm and torso on landing.

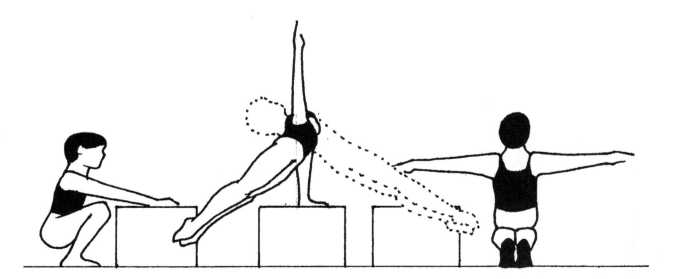

HANDSPRING VAULT LEAD-UPS

Handspring Vault Progression	
Floor Review	***Springboard***
Blocking	Handstand block from springboard
Handstand to flatback	Run, step-hurdle, lunge, handstand to
Block to flatback	flatback
Front handspring	

Review chapter 4's front handspring progression on floor: blocking (page 168), handstand to flatback (page 168), block to flatback (page 169), and the front handspring (page 171).

After your review the floor drills, begin the progression using the springboard:

1. Handstand block from springboard to mat, flatback

2. Step-hurdle, lunge, handstand to flatback

3. Short run, step-hurdle, lunge, handstand to flatback

Many children are able to do a drill long before they are ready to learn the skill that corresponds to the drill. Do not wait until students are ready to learn a handspring vault before they work on these drills. The ability to perform these drills gives gymnasts many physical benefits as well as confidence and self-esteem benefits.

Handstand Block From Springboard

- Facing springboard, kick up to handstand so that the fingers are touching the edge of the board.
- Block, extending shoulders, to "hop," or move handstand forward onto safety cushion.
- Hold handstand position tight as entire body falls forward onto safety cushion.
- Sequence is lunge, lever, handstand, block ("hop"), flatback.
- Assist: Stand beside gymnast and guide the handstand hop by holding gymnast's thighs or lower legs.

VAULT TECHNIQUE

Vaulting may be viewed as a series of skills, all of which build on one another. The success of many basic vaults depends on the quality of the approach, the hurdle, and the preflight. All of these skills build and depend on the combination of skills in a fluid motion.

Once the gymnasts establish the skills leading up to contact with the horse, emphasize vaulting techniques to propel the body on top of and over the horse. These skills are hand placement and flight.

Vault Technique With Hand Placement Lead-Ups

Vault Techniques	
Jumps with hands on horse	Approach, hurdle/rebound, jump with hands on vault (pike, squat, straddle)

1. Stand on springboard, jump with hand placement.
2. Step-hurdle, jump with hand placement.
3. Short run, step-hurdle, jump with hand placement.
4. Long run, step-hurdle, jump with hand placement.

Jumps With Hands on Horse

Jumping with the hands staying on the horse allows the gymnast to feel comfortable with jumping from the springboard and gaining height with successive jumps. They also can feel the different leg positions to prepare for squat, straddle, and flank vault.

Learning Cues for Jumps With Hands on Horse

Verbal/Linguistic

- Stand on springboard and place hands on horse shoulder-width apart with straight arms.
- Jump off the springboard, keeping arms straight and lifting hips above horse in a series of jumps.
- Point feet as they leave the springboard (tuck, straddle, or pike the legs).
- Return to straight body position to land back on board.
- Rebound immediately to continue the series of jumps.

Logical/Mathematical

- Lift hips to highest angle possible (horizontal or above).
- Tuck jump: Close angles of tuck at knees and hips.
- Straddle jump: Open straddle to widest angle possible.
- Pike jump: Close angle at hip in pike as much as possible.

Visual/Spatial

- Watch hands and use handstand hand placement on vault.
- Keep head in line with upper arms by ears.
- Keep feet pointed during tuck, straddle, or pike.
- As hips lift, see tucked legs (with legs together) rising up to chest.
- As hips lift, see legs opening in straddle with knees facing ceiling.
- Turn out legs and keep a round back and hips tucked under in straddle.
- As hips lift, see legs straight and together in pike.

(continued)

(continued)

Bodily/Kinesthetic

- Push down on horse to keep elbows straight and shoulders extended.
- Punch board as hard as you can, driving feet up off the board and lifting hips in takeoff.
- Extend legs before you tuck, straddle, or pike.
- Use enough momentum and height to tuck, straddle, or pike legs.

Musical/Rhythmical

- Use your landing as your takeoff.
- Punch, lift hips (tuck, straddle, pike), rebound (punch), lift hips (tuck, straddle, pike).

Assist

- Stand beside gymnast between springboard and horse (in the straddle vault, move to the other side of horse and reach over to spot).
- Lift hips by placing one hand on the belly and the other on the upper arm for support.

Common Errors

- Hips aren't lifted high enough.
- Arms are bent.
- Head is not in line with ears.
- Punch off board is insufficient.
- In tuck: Tuck is opened.
- In straddle: Back is flat.
- In pike: Head is stuck out, which flattens spine and lowers pike. Legs are bent or apart.

Other Challenges

- Increase the number of consecutive jumps.
- Perform a sequence (tuck, tuck, pike, pike, straddle, straddle).
- Perform jumps up to folded mats for landings without using the hands.

Approach, Hurdle, Rebound, Jump With Hands on Horse

- Approach, step-hurdle, and get feet together and in front on springboard.
- Rebound, reaching straight arms up toward horse.
- Place hands with straight arms on top of horse, shoulder-width apart.
- Use handstand hand placement. Look at hands.
- Keep arms extended and pushed out at shoulders.
- Maintain straight hollow body position in preflight.
- Push down and back with arms as hips come up.
- Lift hips to highest angle possible (horizontal or above).
- Perform a tuck, straddle, or pike jump with hips elevated.
- Bring legs back together before landing back on springboard.
- Assist: Stand beside gymnast between springboard and horse. Lift hips by placing one hand on the belly and the other on the upper arm for support.

VAULTS

Flank Vault

Flank Vault Progression

Vault Techniques	*Vault*
Pike jumps with hands on vault	Three jumps, flank
Approach, hurdle/rebound, pike jump with hands on vault	Flank vault

The flank vault is not a competitive gymnastics skill. However, it is one of the easiest skills to learn and gives gymnasts a feeling of accomplishment. The skill is similar to jumping a fence and does not depend on upper-body strength, upward momentum, or flexibility. In some cases if a gymnast cannot make a tight tuck to squat on or lacks the strength and flexibility to straddle on, the flank is a good beginning vault skill. Also, this is an easy vault to spot: it's the same spot as for a squat vault (just make sure you're on the correct side) but since the flank tends to be a slower vault, it's easier to spot, so it's a great way to train new spotters.

Three Jumps, Flank

- Jump, jump, jump, push, lift hips, flank, land, salute.
- Stand on springboard, place hands on vault shoulder-width apart.
- Keeping legs together, push off with feet and raise hips while supporting with arms.
- Jump off springboard, keeping arms straight and lifting hips above horse for two jumps.
- On the third jump, push down and back with arms, lifting legs to the side in a layout flank position.
- Swing both legs to one side, shifting weight to outside arm. As legs continue to swing toward floor, lift outside arm up to vertical.
- Land on both feet with back to vault.

Flank Vault

- Run down the runway, hurdle onto the board, and rebound off, reaching for the horse.
- Place hands on top of horse, shoulder-width apart.
- Focus on hands, then focus straight ahead.
- Swing legs to one side.
- Stretch inside arm up to vertical and push horse away with support arm. Keep shoulder above other shoulder. Think of making a huge curve over the horse with feet. Think of it as a cartwheel with legs together.
- Keep hip above other hip and do not pike. Keep chest in line with body; do not lean forward to complete flank position as legs pass over the top of the horse.
- Land on both feet with back to vault.
- Sequence is run, hurdle, punch, two arms, swing legs, one arm, land, salute.
- Assist: Stand on back side of horse, reaching in to place one hand under hips and one hand on supporting arm. Help support torso over the horse and guide landing.

Squat-On and Squat-Through Vault

Squat-On/Squat-Through Vault Progression	
Vault Techniques	*Vault*
Tuck jumps with hands on vault	Three jumps, squat-on
Approach, hurdle/rebound, tuck jump with hands on vault	Squat-on

Three Jumps, Squat-On

- Jump, jump, jump, push, lift hips, squat on.
- Stand on springboard, place hands on horse shoulder-width apart with hollow body.
- Keeping legs together, push off with feet and raise hips while supporting body with arms.
- Jump off springboard, keeping arms straight.
- Lift hips above horse for two jumps.
- On the third jump, push down and back with arms as hips come up and forward.
- Jump to land in a squat position on top of horse so that feet land between hands.
- Assist: Stand beside gymnast between springboard and horse. Lift hips by placing one hand on the belly and the other hand on the upper arm for support.
- Other challenges: Try to raise hips and legs higher on the jumps. Drive heels to stretch legs straight in air and keep body as straight as possible before tucking.
- On third jump, squat through.

Squat-On

- Run, step-hurdle onto board, and rebound.
- Reach straight arms up toward horse.
- Place hands shoulder-width apart on top of horse.
- Keep arms straight and maintain straight hollow body position in preflight.
- As the hands contact the horse, push down and back with arms, tucking the legs as hips come up and forward.
- As hips lift, see tucked legs (with legs together) rising up to chest—but do not drop head.
- Get feet under chest, not just under hips.
- Pull knees to chest to land on top of horse in a squat.
- Flex feet at last second to land in squat. Lower hips as feet contact horse.
- Land the feet between hands. Focus on the hands. Look straight ahead once on horse.
- Stretch up to jump up off horse and land vertically.
- Upon landing, lower the arms sideward, downward, then to a forward low diagonal.
- Stick the landing and extend arms to balance with salute.
- Sequence is run, step-hurdle, rebound, hand placement, raise hips, squat on, stand, jump, land.
- Assist: Stand beside gymnast between springboard and horse. Lift hips by placing one hand on the belly and the other on the upper arm for support.
- Other challenges: Try different jumps on dismount.

Learning Cues for Squat-Through

Verbal/Linguistic

- Run, step-hurdle onto board, and rebound.
- Reach straight arms up toward horse in straight hollow body position.
- Place hands shoulder-width apart on top of horse.
- Push down and back with arms as hips come up by quickly pulling the knees to the chest to go over horse in tuck.
- Upon clearing the horse, stretch up and extend body to straight hollow body position.
- Land on both feet in safe landing position, then salute.

Logical/Mathematical

- Sequence is run, step-hurdle, rebound, hand placement, raise hips, squat through, land.
- Take off and land vertically, and keep upper back slightly hollow.

Visual/Spatial

- As hips lift, see tucked legs rising up to chest—but do not drop head.
- Keep chest up and get feet directly under chest and hips.
- Keep space between pointed feet and horse in squat-through.

Bodily/Kinesthetic

- Feel the chest up. Feel legs together.
- Feel a push away with hands on horse.
- Feel feet pointed when going over horse.

Musical/Rhythmical

- Run, step, punch, reach, lift hips, tuck, extend, land, bend knees, balance, salute.
- Pull knees up quickly and think, *Up, tuck, open.*
- Lift body and arms up out of tuck and straighten legs before landing.

Assist

- Stand beside gymnast between springboard and horse.
- Lift hips by placing one hand on the belly and the other on the upper arm for support.
- Move with gymnast throughout vault and landing.

Common Errors

- Safety concern: shoulders riding forward of hands can cause a fall forward onto the head.
- Push and tuck are not adequate to clear horse.
- Push goes back with arms first and not down.
- Weight goes forward.

Straddle-On and Straddle-Through Vault

Vault Techniques	Vault
Straddle jumps with hands on vault	Three jumps, straddle on
Approach, hurdle/rebound, straddle jump with hands on vault	Straddle-on

Remember to spot this vault carefully to prevent gymnast from falling forward. Review the lead-up skills on beam for this vault (chapter 5, page 195).

Three Jumps, Straddle-On

- Jump, jump, jump, push, lift hips, straddle on.
- Stand on springboard and place hands on vault.
- Keeping legs together, push off with feet and raise hips while supporting with arms.
- Jump off springboard, keeping arms straight and lifting hips above horse for two jumps.
- On the third jump, push down and back with arms.
- Lift legs up and open to a straddle position.
- Feet arrive outside of hands in pike straddle on top of vault.
- Assist: Stand on other side of the vault with one leg in front of the other for stability. Reach over horse and hold gymnast's upper arms for support or reach over horse with one hand and place it on gymnast's belly to lift while placing the other hand on the upper arm for support.
- Other challenges: Try to raise hips and legs higher on the jumps. Try to straddle over after third jump.

Straddle-On

- Run, step-hurdle, rebound, hand placement.
- Raise hips while supporting weight with arms.
- Lift hips high before straddling.
- Place feet outside of hands in pike straddle on top of horse.
- Stand and jump from vault.
- Upon landing, lower the arms sideward, downward, then to a forward low diagonal.
- Stick the landing and extend arms to balance with salute.
- Sequence is run, step-hurdle, rebound, hand placement, raise hips, straddle on, stand, jump, land.
- Assist: Stand on back side of horse but reach over to front of horse to assist in preflight by holding upper arms for support. Lift and pull as necessary. Help to stabilize the torso if necessary in the straddle. Continue to hold upper arms, place other hand on back, and step to the side of gymnast during dismount.

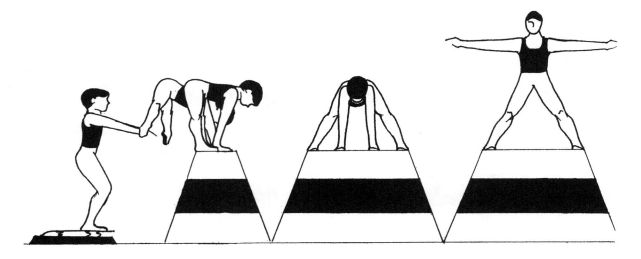

Learning Cues for Straddle-Through

Verbal/Linguistic

- Run, step-hurdle, rebound, hand placement.
- Raise hips while supporting weight with arms and perform a straddle-through by turning legs out in straddle with knees to ceiling.
- Get feet under chest, not just under hips.
- Make straddle wide enough to clear horse without touching.
- Bring body back to straight body position before landing.

Logical/Mathematical

- Sequence is run, step-hurdle, rebound, hand placement, raise hips, straddle through, land.
- Open straddle at end of rebound.
- Keep torso vertical if possible.
- Lift straddle up to highest angle possible.

Visual/Spatial

- Lift hips high before straddling.
- As hips lift above vault, see legs opening in straddle, but do not drop head.
- Get feet under chest, not just under hips.
- Keep the chest up.
- Keep upper back slightly hollow.
- Knees face ceiling in straddle.
- Straddle over: Stay in support long enough to bring straddle over vault. Straddle wide enough to clear mats without touching. Bring body back to straight body position before landing.

Bodily/Kinesthetic

- Push down on horse until arms straighten.
- Feel muscles above knees squeeze tight.
- Straddle legs, bringing heels forward over horse.
- Keep feet pointed, then bring heels forward before landing.

Musical/Rhythmical

- Run, punch, reach, lift, straddle through, land, bend knees, balance, salute.
- Straddle legs quickly after punching.
- Push then pull legs.

Assist

Stand on back side of horse but reach over to front of horse to assist in preflight by holding upper arms for support. Hold upper arms and step backward to move with gymnast through postflight and landing.

Common Errors

- Chest leans forward at an angle, which keeps hips and straddle low and behind mat stack.
- Arms or legs are bent.
- Hips don't lift.
- Arm push is not adequate.
- Straddle is not wide enough.
- Legs don't come together before landing.

Handspring Vault Progression

Handspring Vault Progression	
Short run, step-hurdle, lunge, handspring over mat stack	Short run, step-hurdle, lunge, handspring on mat stack to incline
	Short run, step-hurdle, lunge, front handspring stepout

The gymnast should be able to perform a handspring on the floor (see chapter 4, page 171) and has successfully completed the lead-ups for the handspring (page 167).

Front Handspring Using Springboard and Mats

- Bend arms and legs at 90 degrees to gain power in run.
- Arms circle backward, downward, and up to overhead.
- Punch board as hard as possible.
- Drive feet overhead to vertical handstand on mat.
- When hands make contact with mat stack, handstand should already be at 60 to 65 degrees.
- Just as you make contact with mat, extend shoulders.
- Hold the handstand position as the body rotates around to standing.
- Sequence is run, step-hurdle, punch board, rebound, handstand, stand.

Front Handspring Vault

Note: Make sure that springboard is placed far enough away from horse so that gymnasts can attain the quickest extended preflight and are not forced to pike onto horse.

Learning Cues for Front Handspring Vault

Verbal/Linguistic

- Run down vault runway with fast, even steps using bent arms in opposition.
- Step-hurdle onto springboard and punch by pushing through feet and legs from the rebound into a straight body.
- During preflight, swing arms forward to a completely extended shoulder position to reach up and place hands on horse.
- Maintain a straight hollow body position and keep arms extended.
- Drive the heels backward and upward to rotate the body to an inverted position.
- When feet are directly above hands in handstand position, extend shoulders to block body up and out in postflight.
- Remain in tight straight body position with arms overhead until feet touch the floor.
- Upon landing, lower the arms sideward, downward, then to a forward low diagonal.
- Stick the landing and extend arms to balance with salute.

Logical/Mathematical

- Sequence is run, step-hurdle, punch board, rebound with preflight and arm swing, handstand on horse, block, postflight, landing.
- Reach out (but don't drop arms) in lunge to get the most powerful block that you can.
- At three-quarter handstand, block through shoulders.
- Keep arms in one line—do not create a shoulder angle—to stand up.
- Open angle of legs slightly to stand up in step out.

Visual/Spatial

- Get feet in front of torso on hurdle.
- Keep body hollow throughout.
- Reach your arms as far out in your lunge as possible.
- Reach arms out to vault, extending entire body to create preflight onto horse.
- See hands but do not lift head—look to horse with eyes only.
- Just as you make contact with horse, extend shoulders (block).
- Bring legs together quickly and keep them together.
- Drive feet and legs over the top, drawing with toes a big curve over the horse.
- Keep hips directly above shoulders.
- Keep arms extended overhead.
- Watch hands on postflight to keep chest up.
- Keep arms stretched up after block.
- Keep arms and legs straight throughout.
- Keep chest up (do not round chest) on postflight and landing.

Bodily/Kinesthetic

- Feel the powerful push of the legs in the hurdle lunge.
- Feel the drive of the feet and thighs high overhead to handstand.
- Feel the block.
- Feel tight abdomen.
- Squeeze leg and buttocks muscles, pushing hips forward to keep from piking.
- Feel straight arms by ears throughout handspring.
- Feel a straight hollow body.
- Keep feet pointed until landing.

(continued)

(continued)

Musical/Rhythmical

- Begin arm swing on last step before hurdle.
- Block immediately upon reaching mat.
- Block as quickly as possible by quickly extending shoulders ("pop" the shoulders).
- Bring your legs together quickly for the block, then step out to stand up.
- Rhythm is:

  Punch, block (postflight), land.

  And 1, 2, 3, 4.

Assist

Stand to the side between board and horse. Place one hand on the thigh and one hand on the belly. Another way of spotting is to stand on the back side of horse but reach forward over horse to assist gymnast from rebound by a spot from upper arm and upper back. Beginning vaulters will need both a spotter between the board and the horse and one or two spotters on the far side to hold the arm and support the back through to the landing.

Common Errors

- Run is too slow.
- Feet hit board in the wrong place.
- Rebound is not extended.
- Knees are bent.
- Arms drop in the reach through the lunge.
- Block doesn't happen at all or happens at the wrong time.
- Arms and legs are bent.
- Legs don't come together.
- Chin is tucked so that the back straightens or rounds, pulling gymnast back to floor.
- Back is arched.
- Postflight doesn't happen.
- Hips are piked—hips lift and heels don't drive off the board.

7

Bars

Bars Skills

Grips and hangs	Supports and positions	Mounts
All bars grips Overgrip Undergrip Mixed grip **Suspended hangs** Long hang (H) Tuck hang (LHP) Pike or L hang (LHP) Straddle pike hang (LHP) Chin-hold hang (LH) Bat hang (LH) Sloth hang (LH) **Inverted suspended hangs** Inverted tuck hang (LHP) Inverted pike hang (LHP) Inverted straddle hang (LHP) Inverted straight-body hang	**Parallel bars** Upper-arm support position 　(tuck, pike, or straddle) Straight-arm support position 　(tuck, pike, or straddle) Rear straddle support Front straddle support Hand travel (straight-arm walks) Hand hops **Low and high horizontal bar** Front support Stride support Front support, flank to stride support Single-leg cut to stride support Rear support Stride support, single-leg cut to rear support Cast Cast to single leg shoot-through to stride 　support	**Parallel bars** Jump to upper-arm support Jump to straight-arm support **Low horizontal bar** Jump to front support Pullover mount progression Hips to bar Tucked pullover One-leg kick or running pullover Straight-leg pullover

Swings	Dismounts	Rotational movements
Parallel bars Upper-arm swing Swing from straight-arm support Straddle support travel (forward and 　backward) Scissors with half turn Swinging dips Swing to handstand **Low horizontal bar** Review exploratory swings (tuck, pike 　straddle) Open tuck swing Tuck swing half turn	**Parallel bars** Sit on bar, kick over Rear dismount Front dismount **Low and high horizontal bar** Castaway dismount Underswing dismount Sole circle dismount progression Alternating toe taps Hanging straddle Hanging straddle swing Straddle-on, swing Climb to straddle, swing dismount Jump to straddle, sole circle dismount Cast to sole circle dismount	**Twisting rotations on horizontal bar** Thigh turn 180-degree turn in stride **Horizontal circular rotations horizontal bar** Front support to forward roll Cast to back hip circle Stride press Stride press with resistance Mill circle

(continued)

Bars Skills (continued)

Swings	Dismounts	Rotational movements
High horizontal bar Building a swing (H) Counterswing (H) Regrip (regrasp, or hand hop) Tap swing **Parallel and low horizontal bar** Glide kip progression Suspended swing to glide Kip from upper-arm support to rear straddle support Glide swing, single-leg kip to stride support Glide kip to straight arm support	**High horizontal bar** Swing, rear dismount Swing, front dismount	Front support press Front support press with resistance Front hip circle

This chapter is organized differently than the other chapters because of the different types of bars used in gymnastics. The organization is as follows:

1. Types of skills: grips, hangs, supports, swings, mounts, dismounts, and rotational movements
2. Types of bars: parallel (P), low horizontal (L), and high horizontal (H)

Skills on the high horizontal bar, low horizontal bar, and parallel bars require upper-body strength, abdominal strength, and the ability to perform straight-arm skills with control. Static support and hang positions will help develop the strength required for more advanced skills. Flexibility in the shoulders, hips, and hamstrings is just as important as strength in the performance of bar skills.

When you begin to teach bars, have the students perform hanging and support skills. There is a certain amount of strength and flexibility required to move to more advanced skills. Once you start teaching the swinging skills, the gymnasts get to the fun stage and feel that they are flying!

Equipment: Facilities drive your instruction. In competition, parallel bars are 11.5 feet long and 5 feet to 7 feet high. The width of the bar is adjustable from 16 to 20 inches and should be adjusted to fit the performer. Parallel bars should be slightly wider than shoulder-width apart or elbow to fingertip width plus one, two, three, or four fingers. Swinging moves, strength elements, and flight elements performed both below and above the bars make up a routine.

The high horizontal bar is 8.5 feet high and 8 feet long. A routine consists of swinging moves, changes in direction and grips, and a dismount. Uneven parallel bars consist of two bars. The upper bar is 7.6 feet high, the lower bar is 5 feet high, and the bars are 8 feet long. A gymnast performs skills on both bars and moves from one bar to the other using a variety of skills.

Spotting and safety: Sufficient mats are essential. There should be a soft landing area for dismounts and accidental falls. It can be difficult to spot bars skills. Proper spotting techniques are essential because of swinging momentum, inversion, and strength and flexibility issues. You may need to place spotting blocks or folded mats under the bars so that you can get in a position to assist gymnasts. Whenever possible, the spotting should occur under the bar. Swings in the straight-arm position and skills that propel the body over the bar require at least one hand at the gymnast's shoulder or above the bar.

Check the locking devices on the bars before allowing gymnasts to use the bars. Gymnasts should use chalk to protect the hands when working on the bars. If a springboard is used for mounting, remove it immediately once the gymnast is on bars.

School and outdoor recreation facilities: Many facilities have parallel, low, and high horizontal bars outdoors. They may be used to teach many basic skills if you use proper landing mats and carefully spot each skill. You must also make sure that the bars do not become too hot, which can cause burning and blistering of the hands. Limit the number of repetitions on metal bars because these bars cause much more friction to the hands than regulation bars do.

In this chapter: Typically, the high horizontal bar and parallel bars are used in boys' gymnastics and the uneven bars are used in girls' gymnastics. Both boys and girls should try the skills in this chapter regardless of whether they are considered boys' or girls' skills. In this chapter only skills on parallel bars and a single horizontal bar are used. Most skills on the horizontal bar are taught on a low bar although they may be performed on a higher bar later. These skills provide the foundational strength and body awareness for boys who want to progress to advanced skills on the high horizontal bar or parallel bars and for girls who will later add the second bar for the uneven bars. Adjust the bars as low as practical when first introducing a skill. For most skills, adjust the bars so that the gymnast's feet barely clear the floor mats during the skill.

The skills in this chapter are listed by categories and are not necessarily in progression order. However, the skills within a category are listed in progression order. It is often easier to begin many skills on the parallel bars because there is more stability to support the body weight on two even bars. The terms *front* and *rear* are used often in bar skill descriptions. Usually, the name indicates whether the front or rear of the gymnast is facing or touching the bar.

GRIP POSITIONS

Review All Bars	
Grips	Undergrip
Overgrip	Mixed grip

It's important to use the proper grip when performing bar skills. On a single bar, an overgrip hand placement is used when rotating backward around the bar, an undergrip hand placement is used when rotating forward around the bar, and a mixed grip is used when turning 180 degrees.

The issue of hand grips is controversial. Should the thumbs be around the bar or should they be beside the fingers?

The thumbs usually stop or slow down the rotation. So for most skills, especially rotational skills, you want gymnasts to keep the thumbs by the fingers. But you should also consider the size of a gymnast's hands in relationship to the bar. Be aware that the thumbs by the fingers will not work for some students because their hands are too small. Some gymnasts will need to wrap the thumbs around for a secure grip and may need more instruction and practice on shifting the hands.

Overgrip

- Place hands on bar, shoulder-width apart with palms down and thumbs over bar.

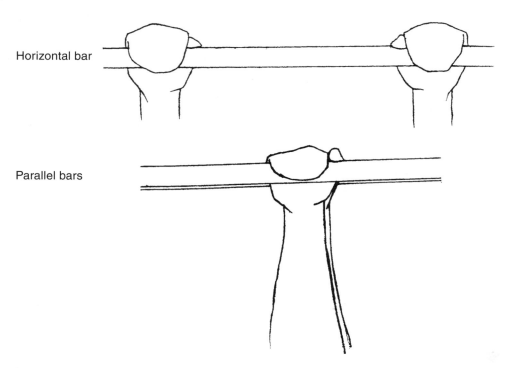

Horizontal bar

Parallel bars

Undergrip

- Place hands on bar, shoulder-width apart with palms under and thumbs up over bar.

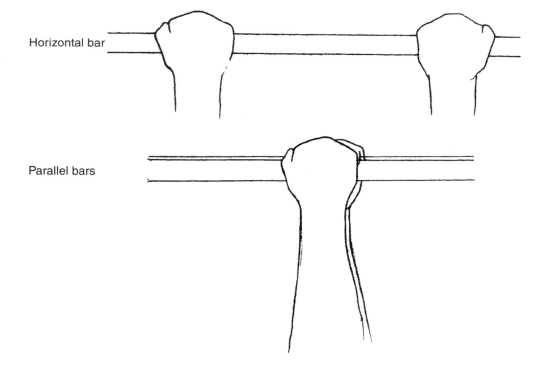

Horizontal bar

Parallel bars

Mixed Grip

- Place hands on bar, shoulder-width apart, with one hand grasping bar in overgrip and the other hand in undergrip.

HANGS FROM BARS

Suspended Hangs

Long hang (H)   Chin-hold hang (LH)
Tuck hang (LHP)   Bat hang (LH)
Pike or L hang (LHP)   Sloth hang (LH)
Straddle pike hang (LHP)

Hanging in different positions from a single horizontal bar or parallel bars helps develop upper-body strength and awareness of supporting the entire body weight from a bar. Even temporarily lifting the feet while suspended helps to develop strength. Once a gymnast gains confidence and strength, he or she is ready to hold the body off the floor for longer periods of time and move to skills in which the entire body weight is suspended.

When you first teach bars skills, have students hang from bars. Tell them that the center of the gravity is between the hands; if they let go with one hand, the center of gravity changes. Have students explore the different shapes and angles they can make while hanging from the bars, and have them discover the feel of the body when legs are tucked, straight, or asymmetrical. They will find that the more segments and angles they have, the more problems they will have in controlling the body and the stronger the muscles must be to hold a body position.

Long Hang (H)

Learning Cues for Long Hang

Verbal/Linguistic
- Use any style of grip.
- Hang under bar, suspending all body weight from hands.
- Body hangs in a straight line.

Logical/Mathematical
- Create a vertical line with your body.

Visual/Spatial
- Keep legs straight and feet pointed.
- Look straight ahead.
- Keep arms shoulder-width apart.

Bodily/Kinesthetic
- Relax and feel a weighted hang.
- Squeeze the bar tightly with hands.
- Squeeze straight legs together.

Interpersonal
- Work with a partner. See that your partner stays straight with tight muscles. Help your partner if necessary.

Naturalist
- Be the moss hanging from the tree.

Assist
- Stand beside gymnast to hold one hand on wrist and one hand on belly. If you cannot hold the wrist because of the height of bar, have one hand on the belly and the other on the back.

Common Errors
- Body is too tense.
- Head is out of alignment.

Tuck Hang (LHP)

- Use any style of grip.
- Assume a long hang, then tuck legs. Keep spine vertical.
- Pull knees up until they touch chest.
- For a challenge, swing in tuck.
- Assist: Stand beside gymnast and hold wrist and under tucked thighs or hold abdomen and back.

Pike or L Hang (LHP)

- Begin in long-hang position using any grip.
- Keep back vertical and lift legs to horizontal (parallel to the floor).
- Feel hip flexors (upper thighs) lifting legs.
- Keep abdomen tight to avoid arching.
- For a challenge, lift pike above horizontal.
- Assist: Stand beside gymnast and hold wrist or lower back and under thighs.
- Challenge: Swing in pike; lift the legs upward until the toes touch the bar in closed pike.

Straddle Pike Hang (LHP)

- Assume a long hang.
- Turn out legs and lift legs to horizontal in straddle.
- Keep abdomen tight to avoid arching.
- Assist: Stand beside gymnast and support wrist and lower leg.

Chin-Hold Hang (H)

- Begin in long hang using overgrip.
- Pull, bending arms until chin is above bar.
- Keep body vertical from head to toes.
- Assist: Stand facing gymnast and support at waist or above knees to assist lift.

Bat Hang (LH)

- Begin in long hang using overgrip.
- Pull feet up to bar in straddle position, placing the balls of the feet on the bar with ankles extended.
- Keep legs straight and head between the arms.
- Assist: Support gymnast in mid and lower back.
- Common errors: Head is back, feet are flexed, knees are bent.

Sloth Hang (LH)

- Begin in long hang using overgrip.
- Pull feet between hands up to bar in closed pike position, placing the balls of the feet on the bar.
- Keep legs straight and head between the arms.
- Assist: Support gymnast in mid and lower back.
- Common errors: Head is back, feet are flexed, knees are bent.

INVERTED HANGS

Inverted Suspended Hangs
Inverted tuck hang (LHP)	Inverted straddle hang (LHP)
Inverted pike hang (LHP)	Inverted straight-body hang (LHP)

Inverted positions are excellent for developing spatial awareness. In all inverted hangs take extra care to assist gymnasts so that they do not fall.

Inverted Tuck Hang (LHP)

Learning Cues for Inverted Tuck Hang

Verbal/Linguistic

- Assume a long hang.
- Lift knees to tight tuck.
- Stay in a tight tuck and lift knees overhead.
- Keep pulling knees up through arms until hips are above shoulders.

Logical/Mathematical

- Keep torso in a vertical line from hips to shoulders.
- Close angles of tuck.
- Maintain a closed tuck throughout.

Visual/Spatial

- Keep arms shoulder-width apart.
- Use undergrip or overgrip.
- Lift knees up to chest.
- Stay in tight tuck.
- See your knees together.
- See your knees lift up between the bars.
- See bar and lower legs coming through grip.
- Keep feet pointed.

Bodily/Kinesthetic

- Feel knees touching chest.
- Squeeze knees and feet together.
- Support feet on bar if necessary.
- Do not drop back backward but keep it in line with arms and shoulders.
- Feel the top of the foot stretch when pointed.

(continued)

(continued)

Musical/Rhythmical

- Movement should be smooth and slow.

Assist

- Stand beside gymnast and reach under bar to place one hand on shoulder and one hand under lower back.

Common Errors

- Knees are not tucked tightly enough to get legs through bars.
- Hips are not lifted.
- Tuck opens.
- Feet are flexed.

Inverted Pike Hang (LHP)

The inverted pike will help build strength for the kip position later.

- Begin in long-hang position using an overgrip or undergrip.
- Lift straight legs to highest possible pike.
- Continue lifting the pike above horizontal and bring legs through arms until hips are above head and legs are in closed pike.
- Legs are horizontal in pike, then they are horizontal again in inverted pike.
- Keep the head inside of the arms throughout.
- Hips are directly under bar and directly over shoulders when inverted.
- Do not drop head back or allow it to rest on upper back.
- Assist: Stand beside gymnast and reach under bar to place one hand on shoulder and one hand on lower back.

 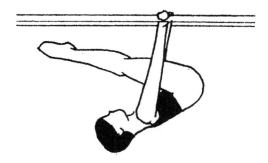

Inverted Straddle Hang (LHP)

- Begin in a long-hang position using overgrip or undergrip.
- Lift and pull open legs to straddle.
- Maintain straddle and lift hips to take feet up outside arms until legs are parallel to floor in piked straddle.
- Legs are horizontal in straddle then they are horizontal again in inverted straddle.
- Spine is vertical in straddle, then vertical again in inverted straddle with hips above shoulders.
- Assist: Stand to the side of the gymnast. Place one hand under shoulder and the other hand on lower back.

 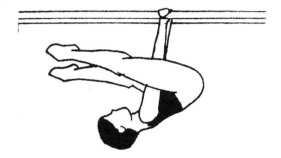

Inverted Straight-Body Hang (LHP)

- Begin in long-hang position using an overgrip or undergrip.
- Lift straight legs to highest possible pike.
- Continue lifting legs with control above horizontal, then straighten hips to a straight-body position.
- Keep the head inside of the arms throughout.
- Assist: Stand beside gymnast and reach under bar to place one hand on shoulder and one hand on lower back.

SUPPORTS

Arm and shoulder strength, balance, and correct body position are essential for supports on the bar. In supports, gymnasts are elevated off the ground and are at more risk for injury than in hangs. Gymnasts should have successfully completed support skills on the floor, folded mats, and beam before moving to support skills on bars. This chapter presents new support positions specific to the parallel bars. The body alignment is different on two parallel bars than on a single bar. Some supports are easier on parallel bars because the weight is equally distributed between the hands and the center of gravity is directly beneath the shoulders and is easier to maneuver.

Incorrect body position is a common error for beginners in all the supports. Beginners tend to push the chest forward, which allows the body weight to drop and puts most of the weight onto the hands. The proper way to release the weight off the hands and into the shoulders is to round out the shoulder, hollow the chest, and tighten the body. This will eliminate pressure on the hands, and gymnasts will be able to hold the support longer. Bent arms are another common error in bars skills. Arms should be straight in support positions.

Allow the gymnasts to explore by placing the heels of the hands on different parts of the bar (back, top, and front of bar). This will allow them to get a feel for how their hand placements affect their body positions.

Supports on Parallel Bars

Parallel Bars	
Upper-arm support position (tuck, pike, or straddle)	Rear straddle support
	Front straddle support
Straight-arm support position (tuck, pike, or straddle)	Hand travel (straight-arm walks)
	Hand hops

Upper-Arm Support (P)

- In the upper-arm support the body is between the bars with the weight distributed in the upper-arm area.

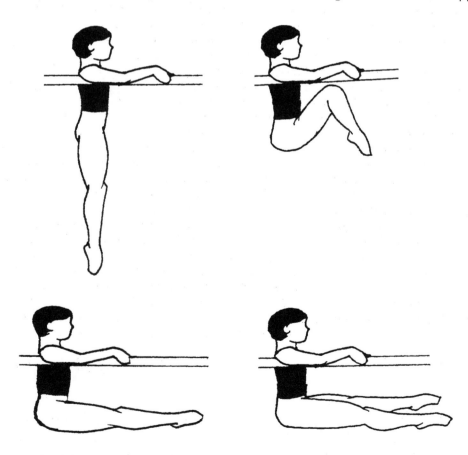

Learning Cues for Upper-Arm Support

Verbal/Linguistic

- Stand between bars with hands in overgrip.
- Place upper arms on bars with elbows flexed and extended out over the bars.
- Shift weight forward and press down until feet are off the floor and upper arms support entire body weight.

Logical/Mathematical

- Sequence is straight-body stand, shift forward, and press down to upper-arm support.
- Bend arms until you create an angle at which your upper arms are in complete contact with bar.
- Keep torso vertical.

Visual/Spatial

- Focus straight ahead.
- Keep shoulders directly above hips.
- Point feet.

Bodily/Kinesthetic

- Press down on bar with upper arms until chest lifts up.
- Squeeze legs together.
- Squeeze muscles above knees.

Assist

- Stand behind gymnast and hold around waist or at hips for support.

Common Errors

- Body collapses through middle of bars.
- One arm presses harder or faster than the other.
- Arms don't push down on bars.
- Chest isn't up.

Other Challenges

- Bring legs up to tuck, pike, or straddle pike.

Straight-Arm Support (P)

The straight-arm support is performed on parallel bars. From the straight-arm support the gymnast may place legs in various static positions such as the tuck, pike, and straddle; or gymnast may bring the legs up in front for a rear straddle support (straddle seat) or bring the legs up in back for a front straddle support (reverse straddle seat). The swing happens from the straight-arm position on the parallel bars.

- Stand in between bars and place hands in overgrip.
- Push on bars to extend arms into supported straight-body position between the bars (shoulders directly over hands).
- Assist: Stand behind gymnast and hold hips to assist in lift.
- Challenges: Bring legs up to tuck, pike, or straddle pike. Bring legs up in front to a rear straddle support. Bring legs up in back to a front straddle support. Perform hand travel or hand hops from a straight-arm support.

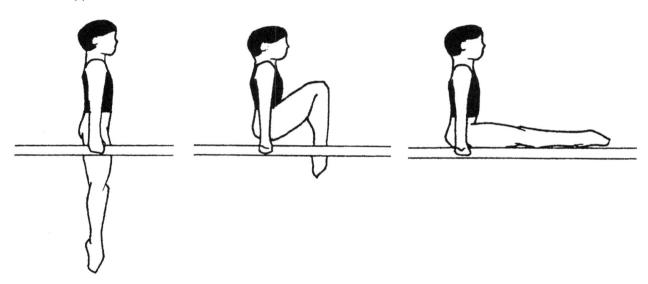

Rear Straddle Support (Straddle Seat)

Some gymnasts may consider the rear straddle support and the straddle seat two different skills. In rear straddle support, hips can be straight; in straddle seat, hips can be slightly piked.

- Begin in a straight-arm support.
- Swing and lift legs forward by flexing at the hips.
- As legs swing above bar level, straddle legs, placing backs of thighs on bars.
- Keep legs straight, hips extended, torso lifted in a rear support.

Front Straddle Support (Reverse Straddle Seat)

Some gymnasts say that the front straddle support has straight hips and the reverse straddle seat has slightly piked hips.

- Begin in a straight-arm support.
- Swing legs behind to place front of inner thighs with legs straight in straddle on bars.
- Keep legs straight, hips extended, and torso lifted in a front support (push-up position with straddled legs).

Hand Travel With Straight Arms

This activity will help develop strength.

- Begin in a straight-arm position.
- Move one hand at a time forward to "walk" down the bars.
- Then try walking hands backward.

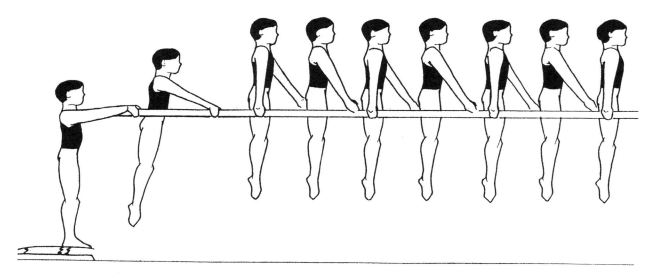

Hand Hops

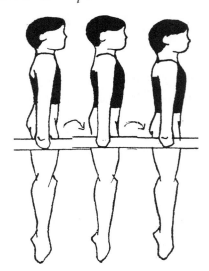

This activity will help build strength as well as teach the regrip skill.

- Begin in a straight-arm support.
- Extend the arms downward by shrugging the shoulders.
- "Hop" the hands forward or backward slightly on bars.

Supports on Horizontal Bar

Horizontal Bar	
Front support	Rear support
Stride support	Stride support, single-leg cut to rear support
Front support, flank to stride support	Cast
Single-leg cut to stride support	Cast to single-leg shoot-through to stride support

Begin all skills on a low horizontal bar. Increase the height of the bar as skill, strength, and confidence increase. Review support skills on balance beam (page 182).

Front Support (L)

The front support is an important skill to master because the proper positioning and alignment of this skill are essential to the success of other skills on bars. For skills such as the front support, pullover, single-leg shoot-through, and front hip circle, gymnasts must understand that the upper body must be slightly in front of the bar. This occurs by maintaining a hollow body position with the shoulders above the bar in front of the wrists. Have gymnasts move their shoulders back and they will discover that they come off the bar.

- Place hands on the bar in overgrip right next to the hips.
- Keep arms straight.
- Keep shoulders in hollow and focus on the bar.
- Keep body weight forward with shoulders in front of wrists.
- Keep legs together and straight.
- Keep buttocks tight and keep upper thighs in contact with the bar.

Stride Support

There are several ways to get into the stride support. Often this is called a stride support press when the entire body is lifted off the bar and supported by the arms. The easiest way to get to a stride support is from a straight-arm front support to flank through to stride. In the transition to the stride support, the gymnast may have the inner thigh on the bar supporting some of the body weight. The gymnast should be able to perform the stride support (see chapter 5, page 184) and the straight-arm front support to straddle seat on the balance beam (page 189) before moving to the stride support on the low horizontal bar. The stride support is used in the flank, leg cut, and mill circle.

Front Support, Flank to Stride Support (L)

The flank is a lead-up for the single-leg cut. The purpose of the flank is to lift the leg and bring it forward without losing support. It is important to keep the shoulders over the bar for balance.

- Begin in a front support in overgrip.
- Swing one leg over (flank) the bar so that inner thigh rests on bar in stride position.
- The same hand as the flanked leg will move to outside of leg so that hands are placed on each side of hips.
- Keep both legs straight.
- Extend arms and lift stride split press off the bar.

Front Support, Single-Leg Cut to Stride Support

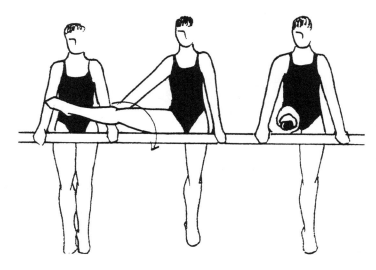

- Begin in front support in overgrip.
- Swing leg quickly on same side over bar to the front.
- Simultaneously lift one hand off bar.
- Immediately replace hand on outside of leg to arrive in stride support.
- Lift the stride support press off the bar. Keep both legs straight.
- Assist: Stand in front of gymnast on opposite side of swinging leg. Place one hand on back to support torso as leg swings to the side. As leg swings to the front, place other hand under leg to keep gymnast from falling forward, or support the other arm.
- Challenges: Perform skill with other leg.

Rear Support (L)

Gymnasts should be able to perform a rear support on the balance beam (page 185) before performing it on the horizontal bar. Initially, the gymnast may sit on a low horizontal bar to practice getting into a rear support. However, the common method to get into a rear support is from a stride support position.

- Sit on bar.
- Place hands in overgrip next to hips with arms straight.
- Keep body straight and tight with the legs together.
- Keep head and chest up and shoulders over the bar in a balanced position.

Stride Support, Single-Leg Cut to Rear Support (L)

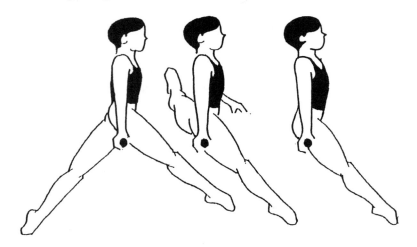

Learning Cues for Stride Support, Single-Leg Cut to Rear Support

Verbal/Linguistic
- Begin in stride support with hands in overgrip.
- Quickly swing back leg forward.
- Lift and replace hand on the bar as leg passes over the bar.
- Leg arrives beside front leg in rear support.

Logical/Mathematical
- Keep torso vertical.
- Don't pike but create a straight diagonal line in rear support.

Visual/Spatial
- Keep arms straight throughout.
- Push until shoulders are down.
- Keep hip down in cut.

- Push hips forward in rear support.
- Focus straight ahead—don't try to watch leg.
- Once in rear support, focus on an upward diagonal.

Bodily/Kinesthetic

- Keep tight buttocks muscles to avoid piking.
- Shift weight onto stronger arm.

Musical/Rhythmical

- Cut leg as quickly as possible.

Assist

- Stand behind gymnast slightly to the side to avoid the swinging leg. Hold gymnast at waist.

Common Errors

- Body leans and falls forward.
- Body pikes and falls backward.
- Chest collapses and body sits back.
- Leg catches on bar during the cut.

Cast

Casting is a clear support skill, which means the weight is on the hands and straight arms and the body "clears," or pushes away, from the bar. Casting is often difficult for boys because they have problems maintaining a hollow body position and they extend the arms so that the bars make contact at the upper thighs instead of more vulnerable areas.

Cast (L)

To practice the correct body position, have the gymnast get in a front support. One spotter will assist in keeping gymnast's arms straight and shoulders slightly in front of bar while a second spotter lifts gymnast's straight, tight body away from the bar to horizontal and returns it gently to front support.

Learning Cues for Cast

Verbal/Linguistic

- Begin in front support (upper thighs touching bar) in a hollow body position.
- Keep shoulders in front of bar.
- Pike lower body to swing legs forward, then swing legs backward and upward.
- Push down on bar, extending through the shoulders to lift the body off the bar.
- At the height of the cast, get shoulders over and in front of wrists. Make a horizontal straight line from shoulders to the toes.
- Legs and torso return to finish in front support.

Logical/Mathematical

- Sequence is front support, cast, front support.
- Torso to toes is one straight body line at height of cast.
- Cast to highest horizontal.

Visual/Spatial

- Use overgrip, keeping arms and legs straight.
- Shoulders must be in front of bar to return to front support.
- Swing your toes to the wall behind you.
- Maintain a hollow body position.
- Focus on bar or hands.
- Kinder cue: Become a teeter-totter—shoulders go forward and feet go up!

Bodily/Kinesthetic

- Squeeze buttocks and tighten abdominal muscles on cast.
- Stay tight in front and back.

Musical/Rhythmical

- Rhythm is:

    Pike, cast (swing).

    And 1, 2.

Assist

- Place one hand under shoulder or arm and one hand under thighs or hips to help with casting.

Common Errors

- Shoulders are not in front of bar; angle of support is incorrect.
- Body pikes too much in cast.
- Loose body causes arching.
- Legs separate.
- Arms are not extended, which can cause body to make contact with the bar at the waist.
- Body is not hollow.
- Hands are placed too wide.

Other Challenges

Jump to support, then cast (come to bar and cast away for several repetitions). Arms must be straight. Cast to squat, straddle, or pike on top of bar. Review these skills on vault (see "Vaults," page 223). This skill needs two spotters. During the cast, one spotter holds the side of one leg to help with the lift; the other spotter stands in front of the bars to keep the gymnast from going over.

Cast to Single-Leg Shoot-Through to Stride Support

This skill is advanced and requires a good cast and flexibility to get the tucked leg in between the arms and the bar. Students can practice by standing and holding a dowel rod or scarf in their hands and stepping over it with one leg.

Learning Cues for Cast to Single-Leg Shoot-Through to Stride Support

Verbal/Linguistic

- Begin in a front support on horizontal bar with hands shoulder-width apart in overgrip.
- Extend through the shoulders to horizontal cast.
- Bend one leg in tuck position.
- Shoot the bent leg between the hands, keeping shoulders in front of bar.
- Finish with legs in stride support press.

Logical/Mathematical

- Sequence is front support, cast, single-leg shoot-through, stride support.
- Make a vertical line from hands through shoulders.
- Push both arms equally to straighten at the same time.
- Separate legs as much as possible while keeping hips square.
- Keep weight distributed on heels of hands with thumbs pressed against index fingers.

Visual/Spatial

- Keep chest hollow and shoulders directly in front of bar.
- Focus on hands.

Bodily/Kinesthetic

- Support weight with straight arms.
- Push down on bar to execute cast.
- Feel inner thigh muscles working to hold legs in straight line in stride support.

Musical/Rhythmical

- Push, hips up, leg through, chest up.

Assist

Stand behind the bar next to the gymnast. Hold the leg that will not shoot through as it swings forward, then back to cast off the bar. Support this leg while the gymnast shoots the other leg over the bar. You may hold the leg with one hand so that you can hold the gymnast's arm with the other hand to support the shoulders. The shoulders must shift forward in front of the bar for a successful shoot-through, but if the shoulders move too far forward, the gymnast will collapse.

Common Errors

- Legs are separated unevenly in stride.
- Back leg touches the bar.

Other Challenges

- Attain a full 180-degree stride split.

MOUNTS

Mounts are skills used to get onto the bars. Many of the same mounts can be performed on the different bars. Sequences and lead-ups are presented to ensure optimal success.

Mounts on Parallel Bars

Parallel Bars	
Jump to upper-arm support	Jump to straight-arm support

Jump to Upper-Arm Support

Review the upper-arm support position (page 244).

- Stand between the bars.
- Jump up between the bars and swing arms over the bars to end in upper-arm support position.
- Challenge: Use a springboard at the end of the bars to gain momentum to go upward and forward. Reach with hands to an upper-arm support position.

Jump to Straight-Arm Support

A basic position on parallel bars is the straight-arm support. To mount or get onto the bars, the gymnast will do the following:

- Stand between the bars or at the end of bars with hands in overgrip.
- Jump, straightening arms to a straight-arm support.

Review the straight-arm support (page 246) on the parallel bars. Practice jumping to straight-arm support then swinging the legs fluidly into the straddle seat (rear straddle support) or reverse straddle seat (front straddle support) as a basic mount variation.

Mounts on Horizontal Bar

Horizontal Bar
Jump to front support
Pullover mount progression
Hips to bar

Tucked pullover
One-leg kick or running pullover
Straight-leg pullover

Jump to Front Support

A basic mount for the horizontal bar is the front support position. Review the front support on the horizontal bar (page 248). To mount or get onto the bar, the gymnast will do the following:

- Face the bar with hands positioned on the bar in overgrip.
- Jump, straightening arms to a front support position.

Never bend arms and move chin close to bar when jumping to front support. The ideal movement is to keep arms straight as shoulders rock up and over the bar. Try to pull the bar down with straight arms as the shoulders lean forward.

Pullover Mount Progression

The same motion is used in the pullover and back hip circle. It is beneficial for the gymnast to perform reverse sit-ups. To get the feel, the gymnast can lie with upper thighs over the bar while the spotter holds her legs. The reverse sit-up should be performed with hands on bar and straight arms, squeezing the gluts and lifting with back muscles to bring the chest up to a front support position.

A successful pullover mount must have the hips close to the bar, a shift of the wrists, and extension of the arms to a front support. The pullover is also a preparatory skill for the back hip circle. The progression for the pullover is as follows:

- Hips to bar
- Tucked pullover
- One-leg kick or running pullover
- Straight-leg pullover

Hips to Bar

Gymnasts must practice getting the hips to the bar. The most common mistake is straightening the arms as the hips near the bar.

- Stand in gymnastics point at arm's length from a bar set at shoulder height.
- Hold bar with hands shoulder width apart in overgrip.
- Step forward on pointed foot and lift free leg.
- Push off standing foot to lift other leg.
- Pull body upward with arms until hips touch bar. Arms should bend 90 degrees or more.

- Return both feet to floor at same time as torso returns to upright position.
- Sequence is grasp bar, push from floor, pull hips to bar, return with both feet to floor.
- Assist: Stand beside gymnast and place one hand on back and one hand under push leg. Shift hands to hips for landing.

Tucked Pullover

- Stand on both feet at arm's length from the bar with hands grasping bar in overgrip.
- Jump off both feet and pull and bend arms.
- Pull chin above bar as legs tuck to pull knees over the bar.
- Pull bar to hips, rotating shoulders backward.
- Shift wrists to the top of the bar to help complete the rotation of the body.
- Finish in a front support.

One-Leg Kick or Running Pullover

- Stand at arm's length in front of bar.
- Place hands on bar in overgrip.
- Walk or run to kick leg high over bar.
- Push other leg off the floor to meet kick leg above bar. Kick to inverted straight-body position.
- Rotate around bar, staying as close to bar as possible.
- Bend arms 90 degrees or more while pulling the bar toward the waist and rotating the shoulders over the bar.
- Shift the grip back to the top of the bar.
- Finish the lift of the torso to a front support position.
- Sequence is grasp bar, run, kick legs over bar as arms pull, shift wrists, front support.
- Assist: Stand beside the gymnast on the front side of the bar. Place hand on gymnast's back and under the push leg to help it join the kick leg high above the bar. Place one hand in front of gymnast's shoulder and press down on back side of thighs with other hand to help gymnast rotate around the bar when inverted.

Straight-Leg Pullover

Learning Cues for Straight-Leg Pullover

Verbal/Linguistic
- From a stand with feet together, grasp the bar in overgrip.
- Lift legs upward and over the bar while pulling with flexed arms.
- Continue to lift the hips over the bar in slight pike.
- When body is inverted, shift wrists and lift chest to finish rotation around the bar.
- Finish in a front support.

Logical/Mathematical
- Sequence is grasp bar, pull with arms, pike, pullover with wrist rotation, front support.
- Place hands on bar shoulder-width apart.
- Maintaining a straight-body position, pull over as close to bar as possible.

Visual/Spatial
- Pull over in slight pike.
- Keep chin over bar; do not throw head back.
- Keep head neutral throughout.
- Watch toes rise over the bar.
- Bring hips over head.

Bodily/Kinesthetic
- Feel muscles above knees tighten.

Musical/Rhythmical
- When body is inverted, shift wrists quickly.
- Keep pullover smooth and continuous.

(continued)

(continued)

Assist

Stand beside gymnast in front of bar. Place one hand on back and the other hand under legs. When body is inverted, shift one hand in front of shoulders and one hand on back of lower legs to press downward and to aid in rotation.

Common Errors

- Head whips back.
- Chest drops.
- Body arches instead of piking.
- Hips aren't pulled to bar.
- Arms don't pull to a 90-degree bend or more (most common error).
- Pull starts out correctly, then arms straighten, which drops the hips away from the bar.

Other Challenges

- Perform straight-leg pullover from a long hang on high bar.

SUSPENDED AND SWINGING SKILLS

Hanging suspended from a bar set at shoulder height and swinging in different positions will develop upper-body strength and awareness of the sensation of holding and swinging the body weight from a bar. Gymnasts and spotters must use extreme caution during swinging skills because of the momentum generated in swinging actions and the increased risk of slipping off the bars. Other precautions include holding the gymnasts' wrists as they swing and having them use chalk when performing bar skills.

The fulcrum of the swing should be in the shoulders and not the hips. In the front swing when the body is in front of the hands, the body pikes, then the hips extend toward the peak of the forward swing. It is a common error to swing mainly from the hips.

It is true that gymnasts must have strength to be successful on bars. However, the great bar workers also use the laws of physics and motion to generate the power for their gravity-defying skills; they don't just need brute strength to "muscle" their moves. To help gymnasts understand this principle, use a weighted string—for example, a washer—tied to a bar. If you pull the washer back taut and release it, it will swing to almost the same distance past vertical. This is a basic pendulum motion, and the farther you pull the washer back, the farther it will swing when you release it (horizontal being optimal). If you pull the washer back to horizontal but leave some slack in the string, it would not even swing past vertical. In fact, if there is enough slack, and the string is thin or the washer heavy, the force of gravity removing the slack could cause the string to break. Relate this to a gymnast who peels off the bar because of bent arms, or the beginner who cannot generate enough swing in a glide to perform a kip because of a shoulder angle during the jump into the mount.

Now take the imaginary string and throw it to wrap around the bar. Notice how the rotational speed increases as the string gets shorter. Remember that the shortening of the radius increases rotation. This same principle applies to hip circles.

Swings on Parallel Bars

Parallel Bars

Swings From Upper-Arm Support
Upper-arm swing

Swings From Straight-Arm Support
Swing from straight-arm support

Straddle support travel (forward and backward)
Scissors with half turn
Swinging dips
Swing to handstand

Swings From Upper-Arm Support

The upper-arm support provides a bigger base of support and more stability for the swinging motion than the straight-arm support provides. The upper-arm swing is used to generate momentum and force to perform an uprise, which is a basic move to take the body from an upper-arm support to a straight-arm support.

Upper-Arm Swing

- Begin in an upper-arm support.
- Generate a swing by piking in front and stretching in back.
- Sequence is upper-arm support, swing forward in slight pike, swing back to straight body.
- Assist: Stand beside gymnast outside the bars. Reach under the bar and provide support with one hand at armpit and follow with light contact at abdomen and back during the swing.

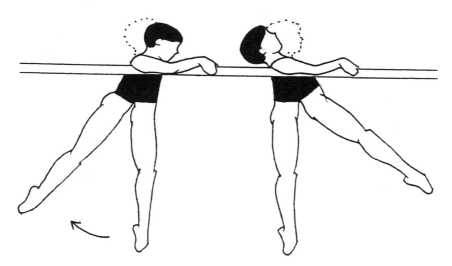

Swings From Straight-Arm Support

Swing From Straight-Arm Support (P)

Learning Cues for Swing From Straight-Arm Support

Verbal/Linguistic

- Begin in a straight-arm support.
- Generate a swing by piking in front and stretching in back; lift legs upward and forward to a pike position then thrust them down and back to a slight arch.
- Repeat to build swing.
- As swing builds, lift the hips in back to a slight pike with legs straight and upper back hollow.

Logical/Mathematical

- Sequence is straight-arm support, swing forward in slight pike, swing back with slight arch.
- Keep body in one line with slight pike and arch.
- Keep arms in vertical line.

Visual/Spatial

- Keep arms straight.
- See feet.
- Keep shoulders directly above wrists.
- Focus on end of bars.

Bodily/Kinesthetic

- Push down on the bars.
- Squeeze muscles above knees.
- Squeeze legs together.
- Feel shoulders elevated at bottom of swing and pressed down at top of swing.
- Drive feet backward on back swing.

Musical/Rhythmical

- Rhythm is 1, 2, 3; 1, 2, 3.

Assist

- Stand beside bar and place one hand on gymnast's back and one hand under thighs.

Common Errors

- Arms are bent.
- Hips are too piked.

Challenges

- Perform a straight-arm support swing to end in a rear support position on one bar, rear straddle support position, or front straddle support position.

Straddle Support Travel

- Begin in a rear straddle support with backs of thighs on the bars.
- Lean forward and shift arms and body to a front straddle support.
- Bring legs together and swing legs forward above the bar to a rear straddle support. Repeat.
- Sequence is rear straddle support, front straddle support, swing, rear straddle support, front straddle support, swing.
- Assist: Stand beside gymnast on outside of bar. Reaching under the bar, place hands on hips of gymnast.
- Challenge: Try reversing the action and travel backward.

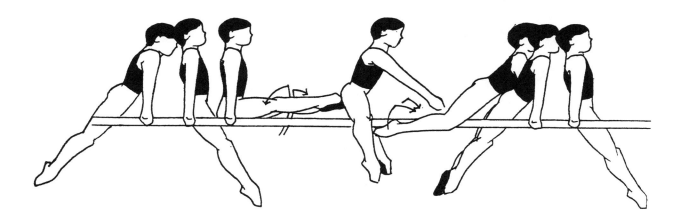

Scissors With Half Turn

- Begin in a straight-arm front support and keep arms straight.
- Generate swing to the height where feet rise above the bars at the top of the back swing.
- Near the top of the back swing, twist the hips in half turn and straddle legs until each leg rests on a bar.
- Release hands, turn torso, and quickly regrasp bars with hands of corresponding legs.
- Finish in rear straddle support facing opposite direction.
- Sequence is straight-arm support, swing forward, swing backward, twist hips, straddle legs and rest feet on bar, release hands, complete turn of torso, regrip, finish in rear straddle support.
- Assist: Stand on side of bar and place one hand on shoulder and at top of swing; place other hand under hips.

Swinging Dips

Dips are strength moves. Before gymnasts work on swinging dips, they should be able to do modified push-ups, push-ups, table push-ups, and modified dips. Gymnasts must also be able to do several nonswinging dips before progressing to swinging dips. To perform a dip, the gymnast stands between the bars and places the hands in overgrip on bars. Gymnast jumps to a straight-arm front support. He or she bends the arms, allowing torso to dip down between bars so that shoulders are still above the bars. Then, keeping the body in a straight vertical line, gymnast extends the arms to return to a straight-arm front support. Sequence is straight-arm support, bend arms to maximum, straight-arm support. Here is the sequence for swinging dips:

- Stand between bars with hands in overgrip.
- Jump to a straight-arm front support and generate a swing.
- Bend arms as you pass through bottom of backward swing.
- Extend arms as you swing forward and upward.
- Sequence is straight-arm support, swing legs forward and bend arms, extend arms, swing backward and bend arms.

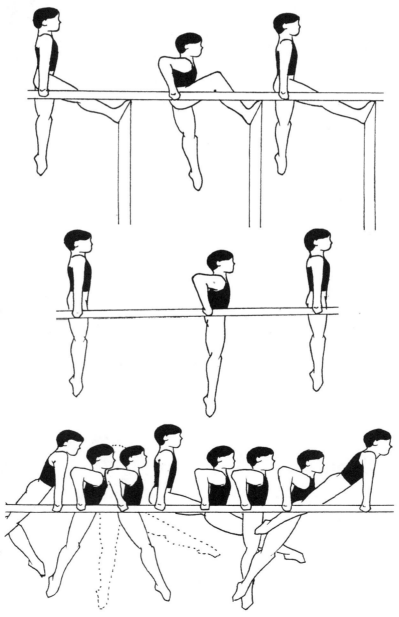

Swing to Handstand

This is an advanced skill and should be spotted carefully.

Learning Cues for Swing to Handstand

Verbal/Linguistic

- Begin in a straight-arm front support.
- Swing high enough to drive hips and legs all the way to handstand at the top of the back swing.

Logical/Mathematical

- Sequence is straight-arm support, swing forward in slight pike, swing back while driving hips to handstand.
- Begin in vertical support.
- Swing in a long arch until body is vertical.

Visual/Spatial

- Focus on bars at beginning of skill.
- Keep head in neutral position.
- Keep arms straight throughout.
- In front swing, watch the ends of the bars.
- In back swing, look between bars at the floor.

Bodily/Kinesthetic

- Feel the swing forward and backward from shoulders.
- Push down on the bars.
- Feel the change in shoulders from pressed down in support at the bottom of the swing to extended in the handstand.

Musical/Rhythmical

- Use the 1, 2, 3 timing of the swing.

(continued)

(continued)

Assist

- Stand on a mat stack beside gymnast and place one hand under shoulder to keep gymnast from collapsing. Place hand on thigh to help drive legs up to vertical.

Common Errors

- Arms are bent.
- Hips lift instead of feet.
- Head sticks out and body arches.
- Legs are bent.
- Momentum is not controlled, which causes handstand to overrotate.

Swinging Skills on Low Horizontal Bar

Low Horizontal Bar	
Review exploratory swings (tuck, pike, straddle)	Open tuck swing
	Tuck swing half turn

Review the swinging skills on page 46 of chapter 2. Try swinging with the body in different positions, turning, and swinging back in a different position. Try to put the skills together and perform combinations in a routine.

Swinging Skills on High Horizontal Bar

High Horizontal Bar	
Building a swing (H)	Regrip (regrasp, or hand hop)
Counterswing (H)	Tap swing

Swing With Hand Hop (H)

There are several parts to the swing on the high horizontal bar. One part is the buildup of the swing to lift the legs higher on each swing. The tap swing (forward swing) happens as part of the buildup. The counterswing is the back swing and the regrip (hand hop) happens at the height of the counterswing.
To build a swing, do the following:

- From a long hang, lift legs upward and forward to a pike position.
- Thrust the legs down and back to a slight arch.
- Repeat to build swing.
- As swing builds, lift the hips in back to a slight pike with legs straight and upper back hollow.

The backward swing is called the counterswing. It happens as follows:

- Swing downward, leading slightly with heels through vertical under the bar.
- Pull downward on the bar and lift the hips to a hollow body position.
- Raise the hips slightly above the bar.

At the top of the counterswing, release and regrasp with hands (hand hop).

The tap swing happens after the buildup of the swing is established.
- Hollow the body at the beginning of the downward swing.
- As the feet approach vertical under the bar, relax the hollow body and open hips to a slight arch.
- Whip or scoop at the near bottom of the swing, which is called the "tap."
- Let the body extend and rise to a horizontal position.
- To reach the top of swing, press and extend the shoulders.

Learning Cues for Swing on High Horizontal Bar

Logical/Mathematical

- Sequence is long hang, build swing, counterswing, regrip, tap swing.
- Build a swing to at least 30 degrees.
- Bring torso to horizontal at the peak of counterswing and forward swing.

Visual/Spatial

- Use overgrip.
- Initiate swing by piking and arching.
- Lift your hips and regrip.
- Release and regrip hands at top of counterswing, never on tap swing.
- Keep legs straight.
- See toes on the pike.
- Watch bar on the regrip.
- Think of "hopping" your hands on the regrip.

Bodily/Kinesthetic

- Feel the hollow body position by keeping buttocks and abdomen tight.

Musical/Rhythmical

- Regrip as quickly as possible.
- Rhythm is:

  Swing, release, catch.

  1 and 2.

Assist

- Stand beside gymnast and place one hand behind thigh and one hand on abdomen.

Common Errors

- Back arches in counterswing.
- Body is not hollow at top of swing.
- Hands don't regrasp.
- Body relaxes too soon for the tap.
- Body doesn't tighten on the upward swing.
- Shoulders don't extend at the top of swing.
- Hands release on tap swing.

Other Challenges

- Count the repetitions of the swing.
- Initiate swing from a cast to underswing.

Swings on Parallel and Horizontal Bars

Parallel and Horizontal Bars

Glide kip progression
Suspended swing to glide
Kip from upper-arm support to rear
  straddle support

Glide swing, single-leg kip to stride support
Glide kip to front support

Glide Kip Progression

The glide kip is an advanced skill that can be used as a mount or part of a transition sequence in a routine. Students must be comfortable with swings and glides before they are able to accomplish the glide kip. A glide is a swing underneath the bar to help gain momentum, and the kip is the actual movement to thrust the body above the bar. There are numerous variations of this skill depending on the type of bar used. The kip is only for gymnasts who have developed strong abdominal and arm muscles; there are lead-ups that will help gymnasts prepare for the skill.

The following is a list of skills that lead up to the kip:

- Back extension rolls (gymnasts should be able to do back extension rolls on floor before the kip on bars)
- Drills for reverse sit-ups
- Jumps to front support with straight arms (emphasize shoulders over the bar)
- Swings from upper-arm support and straight-arm support on parallel bars
- Pullover mount
- Back hip circle
- Mill circle
- Squat-on

Here are drills that lead up to the glide kip mount:

- Glide to target.
- Glide out, straddle back.
- Glide out, straddle back, glide out again. (Partner can help by standing behind and lifting gymnast's hips for next glide. This requires some shifting of the gymnast's hands.)
- Perform a long-hang glide.
- Seesaw shoulders back over the bar.
- Drop kip (gymnast must be able to go from a hang to lift).
- Glide to single-leg shoot-through.
- Glide kip from front straddle support to rear straddle support.
- Glide kip to straight-arm support on parallel bars.
- Glide kip on horizontal bar.
- Long-hang kip on high bar. (This is sometimes easier until glide gets better, but it is harder to spot.)

Suspended Swing to Glide

The glide is a smooth fluid motion in which the body is suspended with straight arms from the bar. At the top of the back swing the body is in pike, similar to how it might look sitting on the seat of a swing. In the forward swing the body fully extends at the hips to a stretched-body position.

Here is a drill to help with hip extension: Have a target for the gymnasts to stretch for and touch with the feet at the end of the glide forward.

Learning Cues for Glide

Verbal/Linguistic

- Stand on mat stack at arm's length from bar set at shoulder height.
- Place hands on bar in overgrip and push hips upward and backward, keeping head between arms.
- Keep chest hollow and arms extended.
- Lift hips up and push feet off floor to swing in pike with feet and legs extended above floor.
- At the completion of the forward glide, the legs are together and the body position is straight with buttocks tight.
- Swing backward and upward through pike again.
- Return to start position on mat stack or floor.

Logical/Mathematical

- Sequence is hollow, grasp bar, piked front swing to straight body, piked back swing, jump, piked front swing, piked back swing.
- Keep equally piked on the front swing and back swing.
- Open shoulder angle at end of swing.

Visual/Spatial

- Keep head down between the arms.
- Keep the chest up.
- Pike only slightly.
- Watch your feet and straight legs glide out in front of you.
- Kinder cue: Pretend you're on roller skates and slide your feet out in a glide.

Bodily/Kinesthetic

- Feel shoulders open but don't arch at end of swing.

Musical/Rhythmical

- Swing should be smooth.
- Rhythm is:

  Swing, swing.

  1, 2, 3; 1, 2, 3.

Assist

Stand beside gymnast in front of bar. As gymnast glides outward, place one hand on back and one hand on back of thigh. As gymnast swings back, remove hand on thigh and place on hip.

Common Errors

- Feet hit the floor because shoulders close or pike is too deep.

Other Challenges

- Perform glide and regrasp at top of back swing to do a series of three to five glides.
- Perform glide and return with legs in straddle.
- Perform glide on high bar from long hang.

Seesaw

The seesaw drill helps the gymnast develop body positioning to keep the hips close to the bar for an underswing. The gymnast begins in a front support, then leans back slowly and concentrates on maintaining a hollow body position, keeping arms straight and bar to hips. Gymnast then teeters back to a front support. The spotter stands on front side of bar and puts an arm around gymnast's hips to "lock" gymnast to the bar as he or she drops the hips. Spotter's other hand is on the leg.

Kip

The kip is a transfer of power—the closing and opening of the hip joint. It is the kipping action of the folding of the body, then the explosive opening of the body, that generates force. The swing provides momentum, then the body folds to a pike, and the explosive opening of the hips causes the force from the pike, which fights gravity and propels the body up. A common mistake is that the gymnast kips too early. The gymnast should not start the kip until he or she reaches the end of the swing and stops, then kip and bring the legs to the bar.

Lifting the upper body up is the end of the glide kip. At the point where the gymnast feels the feeling of dropping back, she must pull (push) the bar down with straight arms as she forces her shoulders back over the bar. When pulling down on the bar, she must shift the hands and drive heels up with buttocks tight and straight.

Kip From Upper-Arm Support to Rear Straddle Support

A variation of this skill is a kip from upper-arm support to straight-arm support on parallel bars.

Learning Cues for Kip From Upper-Arm Support to Rear Straddle Support

Verbal/Linguistic

- Jump to an upper-arm support.
- Generate a swing by piking in front and stretching in back.
- At the top of a forward swing, pike and raise the hips to inverted pike above the bars.
- Push down against bars with upper arms. It may also help to push down on bars with elbows.
- Extend hips and direct legs upward and forward.

- Straddle legs as arms extend on downward part of cast.
- Finish in a straight-arm rear straddle support.

Logical/Mathematical

- Sequence is upper-arm support, swing forward in slight pike, swing back to straight body, swing forward to inverted pike, straddle legs, push, extend arms, and bring legs to a straddle support.

Visual/Spatial

- Keep knees straight throughout.
- Shoot feet up and over torso.
- Lift hips up in inverted pike.
- Push arms straight in support.
- Push down on bars.
- Keep chest up.

Bodily/Kinesthetic

- Feel muscles working to push against bars.
- Feel tight abdomen bringing legs to inverted pike.

Musical/Rhythmical

- Rhythm is

  Swing, pike, push.

  1, 2, 3.

Assist

Stand beside gymnast on outside of bar. Reach under bar to place one hand on back. As gymnast reaches inverted pike, place other hand on back of thigh for support.

Common Errors

- Arms don't push down on bars.
- Kip doesn't happen.
- Legs don't straddle, which causes a fall forward.

Glide Swing, Single-Leg Kip to Stride Support

- Stand on top of mat stack or springboard.
- Jump and perform the best stretched glide possible.
- At extension of glide, pike, bringing both legs quickly to the bar.
- Split legs in stride position so that one goes between arms and is above the bar and one leg goes underneath the bar.
- As the body swings backward, pull forcefully down with the arms, bringing the inner thighs to bar.
- Rotate the body forward and upward to end in a stride support position on top of the bar.

Glide Kip to Front Support

Learning Cues for Glide Kip

Verbal/Linguistic

- Stand on top of mat stack or springboard.
- Jump off both feet and reach to bar in a hollow.
- Bring the hips up and back to get a straight segment between the hands and hips.
- Open the shoulder angle and pike at the hips.
- Catch bar in overgrip and perform the best stretched glide possible.
- At the extension of glide, keep torso horizontal and quickly pike the legs.
- Lift the ankles quickly to the bar.
- As body begins to swing backward, pull down with arms.
- While holding the ankles to the bar, think of pulling the bar along the front of the legs from ankles to thighs.
- Shift the hands onto top of bar to arrive in straight-arm support with body slightly piked and toes slightly in front of the bar.
- Finish in front support by lifting heels back and up to form a straight line from shoulders to feet.

Logical/Mathematical

- Sequence is jump, catch in hollow, glide, kip, front support.
- Start in a straight-body stand slightly more than arm's length from bar.
- Push hips up and back as shoulders stay low.
- Stretch entire body to horizontal in glide.
- At top of glide, keep torso horizontal.
- Bring legs to horizontal line above torso with ankles touching the bar.
- Skill begins and ends in vertical straight-body position.

Visual/Spatial

- See straight legs and pointed feet stretching out in front of you in glide.
- See legs coming up toward bar.
- Pull ankles back to bar.
- Pull down on bar, rising above it with straight arms.
- Think of pulling pants up from the ankles to the hips.

Bodily/Kinesthetic

- Feel body stretch out in glide.
- Push small of back upward and backward as you jump forward to grasp the bar.

Musical/Rhythmical

- Rhythm is:

  Jump, catch, glide, kip, up.

  And 1, 2, 3, 4.

Assist

Stand beside gymnast in front of bar. As gymnast glides outward, place one hand on gymnast's back and one hand under thighs. On back swing, support thighs and push against back so that torso goes up above bar.

Common Errors

- Legs drop as soon as they come back to the bar.
- Arms pull down too soon.

DISMOUNTS

A dismount is a controlled, upright landing from the bars to a stand on the floor. The spotter must be ready to move with the gymnast in the direction of the dismount.

Dismounts From Parallel Bars

Parallel Bars	
Sit on bar, kick over	Rear dismount
	Front dismount

Sit on Bar, Kick Over (P)

- Begin in a straight-arm support in overgrip with body vertical.
- Swing until straight body is above the bar and parallel to floor.
- Center body to sit on one bar while releasing with one hand.
- Push away, releasing the other hand to land vertically.
- Sequence is straight-arm support, forward swing, hand release, rear sit, release, land.
- Assist: Place hands on lower torso for support and guidance.

Rear Dismount (P)

- Start to swing, piking on front swing and extending on back swing.
- Build up the swing until the body is horizontal on front swing.
- When the body is in front swing above bar, shift the shoulders and backs of hips over and past bar.
- Shift outside hand to inside bar and place behind inside hand.
- Release inside hand, keeping outside hand on bar for support.
- Land on both feet and bend knees; stretch up to salute.
- Sequence is swing, forward swing, backward swing, forward swing over bar, transfer hand, release hand, land.
- Assist: Stand beside gymnast on outside of bar. As gymnast swings forward, place one hand on gymnast's inside arm and other hand on back. Follow gymnast up and over bar.

Front Dismount (P)

Learning Cues for Front Dismount

Verbal/Linguistic

- Start to swing, piking when in front and extending on back swing.
- Build up the swing until the body is horizontal on the backward swing.
- Shift hips and shoulders over and past one bar until front of body clears the bar, releasing with far hand.
- Shift outside hand to inside bar.
- Lift inside hand off the bar.
- Immediately lift outside hand off.
- Land beside bar on both feet, bending knees with arms overhead.
- Stretch up to salute to finish.

Logical/Mathematical

- Sequence is swing, forward swing, backward swing, swing over bar, transfer hand, release hands, land.
- Swing until entire body is above horizontal, then release and shift to land vertically.

Visual/Spatial

- Focus straight ahead, then over dismount bar.
- Spot floor, then change focus to spot in front of you.
- Swing high with feet pointed.
- See straight legs swing over bar.

Bodily/Kinesthetic

- Feel arms straight.
- Keep shoulders pressed down.
- Keep abdomen and buttocks tight.

Musical/Rhythmical

- Move shoulder, then hips.
- Swing legs over bar and release arm as weight shifts.
- Rhythm is:

  Swing, release, land.

  1 and 2.

Assist

Stand beside gymnast on outside of bar. As gymnast swings backward, place one hand under shoulder and one hand on thigh. Move with gymnast through swing to prevent collapsing and push legs up to vertical.

Common Errors

- Swing is not high enough.
- Head sticks out and body arches.
- Weight doesn't shift far enough sideways to clear bar.

Dismounts From Horizontal Bar

Horizontal Bar (Low and High)

Castaway dismount

Underswing dismount

Sole circle dismount progression

Alternating toe taps

Hanging straddle

Hanging straddle swing

Straddle on, swing

Climb to straddle, swing dismount

Jump to straddle, sole circle dismount

Cast to sole circle dismount

Castaway Dismount (L)

- From a front support position, swing legs forward, then backward and upward.
- Push down on bar and extend through the shoulders.
- Lift the body to horizontal.
- As the body reaches highest point, push away.
- Release the bar to land vertically with arms above head.
- Sequence is front support, cast, release, land.
- Assist: Stand beside gymnast and place one hand on arm and one hand under thighs to help lift up cast. Follow along with gymnast, keeping one hand on gymnast's arm to guide landing.

Underswing Dismount

The pullover, back hip circle, and underswing dismount all use the same movement pattern and muscle groups. Falling back is a lead-up to the beginning of the underswing dismount and is also a lead-up to the beginning of a back hip circle and drop kip.

Learning Cues for Underswing Dismount

Verbal/Linguistic

- Begin a front support in overgrip with arms straight and thighs close to bar. This skill can also start from a stand with a jump. This provides momentum until the mechanics of the skill are more developed.
- Keeping thighs close to bar, lean the shoulders backward to begin backward circle, lifting legs upward.
- After hips pass under the bar, fully extend body by thrusting hips and legs forward and upward into a hollow body position.
- Release hands and land vertically in safe body position, then salute.

Logical/Mathematical

- Sequence is front support, hip contact, glide under bar, release on front swing, stand.
- Flight is on an upward, diagonal path.

Visual/Spatial

- Keep feet high throughout; don't let them hit the floor.
- See feet lifting in front of you.
- Think of going forward and getting legs up over a barrel.

Bodily/Kinesthetic

- Drive feet and thighs up.
- Feel the pull on bar.

Musical/Rhythmical

- Keep rhythm as smooth as possible.
- Turn hips under as fast as possible to get feet moving toward bar.
- Don't hold on too long; when body is stretched at top of swing, let go!

Assist

Stand beside gymnast on front side of bar. Reach under to place one hand on gymnast's back and one hand under gymnast's thighs to follow through dismount. This maneuver holds the gymnast's hips in contact with the bar as the shoulders shift back.

Common Errors

- Hips drop, which causes piking.
- Feet drop and hit the floor.
- Arms bend as body drops down, then arms bend slightly as body extends to push away from bar.
- Hands hold on too long.
- Hips get too far away from the bar.
- Body doesn't circle enough before shooting out.
- Upper body falls forward on landing.

Sole Circle Dismount Progression

The progression for sole circle dismount is as follows:

- Alternating toe taps
- Hanging straddle
- Swinging straddle
- Straddle on, swing
- Straddle, sole circle dismount
- Jump to straddle, sole circle dismount
- Cast to sole circle dismount

Alternating Toe Taps

This is a hanging skill that places one foot on the bar at a time.

- Stand at bar set at waist to chest height.
- Place right foot on bar outside right hand with leg in slight turnout.
- Return to stand.
- Repeat skill with left leg.
- Sequence is stand, place right foot on bar outside right hand, stand, place left foot on bar outside left hand.
- Assist: Stand in front of gymnast and help to hold the hips up high.

Hanging Straddle (L)

Review the bat hang (page 240) to prepare for this lead-up skill.

- Hang from bar in overgrip.
- Bring legs to straddle and begin to swing.
- Generate a swing big enough to bring feet up to bar.
- Swing with feet on bar.
- Swings should be smooth. Let the momentum of the swing dictate the movement. Don't try to "muscle" the movement.
- Sequence is straddle hang, lift feet up to bar in straddle, swing in hanging straddle.
- Assist: Stand beside gymnast and hold hips. Walk back and forth with gymnast in swing.
- Kinder cue: Tell the students to use "monkey toes," which must hold onto the bar.

Hanging Straddle Swing

In the lead-ups for a sole circle, the first thing you want gymnasts to feel is the control of the swing, because the sole circle generates force. Gymnasts can experience the swing by performing a hanging straddle and having the spotter "swing" the gymnast back and forth.

Straddle-On, Swing

- Get in a straddle with feet on top of the bar and hands in overgrip to practice the motion of swinging back.
- Swing backward, keeping the hands and feet on the bar. In the swing the feet move from the top to the back to the bottom of the bar. Keep the feet in contact with the bar.
- Assist: Lift the gymnast up into straddle on top of the bar, or gymnast may cast to straddle on the bar. With two spotters, the main spotter holds at shoulders and assists the cast of the legs behind the bar. Reach up and spot the shoulders. Second spotter stands to the front and side of the bar facing the gymnast and stops the shoulders from falling forward. When the gymnast does not need the second spotter, he or she is ready to squat on, straighten legs, and perform a pike sole circle.

Climb to Straddle Swing Dismount

- Begin in a front support.
- Climb up to a straddle stand on bar or cast, straddle on.
- Lean back and keep legs straight.
- Swing under bar. Let the fall take you up into the swing.
- At the bottom of the underswing, shoot hips and feet upward and outward.
- Bring legs together.
- Land vertically with arms above head, bending knees on landing.
- Stretch up to finish in a salute.
- Sequence is front support, straddle stand on bar, swing, underswing, release, stand.
- Assist: Stand behind gymnast. Lift gymnast by hips to place both feet in straddle on bar. Release.

Jump to Straddle, Sole Circle Dismount

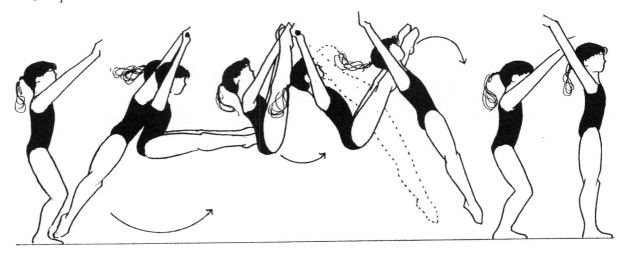

Learning Cues for Jump to Straddle, Sole Circle Dismount

Verbal/Linguistic
- Stand at bar with extended arms in overgrip.
- Jump to bar in straddle position, placing feet on bar outside of hands. Hold position to swing under the bar.
- At bottom of swing, extend hips and feet upward and outward.
- Release bar to land vertically in safe landing position.
- Stretch up to finish in salute.

Logical/Mathematical
- Sequence is jump to straddle stand, half sole circle to underswing dismount.
- Jump to horizontal straddle (torso is horizontal too).
- Keep shoulder angle open and use momentum of swing.
- Land in vertical.

Visual/Spatial
- Keep head inside arms.
- Do not jump high.
- Place feet on bar outside of hands.
- Hold straddle position to swing under the bar.
- At bottom of swing, extend hips and feet upward and outward.

Bodily/Kinesthetic
- Push down on bar; do not bring shoulders to bar.
- Keep muscles above knees tight.
- Shoot feet and hips up and out.

Musical/Rhythmical
- Get feet to bar quickly.
- Rhythm is:

  Jump, swing, stand.

  And 1, 2, 3.

Assist

- Stand behind gymnast holding hips to help hold straddle position.

Common Errors

- Jump is too high.
- Shoulder angle closes.
- Feet don't get to the bar or feet stay on bar.
- Feet and hips don't shoot upward and outward.
- Hands and feet let go too soon.
- Hips don't extend, which causes a fall.
- Feet drop off bar too soon.

Cast to Sole Circle Dismount

- From a front support, cast to horizontal.
- Pike and quickly bring balls of feet to bar in straddle.
- Apply pressure to the bar by pulling the bar against the feet while pointing feet.
- Swing downward, then upward.
- Maintain straight arms and a hollow chest position.
- As the hips rise in the forward swing, release the feet from the bar.
- Bring legs together and extend hips and shoot feet upward and outward.
- Release bar with hands to land in safe landing position.
- Stretch up to finish in salute.
- Sequence is cast, straddle stand, sole circle dismount, land.
- Assist: Stand behind bar beside gymnast. As gymnast casts, hold hips so that gymnast can place feet on bar. Lower gymnast into underswing.

Dismounts From High Horizontal Bar

High Horizontal Bar

Swing, rear dismount   Swing, front dismount

Swing, Rear Dismount (H)

Learning Cues for Swing, Rear Dismount From High Horizontal Bar

Verbal/Linguistic

- Swing on high bar.
- In counterswing, pull down with arms causing a shoulder angle (close shoulder angle slightly).
- Lift hips in slight pike with feet under body. This will segment the body to slow down the swing to prevent peeling off the bar.
- Let go at top of swing to stand up in safe landing position with arms extended.
- Slightly bend knees on landing, then stretch up in salute.

Logical/Mathematical

- Sequence is counterswing, pike, pull down with arms, release, land.
- Create a straight line in the air before landing.
- Keep the angle of the body in the release.

Visual/Spatial

- Use overgrip.
- Stay hollow and piked; don't arch.
- Try to hollow at top of swing (beginners will pike).
- See the bar, release; see the floor, then look up to a spot in front of you.
- Keep head inside arms.
- Keep arms above head.
- Lift hips and let go.

Bodily/Kinesthetic

- Feel body tight; don't arch.

Musical/Rhythmical

- Release late at top of counterswing.

Assist

- Stand beside gymnast and support at abdomen and back. Grab gymnast's arm or wrist on the release.

Common Errors
- Body is arched.
- Release happens too soon.

Swing, Front Dismount (H)

- Swing on high bar.
- In front swing, let go at top of swing to stand up with arms extended.
- Slightly bend knees on landing, then stretch up in salute.

ROTATIONAL MOVEMENTS

Twisting Rotations on Horizontal Bar

Thigh turn	180-degree turn in stride

Thigh Turn

- From a rear support on horizontal bar, turn hands to undergrip and "roll" on thighs, maintaining a straight body to front support.

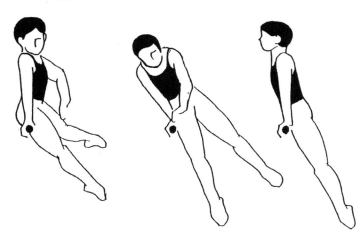

180-Degree Turn in Stride

- Begin turn from a stride position with right leg in front.
- Change the left hand to an undergrip position. Keep arms straight. Keep chest up; don't round back or lean forward.
- With support on the left hand, make a 180-degree rotation to the left. Turn shoulders before hips.
- Focus 180 degrees from front spot in turn.
- Reposition the right hand next to the right hip in an overgrip position
- Upon competition of turn, reposition the left hand to a position outside the left hip.
- Keep split equal.
- Repeat skill to other side.
- Swing leg back to finish in a front support position.
- Sequence is front support, cut or shoot to front stride, lift hand, change grip to mixed, turn body 180 degrees, change grip to overgrip.
- Grip sequence is overgrip, mixed grip, overgrip.
- Assist: Provide control at the hips throughout the turn by standing behind the gymnast with hands on the waist.

Horizontal Circular Movements

All skills that circle the bar need a good spot. The spotter must be in a good position to be able to spot the entire skill. The end of the skill usually needs the most support and attention.

Horizontal Circular Rotations on Horizontal Bar

Horizontal Bar	
Front support to forward roll	Mill circle
Cast to back hip circle	Front support press
Stride press	Front support press with resistance
Stride press with resistance	Front hip circle

In any circling motion the gymnast must understand gravity. When gravity is helping the movement, the gymnast wants to be as big as possible by lengthening the radius. Gravity is a gymnast's friend! On the upswing, gravity is the enemy and the gymnast must counteract the pull of gravity. To do this, the gymnast must shorten the radius.

Front Support to Forward Roll (L)

This skill can be used as a beginning dismount.

Learning Cues for Front Support to Forward Roll

Verbal/Linguistic

- Begin in front support.
- Lean shoulders forward over the bar, flexing arms partially until most of the torso weight is over the bar.
- Flex hips and knees to roll slowly over bar.
- Shift hand placement forward, bringing the heel of the hand around bar during roll.
- Bring feet to mat as slowly as possible to finish.

Logical/Mathematical

- Sequence is jump to front support, roll forward, shift wrists, feet to mat.
- Start and end with body in vertical.

Visual/Spatial

- Get shoulders in front of bar.
- Keep leaning forward until you begin to roll.
- Keep arms straight.

Bodily/Kinesthetic

- Feel weight forward over bar.
- Press shoulders down before rolling.
- Squeeze legs together and keep feet pointed.

Musical/Rhythmical

- Roll should be smooth and compressed tightly around bar.

Assist

Stand beside gymnast in front of bar to place one hand on upper back to provide support and to control head and neck. Place other hand behind gymnast's knees to help control the speed of rotation.

(continued)

(continued)

Common Errors

- Arms are bent so much that abdomen is resting on the bar.
- Legs are bent so much that landing is heavy.
- Arms let go of bar.
- Hands lose grip because they're not shifting forward.

Challenge

- Perform skill with completely straight arms.
- Perform skill from a higher bar.
- Perform skill from a higher bar while keeping arms and legs straight.

Additional challenge

- Try to roll to tuck hang, then open to pike. (Sequence is jump to front support, lean forward, roll, shift wrists, pike when inverted, slowly lower to L hang.)

Cast to Back Hip Circle (L)

The cast to a back hip circle is considered a beginning skill. However, gymnasts should learn the cast (page 251), the forward roll over bar, the underswing dismount (page 280), and the pullover mount (page 256) before learning this skill.

- Begin in a front support.
- Cast and return the hips to the bar.
- Lean the shoulders backward causing the backward rotation around the bar just like beginning of underswing.
- Shift wrists quickly to continue the rotation.
- End in a front support.
- Sequence is front support, cast, swing, circle body backward around bar while shifting wrists, front support.

Mill Circle Progression

The mill circle is also called the stride circle.

Stride Press

Gymnast should practice lifting up off the bar in a stride press. Remind them to strive for as big a split as possible.

- Begin in a stride support with the hands in undergrip.
- Press down on bar to lift the body as high off the bar as possible.
- Open legs into a wide split.

Stride Press With Resistance

In a stride press the spotter stands in front to support the front leg. The gymnast lifts up high on bar in undergrip and presses the upper thigh of back leg against the spotter, who provides resistance on back leg—just like putting the brakes on.

Mill Circle

A common problem with the mill circle is falling forward at the end of the skill. At the end of the circle the gymnast must push down on the bar and lift the chest. This works because the radius is lengthened, which slows down the rotation. The gymnast can also put the thumbs around the bar to slow down the rotation at the end.

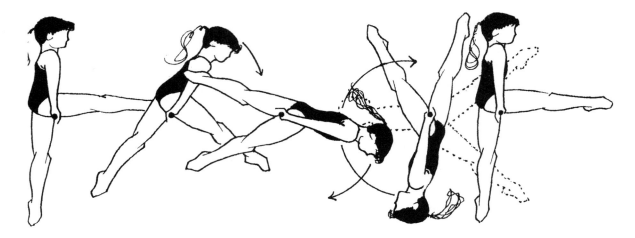

Learning Cues for Mill Circle

Verbal/Linguistic

- Jump to front support on a bar set at waist to chest height.
- Perform a single-leg cut.
- Switch to undergrip.
- Push down on bar and keep hips as high as possible.
- Extend the front leg and lean forward with upper body.
- Circle around the bar while maintaining straight arms.
- Shift heels of hands on top of the bar to finish in stride support.

Logical/Mathematical

- Sequence is jump to front support, single-leg cut, switch to undergrip, circle bar, finish in stride support.
- Start in vertical.
- Use maximum split.
- Rotate around bar in 180-degree split.

Visual/Spatial

- Keep front leg high.
- Place back thigh on bar.
- Lean forward in front of bar.
- Pretend there is an open window in front of you. Lift up and step up and out the window with your front leg.

Bodily/Kinesthetic

- Feel elbows straight.
- Feel knees tight.

Musical/Rhythmical

- Shift wrists on the way up.

Assist

Stand behind the bar next to gymnast. Place one hand under bar on gymnast's wrist with your thumb down and reach the other hand to the lower back to assist the last half of the circle as gymnast works against gravity.

Common Errors

- Circle starts too close to bar, which causes body to collapse.
- Arms are bent.
- Knees are bent.
- Body doesn't generate enough speed.
- Hips pike and fail to stay open on the last half of the skill.

Front Hip Circle Progression

Many beginners have problems with the front hip circle because they do not shift their hands and regrip. The gymnast should regrip the hands as they are returning to the top of the bar.

Front Support Press

- Begin in a front support with the hands in overgrip.
- Push body up high until thighs are on bar and the body is hollow. (Avoid piking.)

Front Support Press With Resistance

In a front support press, the spotter stands behind the gymnast and provides resistance on the back of the gymnast's legs or body to keep him or her from going over. The gymnast will stay in a straight position and move forward to horizontal (with resistance) without changing body position.

Gymnast can also practice going from a stretch to tight pike by squeezing bar between abdomen and legs tightly.

Front Hip Circle

The pike must come from moving the chest and torso up and out in the dropping motion, not by dropping the legs, which stops the rotation.

Learning Cues for Front Hip Circle

Verbal/Linguistic

- Stand at a chest-high bar and jump to a front support.
- Push out so that bar touches thigh and body is hollow.
- Lean forward with arms and stay straight until the body passes horizontal.
- Once past horizontal, quickly make a tight pike with the chest and head to the legs.
- As body begins to pike, rotate wrists by moving grip forward; keep heels lifting in circle.
- Keep arms straight.
- Rotate around bar and return to front support to finish, shifting hands so heels of palms are back on top of bar.

Logical/Mathematical

- Sequence is jump to front support, lean forward with hollow body, roll in pike around bar, shift wrists, front support.
- Fall to a little past horizontal, then tightly pike at hips.
- Keep hips and thighs close to bar to create smallest radius of rotation.

Visual/Spatial

- Use overgrip.
- Push shoulders down so that tops of thighs touch bar.
- Keep hip sockets in contact with bar throughout.
- Keep head in line with body.
- Keep feet pointed.

Bodily/Kinesthetic

- Feel elbows straight.
- Feel legs together and tight.

Musical/Rhythmical

- When body hits horizontal, pike.
- Shift wrists as soon as you pike.

Assist

Stand at right side of gymnast in front of bar. As gymnast starts to pike, place left hand on back and right hand under thigh. Hold gymnast up and apply pressure to assist in rotation around the bar. (If you stand at the left side of gymnast, reverse hand positions.)

Common Errors

- Body is so tight that there is no pike.
- Pike happens too soon.
- Arms are bent (arms must be straight when supporting weight but can bend at the bottom of circle).
- Wrists rotate too late.
- Heels drop when pike occurs, which stops the rotation.

About the Authors

Debby Mitchell, EdD, has been teaching physical education since 1978 and gymnastics since 1987. She is an associate professor at the University of Central Florida, where she is helping to develop a new undergraduate degree program in sport and fitness.

Mitchell is a national leader in technology integration. The video laser disk for gymnastics that she developed over a decade ago was the inspiration for this book. She frequently does presentations at state and national conferences on integrating technology into education.

Raim Lopez, MA, has taught gymnastics since 1981. He is an adjunct professor at the University of Central Florida and a fitness specialist who promotes and sells individualized fitness programs. Previously, he taught health and fitness at the elementary school level.

In 1992, Lopez received an award for the Most Innovative Physical Education Program in Florida from the Florida Alliance for Health, Physical Education, Recreation, and Dance. In 2001, he won the Disney "Teacherrific" Award.

Barbara Davis has been coaching and teaching gymnastics for 20 years. She is coauthor and national clinician with USA Gymnastics' Kinder Accreditation for Teachers (KAT). She has been a clinician for USA Gymnastics since 1984 at state, regional, and national congresses. She has presented twice at the International Scientific Congress at the world championships. She was the technical writer for the text and developer of the verbal learning cues for specific learning styles.

About the Illustrator

Stormy Gunter completed her BFA, specializing in etching, at the University of Central Florida in 1997. She has worked as an artist since her graduation. While living in Kentucky and Tennessee, she has participated in several community art festivals and has won numerous awards for her etchings. Stormy is currently attending the Savannah College of Art and Design as a full time graduate student of 2D animation and is planning on entering the field of independent film production.

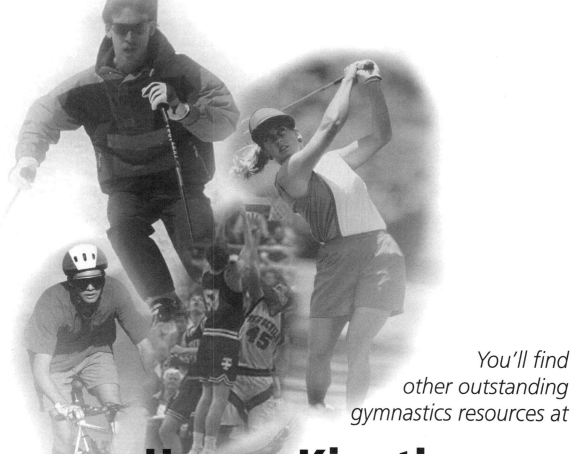